HOLIDAYS
WITH HITLER

HOLIDAYS WITH HITLER

STATE-SPONSORED FUN IN NAZI GERMANY

NATHAN MORLEY

AMBERLEY

First published 2022

Amberley Publishing
The Hill, Stroud
Gloucestershire, GL5 4EP

www.amberley-books.com

Copyright © Nathan Morley, 2022

The right of Nathan Morley to be identified as the Author of this work has been asserted in accordance with the Copyright, Designs and Patents Act 1988.

ISBN 978 1 3981 0796 0 (hardback)
ISBN 978 1 3981 0797 7 (ebook)

All rights reserved. No part of this book may be reprinted or reproduced or utilised in any form or by any electronic, mechanical or other means, now known or hereafter invented, including photocopying and recording, or in any information storage or retrieval system, without the permission in writing from the Publishers.

British Library Cataloguing in Publication Data.
A catalogue record for this book is available from the British Library.

1 2 3 4 5 6 7 8 9 10

Typesetting by SJmagic DESIGN SERVICES, India.
Printed in the UK.

CONTENTS

1	Enchanted Land	7
2	The Nazis Arrive	15
3	The Cultured Worker	26
4	Beauty and Horror	37
5	Hooray for KdF!	42
6	A Mixed Bunch	49
7	Trample on the Hills	55
8	Prora	65
9	Luring the British	71
10	Soaring Above: Aviation	88
11	The Lucrative Olympics	96
12	Let the Games Begin	105
13	Special Presentations	112
14	Hamburg	116
15	Nuremburg's Jolly Gathering	124
16	The Tide Turns	132
17	Follow the Sun	142
18	1939	151

19 The End of an Era	162
20 War	166
21 1940	173
22 Drunk on Victory	180
23 Hitler's Tourists	184
24 A New Europe	194
25 Barbarossa	204
26 1942	209
27 A Change of Fortunes	216
28 Crumbling Home Front	226
29 1944	233
30 Downfall	242
31 A New Type of Tourist	249
Endnotes	253
Bibliography	278
Index	281

1

ENCHANTED LAND

'Beautiful Germany', the popular slogan of the national tourist office, was not an empty phrase or cheap motto coined to catch the ignorant foreigner. During the 1930s, millions of brochures filled with chromolithographic illustrations urged potential visitors to wander along the vine-covered slopes of the Rhine, look up towards the purpling heights of the Black Forest, savour the magnificent natural beauty of Bavaria's mountain scenery or view the cathedral spires of Cologne sparkling in the sunlight. Could there be anything more captivating? For countless British and American excursionists, the answer was a resounding 'no'. Adding to the allure of the landscape, Thomas Cook adopted the slogan: 'Everywhere you will meet with the friendliest of welcomes in Germany.'

By the time our story begins in 1933, Germany's position as a leading holiday destination was secure; its reputation was first forged in the 1800s by young European nobles taking the Grand Tour to soak up history, art and cultural heritage. Such excursions were considered an important way to be educated. At the same time, religious pilgrimages to churches, chapels and shrines continued to attract the faithful and scholars. During a trip to Cologne in 1749, an intrepid English adventurer observed, 'The superstition of this little place surpasses everything of the kind you can imagine.' After crawling belly-down along the shadowy chambers of several ancient chapels, he concluded that Germans were not content with single saints 'but must have whole armies of them'. At the church of St Ursula, that same traveller found the walls and floors filled with coffins and bones. The city of Trier was also sanctified by association with a divinity as the cathedral was said to possess the garment worn by Jesus at the Crucifixion, a nail from the Cross, and three of the thorns that formed his crown.

Some visitors, like Joseph Marshall, a gruff adventurer with an interest in agriculture, arrived simply to explore the landscape. Between 1769 and 1770, he stitched together impressions of a deeply religious but impoverished land. 'I have not seen one chateau in all the country,' he grumpily complained. 'No castle, the residence of some old Baron, no country seat of a private gentleman, in a word, nothing but miserable villages or scattered cottages, the residence of poverty.' Travelling at clip-clop pace, Marshall griped at the windswept, rain-washed flatland stretching 200 miles from the Rhine to Hannover. 'What a contrast this is to travelling in England, or even Holland,' he grumbled. 'In our countries, even the most distant parts of the kingdom, we see seats of all ranks and degrees thickly strewed over the parishes.' Marshall's spirits were cheered, however, on arrival at the countryside near Dresden where a burst of sunshine illuminated the landscape: 'It is all hill and dale, corn, vines, and meadows along the banks of the Elbe ... a more entertaining picturesque scene can hardly be viewed.'

The same dreamy landscape was described sixty years later in the hugely successful *Romantic and Picturesque Germany*, which briefly mentioned the emerging spa trade catering to wealthy guests seeking cures for nervous affections and skin problems. Though somewhat dull and medicinal, such trips soon became an act of recreation and spurred Dr A. B. Granville to pen *The Spas of Germany*, the first major manuscript exploring health tourism. Published in 1837, the book fell into the laps of royalty, the powerful and the well-to-do. Written in the form of a travel guide, it included details of hotels, expenses, places of amusement, comforts and discomforts and, most importantly, testimonies of those 'taking the water'.

In 1836, the Wildbad Spa in the Black Forest welcomed 800 wellness seekers displaying every form of muscular, nervous, and lymphatic disorder, 'most of which were entirely, and others partially, cured' according to Granville. He told how a dull-eyed fourteen-year-old lad, so sick that he had to be carried to the baths from his bedroom, was able to cross the street from the hotel to the bathroom on crutches within a month. 'And this day,' the boy's mother gushed, 'ten weeks after our arrival, he has thrown those supporters away, I trust for ever.'[1]

As word spread of spas providing a cure-all, visitors from across Europe flocked to try the region's waters and sanatoriums. Newspaper adverts promised that 'taking the water' could relive gout, rheumatism, liver and kidney disorders, and even depression. Russian author Ivan Turgenev made a pilgrimage to Baden Baden to bask in the 'restorative power of fresh air and rest'. In a letter to Gustave Flaubert, the French novelist best known for his masterpiece *Madame Bovary*, Turgenev described the most magnificent trees he had ever seen, which did 'wonders for the eyes and the soul'.

Over time, the growth of the railways gave way to the creation of new destinations like Garmisch-Partenkirchen, south of Munich, a winter playground famed for its unsullied air. By 1874, the resort boasted an international telegraph station equipped to take bookings from clients in Britain and the United States. On sprawling plateaus, other new resorts boasted grand hotels, pensions, restaurants, tree-lined promenades, botanical gardens, concert halls, banks and even casinos. The Prince of Wales took his well-earned (and well-publicised) holidays at German health resorts, as did Princesses Victoria and Maud, who went through a course of baths and waters annually. The Princess of Wales paid a visit to the Bavarian spa town of Woerishofen, where the successors to Father Kneipp, one of the forefathers of the naturopathic medicine movement, continued to operate his cure of walking barefoot in dewy grass and streams whatever the weather.

By 1863, wealthy Germans were queuing to use the services of Carl Stangen's new travel agency,[2] a local imitation of Thomas Cook, offering accommodation and transport by ship, rail or stagecoach at a flat rate. Like Cook, Stangen chartered trains, cut deals with hotel proprietors for quality rooms and promised customers the elimination of the obligation to tip and annoying customs procedures. As a bonus, Stangen's international travel coupons and traveller's cheques attracted the wealthy, scholars, artists and military sorts to take his first excursion to Norway in 1875. Trips to Austria, Italy, Spain and Switzerland followed as did the construction of Stangen's purpose-built office, decorated with an oriental stylized façade, at 72 Friedrichstrasse. Known as the 'Arab House', it became the first port of call for anyone interested in travel. By 1899, Stangen had chalked up 686 excursions traversing the globe, including regular visits to Palestine, Egypt and the Chicago World's Fair.[3]

A similar picture was emerging across the border in Austria, where travel pioneer Gustav Schrökl developed 'railway pleasure trips' chugging out of Vienna station to Linz, Wels, Salzburg, Steyer and Admont. Before long, Schrökl had added a 'great journey to free Switzerland'.[4] The travel buzz intensified when mountaineer Anton Silberhuber authored several tour guides as well editing the *Austrian Tourist Newspaper*, which promoted trips to Egypt, Palestine, Syria, Greece, Turkey and Bosnia. Holiday traffic proved so lucrative that the Austrian railway company began promoting mini-breaks by offering cut-rate tickets from Vienna to Görlitz, Dresden, Berlin, Hamburg, Budapest and Brno, valid for fourteen days on any route (except express trains) with a 50-pound baggage allowance.[5]

By the latter part of the 1870s, the great summer holiday as we now know it was beginning to emerge. Spearheaded by Thomas Cook, British tourism to Germany continued to grow with visitors spread far and wide. Over time, the actual process of getting to Germany became easier, faster and cheaper. Many English visitors armed with vast trunks – and in some cases even servants – booked passage on luxurious paddle steamers plying the Rhine between Rotterdam and Mannheim, gently gliding through 400 miles of the finest scenery from the coast to the heart of Central Europe. Dr J. William Kay was lucky enough to enjoy a stopover in Cologne in 1872, where he admired the grandeur and beauty of the cathedral. 'They have been six-hundred years building it, and it is a long way from being finished yet,' he marvelled. Much concerned with social improvements, Kay explored the slums of the town but found them so smelly that 'all the eau de Cologne in the universe could not dispel'.[6]

> In the evening, I went to a cafe with a large garden behind it. There were hundreds of people of both sexes and of different grades in life. I saw neither drunkenness nor rowdyism. The people were drinking beer or light Rhine wine. There were no bad women in the place; those members of the sex there were evidently with their husbands or brothers, and many had brought their children.[7]

As the curtain fell on the Victorian age, travel stalwart Carl Stangen reached the high-water mark of greatness and was lauded for helping the German name to be 'respected in the Orient and not just like a travel guide, but like a teacher ... a man showing Germans the wonders of the Orient'. As age took its toll, Stangen began editing *Der Tourist* and *Stangens illustrierte Reise und Verkehrszeitung*, which gained appreciative readers when he commissioned renowned writers, including Franz Jaffe, to pen features on places such as the Chinese quarter of San Francisco, with its opium dens,[8] and London's Whitechapel, famed for the Ripper murders, dark nightlife and pickpockets.[9]

After Sundays became non-working days in 1890, Stangen made room for domestic trips also. The right to paid holiday leave – in addition to Sundays and public holidays – was only won after countless strikes and drawn-out collective bargaining. 'One of the peculiarities of our time is mass travel,' noted novelist and poet, Theodor Fontane, the first master of modern realistic fiction in Germany. 'Now anyone and everyone travels ... modern man, more strenuous as he becomes, also needs greater relaxation.'[10]

Over time, as more employers realized the benefits of a contented workforce, leisure organisations emerged to cater for the workers. 'The Friends of Nature' promoted 'a feeling for the outdoors' through regular hikes and rambles, while a plethora of small independent agencies sprang up offering daytrips and multiple-day excursions. New municipal tourist boards emerged to promote domestic travel to their towns; many of them, including Berlin, were sold as being somewhat exotic or exclusive. Thus, by the start of the twentieth century, the essential flavours of tourism had been developed: sightseeing, spa retreats, bathing trips, boat excursions, mountain and winter sports holidays.

The travel scene expanded further when the major steamship companies – Hapag and Norddeutscher Lloyd, originally founded to run immigrants to the New World – hit financial straits and launched luxury trips, giving birth to the lucrative pleasure cruise. By the time Carl Stangen died in 1911, his agency had been sold to Hapag and operated as the Hamburg America Line, running steamers on fifty routes.

As the number of travel agencies increased, Baedeker's pocketbooks gained a reputation as travel guides of 'unquestioned supremacy'. International editions included *Handbook for the Riviera, London and Its Environs* and *Italy from the Alps to Naples*.[11] These books, bound in red leather, provided exhaustive coverage on hotels, steamer connections, rail timetables, passport and visa regulations, currency, monuments, museums and local customs. 'It is a mistake to think of Baedeker as matter-of-fact and unemotional,' observed a reviewer for *Britannia and Eve*. 'Baedeker has the time and patience to plumb the deepest recesses of the soul.' Some travellers praised the guides for their honesty. For example, in a summary of the Holy Land, the inhabitants of Jericho were described as 'obtrusive' and travellers were warned to be on their guard against thieves. To add insult to injury, the summary poured ice water on the so-called entertainment: 'The villagers usually crowd round travellers with offers to execute a "fantasia" or dance accompanied by singing ... both of which are tiresome.'

The solid growth of tourism came to a halt during the First World War between 1914 and 1918. Perversely, when the conflict ended, victorious British troops were the first enjoy the benefits of the German landscape when they marched into the Rhineland to begin a decade-long occupation. Almost immediately, Cologne morphed into an extension of the British Empire as 12,000 soldiers – many with family in tow – decamped for an untroubled existence as though they were in Aldershot or India. The British military government set up comfortably at the Excelsior Hotel opposite the Gothic cathedral. By 1922, thanks to hyperinflation, British families were enjoying the luxury of once expensive German holidays at bargain prices, given the strong British pound and weak German mark. Americans, too, found that Germany was much more comfortable from traveller's point of view than France.

Moreover, except in the very large towns, Germany was considerably cheaper. 'During the summer, I travelled extensively on the Continent and concluded that France shows signs of ceasing to be the premier tourist country of Europe,' a special correspondent of the *Northern Daily Mail* asserted. 'I think that change is partly due to the very astute advertising of the German travel agencies. They have sent their propaganda into every quarter and whittled down the old belief that the British would not be welcomed in their cities.'

> In places like Berlin, Dresden and Munich, they have encouraged their police to talk English so that they can assist Americans and Britishers. In all the big hotels and restaurants, you'll find English notices cheek and jowl with German notices. At all important railway stations there is an interpreter that really can talk English intelligibly and not the jargon which frequently baffles travellers when approaching interpreters elsewhere.[12]

Tourism grew hand in hand with the rise of trade unions. By the mid-1920s, three federations dominated the landscape. The largest, the Allgemeine Deutsche Gerwerkschaftsbund (ADGB), represented semi-skilled industrial workers; the Hirsch-Dunckersche federation looked after white-collar employees; and the Christian unions represented skilled Catholic workers. Over time, all three federations fought for better wages, working conditions and other benefits including an eight-hour day and more leisure and educational activities. Hiking, already popular before the war, blossomed along with the thirst for betterment and education. Department store travel offices such as Tietz, Wertheim and Kaufhaus des Westens and local newspapers and journals helped drive an increase in the number of people taking day trips.

The German national rail network, the Deutsche Reichsbahn, opened the Reichszentrale für Deutsche Verkehrswerbung to tempt travellers to explore the country. Working together with seaside and mountain resorts, they commissioned iconic illustrative posters that helped shape the way the public viewed Germany, as well as producing the *Deutsche Verkehrsbücher* travel guides.[13]

2

THE NAZIS ARRIVE

On 30 January 1933, Germany's president, Paul von Hindenburg, appointed the Nazi leader Adolf Hitler as Chancellor of Germany. Recognising the economic and psychological importance of tourism, the Nazis established the Reich Committee for Tourism (RAFV) to kick-start the holiday trade, which was still reeling from the Great Depression. In Munich, for example, the number of arrivals had dropped from 594,000 in the summer of 1930 to just 395,000 in 1933.[1] In an effort to give domestic tourism a leg up, Hermann Esser, a Nazi member of the Bavarian cabinet, demanded civil servants spend their vacations on home soil, saying it 'cannot be tolerated that persons paid out of public funds should spend their holidays abroad'.[2] His cause was boosted when Hitler slapped an astronomical RM1,000 fee on visas for German tourists hoping to visit Austria, a reprisal for anti-Nazi measures taken by Austrian Chancellor Engelbert Dollfuss. At the stoke of a pen, Hitler killed German tourist traffic to Austria, which represented about 52 percent of its total.[3] Revelling in the development, Hermann Esser sniffed that if Dollfuss didn't welcome Nazis (he had banned the party) then 'Germans had no wish to impose their sight upon them'.

To prevent Germans sneaking into Austria via backdoor routes through Switzerland, passports were specially endorsed for countries. At the same time, Nazis organised mini-riots in several Austrian resorts to create further mischief, with details carried across the world by the press. This first major effort by Nazis to exert influence over a neighbouring country also became a test of the world's attitudes toward the new regime in Berlin. 'The consequent excitement all over Austria, and especially Tyrol,' wrote one correspondent from Innsbruck, 'reveals how much the country depends on tourism, and people tell me that if Hitler had wanted to alienate sympathies which were being won for union he could not have done so more effectively.'[4]

Desperate to remedy the situation, the Austrian government set aside half a million schillings to attract visitors from Hungary, Yugoslavia and Czechoslovakia, while also unveiling a scheme for new casinos in Salzburg, Semmering, and Baden-bei-Wien. Workers in the nation's tourism industry were encouraged to learn foreign languages, and a bumper crop of glossy new brochures gave readers a peek at the beauty of the Alps, using coloured landscapes – a distinct departure from the flimsy monochrome efforts produced beforehand. One of the more lauded publications, the *Illustrated Tourism and Travel Newspaper*, was mailed to millions of homes across the continent. Additional support came from the British Workers' Travel Association (BWTA), which furiously denounced Nazi tactics and, in an act of solidarity, sent members to holiday in Tyrol and Vienna 'because of the bold stand being put up by Chancellor, Dr Dollfuss, against German aggression'.[5] Acres of print space were devoted to letters sympathetic to Austria's plight from notables including Marie-Louise de Rothschild, who, giving her best shot at drumming up tourist traffic, provided a masterly example of how to influence readers.

> This charming country (Austria) offers magnificent scenery, its lakes, mountains, and forests are some of the finest in the world, the climate excellent, and the people most hospitable and friendly. At the present time the rate of exchange very favourable, thirty Austrian schillings to the pound and pension rates work out most reasonably. Those who visit Austria this year will serving a double purpose: not only will they have a very enjoyable and

comparatively inexpensive holiday, but will also help the most courageous Austrian Chancellor in his fight for freedom and independence for his country.[6]

The campaign worked. Austrian writer Willi Frischauer had clear memories of British tourists crowding hotels, packing dinner dances and small country inns, cherishing Tyrolean hats and the dirndl, the local costume of the Austrian peasant girls. 'Every item they bought, every penny they spent went towards the ten million pounds which Austria derived from its main industry – tourist traffic,' Frischauer gushed. 'Every English penny helped to save Austria from economic collapse, which had threatened since Hitler began to attempt to ruin the country and thus force it into surrender. Every Austrian knew that, and was grateful to the English and welcomed them as friends and saviours.'[7]

Before too much time passed, cheaper train fares and hotel discounts also helped boost domestic tourism in Austria. New brochures such as *Das Billige Wien*, published during the height of the boycott, promised to 'fiddle ways and means to make holidays in beautiful Vienna pleasant and cheap'. Within its sixteen pages it recommended budget hotels, museum offers and, remarkably, a list of health food cafes, vegetarian restaurants and temperance establishments. Pre-made itineraries included visits to museums, the opera, the Philharmonic, the Vienna Boys' Choir, libraries and picture galleries famed throughout the world for their treasures. Two-for-one discounts were offered on tours of the royal palaces at Schwarzenberg, Schonbrunn and Belvedere Park, the latter a green oasis laid out in terraces and studded with fountains. At the same time, in anticipation of budget travellers, cheap souvenirs became available in abundance. Plaster casts of Vienna's Spanish Riding School horses were sold in every curio shop, as were models of Viennese trams in tacky metallic gold, embroidered traditional lederhosen and darling dirndls.

Over in Germany, the heavy Nazi hand came down. Union meetings were broken up, newspapers suppressed and political opponents intimidated. Just before a general election was due, the home of the German parliament, the Reichstag, was mysteriously burned down on 27 February 1933. Hitler proclaimed 'the Bolsheviks' struck the match and issued warrants for the arrest of scores communists and socialist deputies. Soon after, the new Reichstag passed an Enabling Act giving Hitler powers of dictatorship and then dissolved itself.

One of Hitler's first acts was to appoint forty-three-year-old Nazi disciple Robert Ley as the head of the 'Action Committee for the Protection of German Labour'. Within a matter of months, Ley forcibly dissolved unions and absorbed their assets into the Deutsche Arbeitsfront, known as DAF.[8] In typical Nazi fashion, a brutal crackdown exacted a terrible price from prominent former union leaders. In Berlin, Theodor Leipart and Peter Grassman were humiliated by being beaten, forced to run long distances and do knee-bends. 'In paralyzed wonder, the overpowered workers looked on at their own ruin' was how one observer later summed it up.[9] This show of force set the tone for what followed as opponents were weeded from the workforce, aided by a 'List of Outlaws' naming those previously active in combating national socialism.[10]

Despite assurances to the contrary, DAF did little to improve workers' rights.[11] Workers could not strike, bargain for wages or leave their jobs without permission. The entire system was clearly intended to keep Germany a low-wage country founded on notions of efficiency and lots of hard work. Over time, DAF penetrated almost all areas of economic and social policy with a bureaucracy of 44,000 full-time and 1.3 million volunteer employees. For the sake of good publicity, Ley often threatened employers over all manner of subjects. With increased mechanization, he reminded factory bosses that 'men are our most valuable goods' and warned managers who dared to 'rate machines higher than men' that they would have the opportunity to study a contrary opinion in concentration camps.[12] With this kind of phony rhetoric, Ley presented himself as a kindly benefactor for the working man, unmoved by wealth and power. He often staged spontaneous factory walkabouts for the newsreels where he happily exchanged pleasantries with workers, though he cared little for them. Hjalmar Schacht, head of the Reichsbank, thought him a notorious drunkard with elastic morality 'given to every kind of erotic excess without the slightest sense of responsibility'.

Made of Rhineland peasant stock, Robert Ley opened his eyes to the world in the tiny hamlet of Niederbreidenbach in 1890, the seventh of eleven children of farmer Friedrich Ley and his wife Emilie. At the age of six he was shaken when his father committed insurance fraud by setting fire to his own farm, an incident which gave Ley a lifelong fear of poverty. Although highly strung, he was academically gifted and studied chemistry at university before joining the Army Air Corps during the First World War, where he received a head injury which caused a stammer and bouts of muddled behaviour, aggravated by heavy drinking. The injury also led to a paralysis of his left leg, leaving him dependant on a brace and walking stick.

Ley's other fundamental characteristic was his anti-Semitism, which was profound and particularly strong. Throughout his career, he preached hatred of the Jews and advanced the implementation of German racial theory by giving less housing, less food and fewer cultural facilities to inferior races. Having gained a doctorate in 1920, he had begun work as a food chemist for the IG Farben company in Leverkusen, an area still under French occupation. Along the way, he moved steadily towards the Nazi Party. After joining he became unswervingly loyal to Hitler, as he later recalled:

> An inner voice drove me forward like hunted game. Though my mind told me differently and my wife and family repeatedly told me to stop my activities and return to a civil and normal life, the voice inside commanded: 'You must. You must,' and I obeyed that irresistible force. Call it mystic, call it God?[13]

Most striking of all, however, was Ley's sense of purpose. Hitler referred to him as 'the greatest idealist' in his administration and backed his election to the Prussian Diet on the Nazi ticket in 1929. A year later, he joined the ranks of the Reichstag and was put into a role overseeing the organisation of the Nazi Party, holding this responsibility until the downfall of Nazism.

By the peak of his career, Ley had arranged a relatively pleasant life for himself, owning a home in Berlin's exclusive Grunewald district, a country seat and a small retreat in the Alps. However, he allowed himself no leisure other than daily liquid lunches. Each day he would work, or discuss work, until the early hours. When he got very tired, aides remembered, he chatted more and achieved less.

As the head of the DAF, Ley held the purse strings to enormous assets, bolstered by 4 million members contributing RM184 million annually (compulsory contributions deducted from wages). On top of that, the former unions had amassed a vast strike fund in addition to owning hotels, banks, hostels, co-op stores, a property portfolio and various other businesses. For the most part, this windfall was sufficient to cover the expenses of the Nazi Party while leaving plenty in reserve for DAF activities.[14]

Throughout the spring and summer of 1933, the Nazis made their presence felt as a significant force in daily life. The gates opened at the first concentration camp at Dachau, the Jewish population was harassed and brutalised, Jehovah's Witnesses were persecuted and officers of the Gestapo, the shadowy secret police, made their first appearance on the streets of Berlin.

As curtain raiser for the decade to come, 20 million Germans were prodded into the DAF, which was busily creating 'soldiers of labour' devoted to the Führer and Nazism. Using carrot-and-stick methods, DAF rolled out plans for Kraft durch Freude (KdF; in English 'Strength through Joy'), an organisation designed to promote mass leisure, sport, tourism and healthier workplaces based on the achievements of Dopolavoro (OND), the Italian after-work foundation. OND, according to its head, Corrado Puccetti, was aimed at providing support in economic, physical, hygienic, sanitary and cultural areas – or, as he said, a noble expression of fascist community work.

Concerned at being seen as a blatant OND rip-off, Robert Ley abandoned plans to call his version 'after work', deciding instead on a name expressing 'motivation and strength' to equip the German people for harder, more strenuous work. The organisation would work through channels such as Holidays and Travel, Sport, Beauty, Labour, Culture and Evening Leisure.

The Nazis Arrive

In one of his most notorious speeches, given at the launch of KdF in November 1933, Ley offered a glimpse of his thinking. 'We can and want the eight-hour working day,' he explained. 'We may be forced to increase the pace of work in certain areas in order to become exportable again. That is why we want and have to give working people complete relaxation of their body and mind in their free time.'[15] He detailed, at some length, exactly what he had in mind:

> We alone have the duty of removing fatigue from the people, to steel their nerves and to provide them with a release from tension. For this, we must offer the very best. We are certain of one thing and that is that the German people should be given the right to participate in the rich and magnificent culture of German music, theatre, cinema and art. They should be able to share the beauty of the countryside and the pleasures of physical exercise. In a word, to enjoy the joys of life. This programme should elevate the personalities of all men, especially the workers. It should destroy the inferiority complex of the working man. It should set things right and remove false attitudes and beliefs, such as the belief that a feeling for art and culture is dependent upon wealth and knowledge. Thirdly, this programme should remove boredom from man. From this boredom arises stupid and evil ideas which lead many to a concept of homelessness, and a feeling of complete uselessness. Nothing is more dangerous to any state than that.[16]

An enthusiastic audience – including Hitler's propaganda chief, Joseph Goebbels, perched in the front row – gave Ley a rapturous round of applause. Speaking on the same stage, Goebbels predicted the KdF would do 'very great work'[17] and level social inequalities to create a great *Gemeinschaft*, offering every German, regardless of class and income, the same rights to rest and relaxation:

> If the work which we begin here today stands under favourable stars, it should be a decisive force for the social development of all German people. This work already has precedents in other states, but I believe it would be wrong for us to follow blindly these

models. We are convinced that this work should be stamped with a distinctly German and National Socialist flavour. It is a matter of organizing leisure in such a way as to recognize the principle that the state is actually bound up with the people and that the people must not be left isolated, that not only work but also leisure must be organized.[18]

For his part, Hitler proclaimed KdF's primary aim as strengthening the body and soul of the German people. 'I can make policy,' he said, 'only with a people who do not lose their calm.' To attain this goal, KdF would serve the entire nation. Nobody was forgotten.

In all, about 37 million people were potential beneficiaries of the organisation which quickly penetrated the veins of society, spreading national socialist ideology through roll calls, workplace slogans and parades. KdF activities were promoted as beneficial for the mind and body. 'Our work tempo is very fast,' said Herbert Warning, head doctor at Focke-Wulf's factory in Bremen. 'The "life struggle" of our nation is extremely hard. We are therefore obliged to make our vacation a true source of relaxation.'[19]

Over time, factories appointed a 'KdF-Wart' (representative) to promote outings and cultural programmes as well generating enthusiasm about forthcoming trips. Further publicity came with uncritical radio exposure and DAF's wireless receiver – installed at workplaces – serving a captive audience. In order to instil a feeling of 'community', staff, managers and company directors were harangued into sitting on the shop floor to hear important broadcasts or join in collective 'sing-songs' during the 'KdF Song Book Hour'. Many employees stood before microphones to give accounts of their early KdF adventures. In Hannover, workers spoke of a weekend jaunt to the Reemtsma cigarette plant and Lindener Brewery, whilst workers in Berlin told how they had enjoyed outings to the zoo and the Wannsee lido. Some folks who had never left their home towns nor had knowledge of the wider country were shown forests and beaches, prompting free acknowledgement in the exiled Social

Democratic Party's reports that KdF's daytrips and evening social events were well attended.

> They provide light entertainment, even if visitors always also had to swallow a lot of Nazi-nonsense. But they are inexpensive opportunities to find easy relaxation. They also offer the opportunity to very casually meet up with good old friends and animatedly discuss, with a glass of beer, exactly the opposite of what the evening's organizers had aimed for.[20]

With a plethora of new 'Nazi holidays' falling throughout the year, the 'KdF-Wart' had half a dozen new red-letter days available to arrange outings. For starters, 30 January marked the 'day of taking power', followed on 24 February with a celebration commemorating the Nazi Party's foundation. On 16 March, ceremonies marked 'heroes' day', while Hitler's birthday on 20 April saw organised parades take place throughout the Reich. 'Labour day' fell on 1 May and mothers' day followed on the second weekend in May. In addition to that, the 'movement's day', commemorating the failed putsch of 1923, was held on 9 November, and the Christmas holidays spread through mid-December. The Harvest Festival, which the Nazis made a legal holiday, was marked annually as a major event mainly targeting farmers and the rural population. On top of that, the Teutonic festival of summer solstice – celebrated on the shortest night of the year – became part of the Nazi effort to revive Germanic customs and supress Christianity. Alongside numerous smaller venues, the solstice was even celebrated at Berlin's Olympic Stadium, dominated by folklore performances and camp fires. At one festival, 25,000 Germans ascended the Hesselberg mountain to hear Julius Streicher, the anti-Semitic *gauleiter* (district leader) of Franconia, declare:

> When we look into the flames of this holy fire and throw our sins into them we can descend from this mountain with clean souls. We have become our own priests. We approach nearer to God after climbing this mountain. Let people abroad criticise our worship as much they like. The fact remains that God has always accompanied

Germany on her way even thousands of years before there were prophets or churches. The time will come when Germans will climb the sacred mountain not once a year, but whenever they feel the need of worship which formerly drove them into the churches.[21]

In that first year, KdF occupied an astonishing amount of Robert Ley's time. He was especially thrilled to open an office for the Beauty of Labour, designed to make hygienic and aesthetic improvements to workplaces by building new canteens, sports facilities and restrooms. The KdF's Horst Dressler-Andress hoped spotless factories would also encourage workers to be clean and bright, and 'take pleasure in beautifying and looking after his family home'.[22] According to Albert Speer, a young architect assigned to the Beauty of Labour section, Ley dreamed up the scheme after travelling through the Dutch province of Limburg where he spotted a number of 'mines conspicuous for their neatness and cleanliness and surrounded by beautifully tended gardens'.

Work fatigue, according to DAF research, depended on a multitude of conditions, including noise, temperature, humidity, lighting, equipment (material and tools) and general conditions (working hours and breaks). An early campaign for better lighting of factories and offices used the slogan 'Good light – good work', while attempts were made to improve ventilation using American air conditioners. Speer's efforts were prodigious and more influential than many at the time acknowledged; he led with a sense of hard work, creativity and artistic flexibility. In later years, he remembered the Beauty of Labour office as an extremely gratifying project, 'at least for me personally':

> First, we persuaded factory owners to modernize their offices and to have some flowers about. But we did not stop there. Lawn was to take the place of asphalt. What had been wasteland was to be turned into little parks where the workers could sit during breaks. We urged that window areas within factories be enlarged and workers' canteens be set up. What was more, we designed the necessary artefacts for these reforms from simple, well-shaped

flatware to sturdy furniture, all of which we had manufactured in large quantities. We provided educational movies and a counselling service to help businessmen on questions of ventilation and illumination.[23]

There were, of course, the occasional gimmicks designed to attract press attention, such as when workers at a Leipzig factory stopped hearing the howling of work sirens and were instead summoned to work by the clanging of a beautifully crafted church bell installed on the top of the building. 'This work bell expresses the Germans' idea that daily work is the sublimest prayer,' the local DAF leader declared. 'The bell is to add to the beauty of work.'[24] Despite Ley's sincere intentions, the success of Beauty of Labour was, at best, sketchy. Whilst many businesses embraced the scheme, some sought the cheapest options to appear compliant. One disgruntled factory manager felt the need to 'do something' to improve his premises but without spending anything, as an employee recounted:

> He therefore approached the workforce with the request that they should clean up the factory yard during the evening, create some flower beds and plant them with flowers. This happened. The purchase of the flowers was the only thing that caused expenses. Of course, the cleaned-up factory yard changes nothing in our relationship to work and the company.[25]

When confronted with negative comments about the scheme, Ley published figures claiming industry had spent RM40 million on workplace improvements, much of it on new lighting.[26] Furthermore, he highlighted that greater creativity was urged by village councils with a beautification campaign to encourage the removal of ugly signs, open dumps, litter and unsightly telegraph cables. At the same time, volunteers were also urged to pitch in for the maintenance of villages by laying out new parks and planting flowers in the main streets.

3

THE CULTURED WORKER

Within six months of taking power, the Nazis set about discovering how workers occupied their leisure time by surveying 42,000 employees at the Siemens electrical factory in the north-west of Berlin.[1] It was a straightforward survey, comprising a series of questions about their lives asked at the factory gates. The results were surprising. They revealed that only a handful of the workforce pursued organised forms of leisure, with just 50 percent of respondents dabbling in sports, 67.9 percent admitting to seldom travelling outside Berlin and 84.5 percent revealing they never went to the theatre or only attended once a year.[2]

This insight helped shape the direction of KdF. Almost immediately, the organisation began rolling out education programmes, excursions, sports activities and social evenings held either in the factory canteen or at a local pub. KdF established the Amt Ausbildung – later known as the Reichsamt Deutsches Volksbildungswerk – offering evening courses in science, languages, practical mathematics and arithmetic, handicrafts, commerce, animal care and flower arranging. Amateur musicians, painters and sculptors were encouraged to form groups and societies.

DAF also assumed influence in the field of vocational and professional development and introduced correspondence study programmes to attract shift workers and those in the countryside. Over time, adult education classes included tours to regional landmarks, libraries, municipal offices and, as the account below shows, local prisons:

> These prison tours belong to the most popular and most heavily attended 'educational activities' offered by KdF. Ladies are excluded so that the pleasures of sensationalism are not reduced. It is this titillation of the sensations which assures such heavy participation in these tours. We visited a prison in X. It had about one thousand men of which about three quarters were political prisoners. All one-man cells were occupied by three men. The spectators saw the whole operation, prisoners at work, eating, everything. But no one could speak to the prisoners. The director, who was our guide, was a young S.S. man and explained to us, 'We will not be able to afford the luxury much longer of providing prisoners with collars on their shirts and fibre mats on the floors.'[3]

'For us,' wrote Ley, 'everything centres on the German man and woman, all our efforts are concentrated on the development of their energies and gifts to serve a mighty and proud people of the future.'[4] This, he said exultantly, ranked higher than any other priority. 'We shall do our best to make German men and women, once more, mentally and intellectually productive, to awake their talents.'

> And so, our efforts are concerned with every minute at the disposal of the workers. We are always at their disposal. Our will is at one with theirs both during and outside working hours. Since it is our duty to care for the proudest possession Germany has: the hearts of its workers.[5]

Unsurprisingly, a common denominator among the factory evening classes was regular visits from lecturers to give talks on racial, political or economic problems presented in the Nazi viewpoint.

On the cultural front, money was directed at a permanent 'People's Theatre' (Theater des Volkes) in Berlin where drama, opera and musical comedies were presented nightly. Opening with Schiller's *Die Räuber*, the mission of the theatre was to 'move the individuals in the audience to a sense of greatness and unity through the presentation of classics and performances reminding them of the traditions of German literature'.[6] Decked out with ruby red seats and flax papered walls, the grand complex could hold 3,200 people. With an ample supply of uniformly priced tickets, lots were drawn before performances; the lucky were escorted to plush boxes, while others were seated in the pit, stalls or back of the horseshoe-shaped gallery. Alongside the People's Theatre, an opera house and various provincial theatres fell under the control of KdF, but as author Bertram de Colonna discovered, KdF beneficiaries could bag seats at almost all theatres, even for the most exclusive hit shows:

> This is done as follows. When managers expect to have, say, 100 seats, free, they sell them to the Worker's Front for a block price, as they stand. These are distributed by drawing lots. Thus, two adjacent seats may easily have cost 15s. and 10d. the latter through the organisation (KdF), the former at the box office.[7]

In an effort to provide 'quality experiences' for rural audiences, KdF deployed touring troupes to descend on village halls and school auditoriums in remote farming communities. There was great enthusiasm for the 'Germany is singing again' campaign – similar to the British show *Opportunity Knocks* – which found amateur talents hidden throughout the country, leading to a radio series and the birth of several musical ensembles. 'The KdF's work is brought through to the last village, to the farthest patches of our fatherland,' *Arbeitertum*, the DAF mouthpiece, gushed. 'Our Reichstheaterzug performs in the village pubs, in gymnasiums, in the open-air during the summer months, and even in factories – and that, by the way, in a manner as colourful and entertaining as the variety shows in cities!'[8] Another dramatic form, the so-called *Werkspiel*, saw actors join workers to create joint productions performed on the factory floor. One such show was held in the courtyard of the vast Dynamo-Werke at Berlin-Siemenstadt.

The Cultured Worker

A member of the audience observed it was not a matter of great poetry 'but of the choric form and the employment of the amateur players, who were guided by select professional actors. This caused the production to be a success.'[9]

By the close of 1933, German theatre had been remoulded in accordance with national socialist theory, leading to Ibsen, Strindberg, Wedekind, Toller, Werfel, Hasenclever and Shaw being swept from the stage. Even Shakespeare productions were 'tweaked' to conform the Nazi thinking. On one occasion, audience members were stunned to discover a production of *A Midsummer Night's Dream* had the 'un-Nordic' melodies of Mendelssohn removed and replaced with a local composition.

For the right people, the theatre became a lucrative profession. Hermann Göring pulled strings to ensure that his girlfriend Emmy Sonnemann, a second-rate actress from the provincial stage, was installed at the prestigious Prussian State Theatre in Berlin, which fell under his control. She was paid handsomely to star in *Schlageter*, a political drama dedicated to Hitler by its author Hanns Johst. In typical Nazi fashion, the play was showered with sparkling reviews and played to packed houses. The newspaper of the Nazi Party, the *Völkischer Beobachter*, called it 'the first drama of the German revolution'.[10] Only one critic, Herbert Ihering of the *Berliner Tageblatt*, dared give it hostile reception. He charged that Emmy's acting was not up to scratch and lacked the 'final melting together of role and actor', a remark which, surprisingly, left him unscathed.[11] (During contract negotiations, Göring had told opera star Lotte Lehmann that no critic would be allowed to write bad notices about her on pain of liquidation.)[12]

Soon after, a coveted title role was pencilled in for Emmy in *Minna von Barnhelm*, a comedy dealing with love and honour in eighteenth-century Prussia. Given that Minna was written as a waiflike beauty, it was a ponderous spectacle of miscasting. At forty years old and weighing about 170 pounds, Sonnemann was hardly suited to a role designed for a much younger woman. Again, after a glittering first-night party, the critics were rhapsodic and again, only Ihering was brave enough to mention a 'certain uncertainty and bias of the tone'. This time, he was rewarded by being kicked out of the National Writers' Chamber.

By 1934, nothing could stop KdF's quest to provide highbrow culture to the working public. That year, the Music of Great Masters project brought 'outstanding works by famous composers' to factory dining halls, performed by leading orchestras. The Berlin Philharmonic gave special KdF concerts within their regular season,[13] an idea which won widespread applause, including from the African American socialist W. E. B. Du Bois. In his memoirs he tried to capture his experiences, recalling the warmth and respect he was awarded during a trip to Germany and highlighting how the cultural offerings 'unavailable to the working man in the USA' made a great impression:

> I am bathing myself in music. It is cheap – the best orchestra seats for one and two dollars and the gallery for 50 cents. I have heard since Bayreuth, Bizet's *Carmen*, Rossini's *Barber of Seville*, Mozart's *Marriage of Figaro* and *Magic Flute*, Wagner's *Flying Dutchman* and – unforgettable night – *Tristan and Isolde*, Verdi's *Rigoletto* and *La Traviata*, Massenet's *Manon*; with the beautiful dream sung well, but not so divinely as Hayes sings it. And last night, the Ninth Symphony – there where the hoarse horns and dead strings suddenly become human voices, in the noblest hymn to Joy man ever wrote for God. These classics of popular music, without knowing which one cannot talk to civilized folk, are practically unheard of for most Americans. They should be part of the education of every man of culture. They are costly luxuries for the most part in America, and unappreciated at that. Someday, no school curriculum will be complete without such compulsory courses in the world of music and drama.

As Du Bois notes, there could be no doubt Germany was enjoying a musical golden era. In Berlin, the Philharmonic was directed by the world-renowned Wilhelm Furtwangler, whilst the youthful Erich Kleiber was in charge of the State Opera. Across town, Bruno Walter ran the Deutsche Oper and Otto Klemperer staged magnificent productions at the Kroll. The endless number of world-class solo performers living in the city included Rudolf Serkin, Ferruccio Busoni, Adolf Busch, Arthur Schnabel and even the child prodigy Yehudi Menuhin. Given this abundance of talent it was little wonder Germany marketed itself as the world capital of music, boasting that few countries enjoyed the same level of musical talent and diversity.

'You will hear music everywhere,' the Reichsbahnzentrale pamphlet *Welcome to Germany* promised. Visitors, it assured, would be left enchanted by the zither playing down in Bavaria, the accordions on the coast and the sound of guitars and folk songs 'wherever they encountered young people'. 'Germany,' readers were informed, 'had a long-standing history' with the great composers and offered everything from full world-class orchestras to piano concertos and string quartets. In addition to the principal attractions, music lovers were encouraged to visit the Gewandhaus Orchestra in Leipzig, the Gurzenich concerts in Cologne, the Richard Wagner concerts at Bayreuth and the festival weeks in Munich.

> And when you remember that Germany is the home of Handel, Bach and Beethoven, of Mozart and Lortzing, Schumann and Schubert, of Richard Wagner, Hans Pfitzner, and Richard Strauss, you will no longer feel any doubt that even a purely musical tour of Germany would be well worth while.[14]

From time to time, the KdF wasn't above a little pandering for those seeking ostensibly lowbrow entertainment – a phenomenon which was not lost on the Gestapo, who kept special watch on unsavoury comedians and crude cabaret performers, as the following police bulletin from Potsdam attests:

> Unfortunately, at times it could be detected that the jokes, which were presented by the so-called 'announcer', were of very low quality, which caused irritation among many in the audience. It cannot be the task of KdF, mainly out of concerns for provision of work, to provide employment, which is undesired from a cultural-political standpoint, for those artists which grew up in the

atmosphere of Jewish Cabaret. Everything which looks like Jewish chaffing must not be promoted by a Nazi organization. The best form of humour is the funny tale or the anecdote, especially the one in dialect. It can be bawdy, but not purposefully piggish.[15]

Authors of the reports sent to the exiled SPD leadership abroad often winced at the poor standard of some KdF offerings. 'Now theatre, then political cabaret (and what crap)' and shortly afterwards a series of limp comedy shows. On one occasion, the KdF in Westphalia advertised an 'original Negro choir' from Honolulu as being set to perform. 'The music is provided by a Nazi band,' the report observed. 'Probably these Aryans are blacked up with shoe polish. If it weren't so bitterly sad, you could laugh.'[16]

Alfred Rosenberg, the tall, cigar-smoking Nazi ideologist, thought KdF emblematic of everything that was wrong with the party apparatus. Speaking after the war, he lamented that the KdF was a textbook case of how not to run a complex organisation.[17] 'Kraft durch Freude took over a number of musical comedy and even vaudeville theatres, quite without rhyme or reason,' he explained, 'but instead of assisting enterprising, gifted individuals, it turned into a cultural trust with paid officials, and soon began to exhibit all those unpleasant side traits that accompany the assignment of posts and parts.' He complained that at every annual KdF meeting, Ley appeared with record-breaking figures on performances and attendance. 'Artistic values were bandied about like so much mass-produced confectionery. I remember Kraft durch Freude weekends, when the Ninth Symphony was played in the morning, a museum was visited during the afternoon, and *Tristan* was performed at night.' Given this level of animosity, it is worth noting that Rosenberg was in charge of a separate and rival unit organising cultural events, the Nationalsozialistische Kulturgemeinde (National Socialist Culture Community).

In Berlin, KdF arranged discount tickets for the Scala variety theatre which featured amateur turns alongside famous musical acts (including the Paul Whiteman swing band), comedians, dancers, clowns and vocalists. 'At the Scala I saw Grock, the great clown, desperately trying and always failing to construct a human bridge with the dubious help of a confederate,' recalled teenager Peter Fröhlich. 'Their ever repeated announcement that they were about to perform this feat – "*Eine Brücke! Eine Brücke!*" – still sounds in my ears. At the Scala, too, I saw Rastelli, the world's most remarkable juggler, performing virtual miracles such as balancing three soccer balls, one on top of the other, on one foot.'

In its quest for a healthy population, KdF was keen to promote sport within the workplace and embarked on a plan to offer a vast range of outdoor leisure pursuits. Encouraged by some of the larger companies like Bosch, Krupp and Siemens, which already provided sports facilities for employees, Ley, too, believed physical activity essential to social development. 'It doesn't matter how high a person jumps,' Ley said on getting workers into the playing fields, 'what matters is that he jumps at all.'[18] Germans, he added, must learn to participate in sport to a much greater age, not stopping when they reached thirty but going on until they were fifty. Holding a newspaper cutting in one hand and smoking a French cigarette with the other, Ley explained that the British even 'played games even at the age of sixty'.[19]

To kick the nation into activity, large amounts of money were ploughed into building sporting facilities in the Harz Mountains, Bavarian forests and at inland lakes. Funds were also directed to institutions for the training of sports teachers at Berlin University and the Reichs Akademie for training leaders of sport. Members opined that to belong to a KdF sports club was a grand thing, as good as any private society. Participants got to know their workmates, enjoyed social evenings and, as many party commentators pointed out, the playing field became not only a barometer of worker's health but the place to 'level up' society. 'No birth title and no academic degree help with the classification in sport,' explained Hans Von Tschammer und Osten, the head of the KdF Sports Office. Only the 'really capable', he said, would gain the approval of others.

> On the sports field, a simple worker is often far above the general manager, and the young servant sometimes becomes master of

the landlord. And that is a good thing, because when one group of national comrades is freed from feelings of inferiority, but the intrinsic worth of their national comrades are revealed.[20]

By late 1933, most factories had appointed sports organizers to arrange gymnastics, football, swimming, tennis and skiing events.[21] Whilst participation was voluntary for adult employees, clusters of well-drilled younger workers were obliged to do at least two hours of physical activity per-week within company time. To take part, workers paid RM1 for a 'Sports Card' on top of a small fee for the classes. Understandably, pastimes such as skiing, ice-hockey, riding, fencing, golf, and tennis – formerly unattainable luxuries for many – were in demand.[22] Inexpensive kit for all these sports was provided at prices within the workers reach. Special Kraft durch Freude skis, roller skates and tennis rackets were available, whilst yachts, canoes, and even wooden gliders were provided by the movement. Skiing lessons were held on artificial snow, and those taking the courses usually signed up for holidays in the mountains during the winter. Among the KdF departments, Ley insisted the sports unit played a particularly important role.

> It has the noble, but also indefinitely difficult task, of making the leisure time of the German worker within the leisure-time organization a source of strength through recreation that produces joy. Thus, it greatly contributes to boosting the life energies and the performance of the people. Through education and training it takes part in the unified formation and creation of the German man, whose ideal resides in the harmony of body, mind and soul. For the sports department, physical exercises are not only a means to keep the body healthy and fresh, but also the foundation for mentally and spiritually healthy interior development. That is why its exercise courses attach particular importance to educational, personality-building moments and thus have a deeper sense than mere physical exercise.[23]

As an incentive, many workers aimed at obtaining a Reich sport badge, an idea initiated at the turn of the century and revived by the Nazis. By 1934, over 300,000 badges were won each year. Although rather large and ugly, they were worn by men over their breast pockets. The ordinary badge was bronze and could be won by men and women aged eighteen to thirty. The silver badge could be won by people from thirty to forty; and anyone over forty years of age who won a badge received a gold one. The examinations were the same for everybody and were held all over Germany every fourth Sunday.

As time went on, new activities were added to the programmes including map reading, taking cover from an air attack, getting through woodland undetected, judging distances and shooting. 'In spite of the fact that we live today in peaceful times, it should be self-evident that every man should be able to handle a shooting weapon,' a KdF information pamphlet informed. 'Beside its obvious usefulness, it is also a pure pleasure to practice with a precision weapon.'[24]

KdF figures show that during 1934, 633,000 people took part in sporting activities[25] (170,000 signed up for swimming during the summer months). As *Arbeitertum* proudly noted, the addition of new facilities, such as swimming pools and running tracks, pushed that figure up to 3.3 million in 1935.[26]

Impressed by the figures, a British Board of Education deputation paid a visit to Germany to get a first-hand view of the KdF sports programmes, noting that the 'whole population is under the legal or moral obligation to train'.

> Great as the achievements in the field of physical education have been up to the present, they are determined to make them greater still in the future, and it will not be owing to any lack of energy and determination on the part of these young men if they do not eventually succeed in getting the sort of Germany that they so ardently desire and that National Socialism considers that it requires.[27]

Remarkably in a country where the disabled constantly risked ridicule and ostracism, KdF embraced the idea of providing sports for the blind. At Augsburg in Bavaria, thirty men and women took part in gymnastics, wrestling, swimming and track-and-field athletics. (The National Association of Hard of Hearing Germans was also admitted to the DAF, and thus its members were beneficiaries of KdF activities.)

Separate from the KdF scheme, Reich Minister for Food and Agriculture Walther Darre founded a special school for promoting physical fitness among the young at Burg Neuhaus. Every four weeks agricultural workers, both male and female, found 'recreation from their daily work to return invigorated to their labours'.

> One might almost say these young fellows and girls had become different beings, their eyes shine, there is a spring in their walk and their whole bodies seem to be more supple. But this is the main object of this wonderful sports centre, to liberate the young countryfolk from the heavy carriage and expression which is the result of agricultural labour having often a very one-sided effect. Every different type of sport is carried on at Burg Neuhaus and, in addition, dancing takes an important place in the day's programme. The fine old folk-dances, which were long forgotten, are re-awakened to new life. The couples dance round on the big meadow to the strains of the old folk melodies.

4

BEAUTY AND HORROR

According to guidebooks, visitors to Berlin Zoological Gardens – Germany's oldest and most illustrious zoo – were able to admire 433 species of mammals including hippos, antelope, a yawning Asiatic lioness and giant Indian elephants. Set inside an exquisite walled-in garden, the gardens boasted lovely walks passing ornamental pools, sculptures and artificial ruins. From the summer of 1933, discounts to enter this oasis of calm were extended to various Nazi organisations, having previously been given only to military personnel.

As the year unfolded, a rather uneasy mixture of Nazi welfare events and performances from the SS and SA bands began to occupy the open-air dancing pavilion and restaurant nestled in the rock gardens. For some, the brassy sounds of the 'Horst Wessel' march – given an extra helping hand by Nazi sing-songs – hardly created a tranquil atmosphere.

But, having worked up an appetite for Hitler, Lutz Heck, the scientific director, was quick to bring the zoo into line with the goals of national socialism as he loftily described the Nazis as a 'natural science government' led by a strong leader who applied laws to state policy. Over time, together with the board of directors, Heck engineered the behind-the-scenes removal of Jewish board members (no mean feat given that one-third of the shares were held by Jews) and 'helped' the works council dissolve itself. His nationalist fervour also spurred him to build a 'German Zoo' in Prussia displaying only indigenous animals such as wolves, bears, boars and weasels.

If anything it is surprising that it took so long for the zoo to prohibit Jews from buying season tickets, but by 1937 steps were being taken to completely ban non-Aryan visitors and the policy came into effect in late 1938. 'The zoo has always been important as the lungs of Berlin, offering fresh, clean air,' Hans Ammon, co-director of the zoo, gleefully told a board meeting when the ban was implemented. 'I find, though, that since November 1938, our air here has become much cleaner than it had been.' (Until recently, the zoo's official history made no reference to any such undignified episodes.)

The persecution of Jews quickly evolved to a point where district leaders across Germany set their own agendas. For example, in Neustrelitz, a small-town community in the Mecklenburg Lake District, hotel owners – acting in concert with the local tourist board – posted signs announcing that 'the admission of Jews is unwelcome', sparking similar actions elsewhere. Before long, prejudices had spread to the railways, holiday resorts, and the shipping industry, which experienced a notable decline in Jewish passengers.[1] As a new liner of the Hamburg America Line, the *Potsdam*, rolled down the slipway, the company expelled all Jews from its board and management positions. Deeply alienated from the general population, Jews taking long-distance voyages began opting for British or French liners where courteous treatment was afforded. In just one weekend, a Hamburg America vessel leaving New York saw sixty Jewish passengers cancel their reservations and switch to foreign liners. Prior to the Nazi regime, 70 percent of Jewish Trans-Atlantic passengers used German ships, providing a huge source of hard currency.

Before long Jewish youth groups were forbidden from using public sites and hostels, private tennis courts would not accept Jewish members, and restaurants and cinemas began hanging signs in their windows declaring they served 'only non-Jewish clients'. Many cafes and *Konditorei* (sit-in bakeries) were similarly off-limits. 'The owners were doubtlessly happy, because they did not want unpleasantness,' a former Jewish customer lamented. 'We encapsulated ourselves and spared ourselves personal hurt.'[2] Jewish visitors to the Baltic seaside resort of Misdroy were the victims of anti-Jewish demonstrations when crowds gathered outside hotels and boarding houses shouting, 'Out with the Jews.'[3] More than once, jackbooted Nazi thugs – many armed with pitchforks – invaded the Wannsee lido to make sure only Nordic blood was being cooled in the Prussian waters. In response to the threatening war cry 'Jews clear out', scores of-bathers hastily donned their clothes and fled. The cleansing of Wannsee received enthusiastic support from Joseph Goebbels, who owned a home on the nearby island of Schwanenwerder. Many of the island's plots with private houses that had belonged to Jews were forcibly sold to prominent Nazis at bargain prices.

Goebbels installed himself at Inselstrasse on the north shore of Schwanenwerder in a private house with landscaped gardens, guest cottage, garages and boathouse. For convenience, his lover, the dazzling Czech film star Lida Baarova, lived across the road with the actor Gustav Frohlich. Albert Speer and his family later moved onto the island, as did Hitler's doctor, the morbidly obese Theodor Morell, who waddled around his mansion at Inselstrasse 23.

Across the country, the same thuggish tactics used against the Jews at Wannsee lido were copied at other municipal baths and in coast and mountain spas. Sometimes these incidents were reported; mostly they were hushed up. The violence, though, aroused loud commentary in the foreign media. For example, a fight between Nazis and former Jewish servicemen at a garden restaurant in Berlin received widespread coverage. 'Hearing of the presence of the Jews,' an international wire report stated, 'the-storm-troopers decided to beat them up and proceeded to do so with the help of leather belts.' At the same time, Nazi hooligans smashed windows and bullied Jews in the cafes of Kurfürstendamm, one of the finest shopping streets in Europe. A correspondent from the *Morning Post* witnessed storm-troopers hounding a frightened Jew and his still more terrified wife out of Kurfürstendamm into the adjoining Meinekestrasse:

> In the comparative darkness of this side street the storm troopers struck at the Jew's face till he shrieked for mercy. One could hardly believe that the very persons who boast that they have given back Germany her honour could perpetrate such a cowardly assault.

Shortly thereafter, attacks occurred at the Cafe Bristol, where thugs struck Jews and hurled their drinks and ices out of the window. What is more, the popular Café Kranzler and the Kempinski restaurant were also 'purged' while the windows of the Balsam Ice Cream Saloon were smashed to smithereens. Jews who tried to escape by car and taxi were frequently surrounded and abused. Countless foreign tourists, some of whom were said to have 'been molested at the height of the riots', were left horrified.

A stark glimpse of anti-Jewish sentiment can be found within the pages of the *Nordische Rundschau*, which screamed, 'The Jew is our enemy.' Under the banner headline 'They bought from Jews – Thoughtlessness or Maliciousness?', the newspaper sought to shame those who continued to use Jewish shops:

> This should be practically common knowledge. We deliberately say 'should' but the pictures on this page prove otherwise. They were snapshots we were able to take during a very brief stroll in the streets of Kiel and are doubtless the best evidence that there are still plenty of Germans who either shop in Jewish businesses quite 'thoughtlessly' or despite the information provided in recent years about the Jewish peril or the Jews' true nature violate the foremost law of National Socialism, which makes it a sacred duty of conscience and blood for every German not to take their money to the Jew.[4]

It seemed a good moment for Hilde Rohlén to leave Berlin. For a start, as a Jew, she had seen the warning signs months if not years before. 'In the spring of 1934, my then fiancé Norbert Wohlgemuth fled to Stockholm,' she explained. 'He had left

Germany via Rostock with an excursion boat to Denmark and from Copenhagen booked himself on the cheapest boat to Stockholm. In July, I followed him by train from Berlin.' (In 1934, no visa was required for a European to travel into Sweden and stay there for three months.)[5] Many fleeing on tourist routes took with them only what they could carry. Those with the time and money packed more of their possessions and left via the traditional steamer routes to America, Palestine, Britain or the Orient.

In due course, the economic boycott against Jews resulted in a new exodus and caused a drain on the country's capital. Official figures of Jewish and political refugees (described as 'emigrants') fleeing were published in the *Völkischer Beobachter*, which stated that 90,000 Jews had speedily decamped abroad since the Nazis rise to power, along with 20,000 non-Jewish political refugees (social democrats, communists, pacifists and Catholics). The capital loss to the Reich was put at RM32 million by the Economics Ministry and RM80 million by the *Völkischer Beobachter*.

Surprising as it may seem to us, around 10,000 Jewish refugees would make the fatal decision to return to Germany.

5

HOORAY FOR KDF!

With its promise of cheap and cheerful holidays, KdF set the tone for a new era in tourism while simultaneously providing a boost for the Reichsbahn, which was reeling from the depression and competition from cars and air travel. In an attempt to attract passengers back with cheaper fares and aggressive marketing offers, the Reichsbahn launched the 'Flying Hamburger' in spring 1933, creating a global sensation as it sped at 100 miles an hour between Berlin and Hamburg to become the fastest train in the world. Less than a year later, on 18 February 1934, the Reichsbahn's first major KdF assignment saw 1,000 factory and office workers march in the wake of a brass band to Berlin's Friedrichstrasse station to board a chartered train destined for Berchtesgaden, a village nestled high in the Alps. 'The tourists marched smartly in fours, with suitcases swinging in their hands,' a *Times* correspondent declared enthusiastically.

> The station was gaily decorated with flags, Nazi bands played military marches, a choir sang German folksongs. Several government officials' delivered short addresses. Dr. Robert Ley, leader of the Labour Front, said German 'workmen who had been made homeless by the former regime and were now under Nazi rule would get to know their beautiful Fatherland and taste the

joys of comradeship'. He accompanied the excursion as far as Munich.[1]

The Nazi press roared with enthusiasm of how Bavaria – till then a destination restricted to the wealthy – was accessible to everyone.[2] As the first KdF train pulled into Berchtesgaden, a welcoming committee was dispatched clutching small paper flags. Those first KdF pioneers gambolled their way through thirteen days of pleasure hikes, museum trips and excursions to lakes and richly decorated castles. 'It wasn't only the grandeur of the mountains which pleased us,' one of the first excursionists beamed, 'it was also the ease with which we quickly became friends with the Bavarians. "You Prussians aren't nearly as cold-nosed as they say you are," one of them remarked to me. And we quickly became brothers.'[3] Over time, thousands of holidaymakers and many youth groups took similar trips. Teenagers Hans and Grete Döpke found the fresh air and sunshine of Berchtesgaden breathtaking, as they excitedly told their mother:

Ms. Dora Döpke
Hannover-Buchholz
Podbielskistraße 220

Berchtesgaden, June 25, 1935

Dear Mom!
We currently have a magnificent weather and we have made good use of every minute. Today we spent the entire day sunbathing at the swimming pool pictured on the other side [of the card]. We look like half-negroes. [Eli/Efi][4] likes it more and more here so that it will be hard for me to bring her back home again. Until the next letter – the best regards to you and Ewald from your children Hans and Grete.[5]

Apart from the novelty of being on holiday, the mood was raised by a pilgrimage to Hitler's Berghof, nestled in the hills above the town amid flocks of grazing goats. A Baedeker guide described it as a 'stately mountain retreat in one of the most picturesque spots in Europe sixty miles along the motorway from Munich, near the Austrian border'.[6] Occasionally, Hitler could be seen sipping tea on his patio served by his white-jacketed valet, Heinz Linge, who thought the Berghof resembled a hotel. 'While Hitler worked during the mornings,' wrote Linge, 'the guests amused themselves, sunbathing in deckchairs, playing table-tennis, chatting on the terrace or rambling in the magnificent mountains.' Hitler's mistress, Eva Braun, keen on photography and filming, 'would always be involved in one way or another':

> On the first floor of the rebuilt Berghof were his study and the bedrooms for Eva Braun and himself. There were twelve other guest rooms for visitors. The permanent house-staff lived in, near the guests. All rooms had valuable paintings on the walls: originals such as those by von Lenbach, Defregger, Grützner, Waldmüller, Spitzweg, Stuck, Titian and Makart were Hitler's favourites. In the basement was his 'sports centre', a bowling alley. Hitler, who had no interest in sport except for the expander under his bed, loved bowling, although he did not want this known about.

Adorned with hand-carved Alpine-style furniture, Hitler's study provided an astonishing vista of the misty valley to the mountains across the Austrian border[7]. On a small path – still visible today nestled amongst wildflowers – 'KdF pilgrims', as the locals called them, disgorged from diesel-belching charabancs and waited hours and even days for Hitler to appear. As soon as tourists caught sight of him, Martin Bormann recounted, 'people stood at the fence' in reverence.[8] Securing a handshake or nod from the 'leader' was considered the greatest of accomplishments, whilst some admirers collected cobbles from the pathway like holy relics.[9]

For propagandists, the mountain retreat showed Hitler firmly connected to the working man 'as a person like you and I, who lived modestly and in harmony with nature, full of affection for the simple folk, for children and animals'.[10] The book *Hitlers*

Wahlheimat went a step further, presenting him as a lone seer against a majestic mountain backdrop – a great and respected statesman and people's chancellor.¹¹ The international press ran a steady stream of saccharine stories from journalists including William George Fitz-Gerald – using the name Ignatius Phayre – who described the Berghof as the home of a 'wayward, emotional bachelor whose table is meatless and wine-less, and who never smokes'. Fitz-Gerald added that Hitler acted the good neighbour to 'simple folks' in the hamlets round about him. 'He calls in person at the cottages to invite small boys and girls to the "funfairs" he gives each weekend on his cherry-orchard lawns.' After encountering a group of Hitler Youth on a hike to the Berghof, journalist Alexander Powell stumbled into a jamboree of Boy Scouts pottering around Hitler's garden. 'They had asked permission to call on the Führer, and he had asked them to the villa for tea, which consisted of enormous quantities of ice-cream and cake. Oh, boy, how those youngsters ate.'

Many visitors, like British tourist Frances Jean Crossie, found it hard to disagree with such glowing accounts. She caught a glimpse of Hitler during the Bayreuth Festival, which left her glowing with enthusiasm:

> I really was very impressed. The crowds were trying to cheer him, but they could not. Tears were rolling down the cheeks of the majority and even I had some difficulty in keeping down the lump in my throat. I thought 'Why should this be?' But I could find no explanation. The Deutsche people love their Chancellor more than life. They would follow him to the ends of the earth; die for him, if he so willed it and Hitler knows this.¹²

During the first few years of the KdF, the enthusiasm of visitors, the interest of the press and the buzz around Berchtesgaden had never been more intense nor would it ever be so again. A popular picture-postcard showed Hitler lounging on a garden seat on the terrace with the caption 'A quiet hour at Berchtesgaden'. In another version, a little girl was sitting with him. Before the town became a synonym for Hitler's mountain retreat, older guidebooks peddled a 'summer resort' noted for woodcarving and salt mining in a 'picturesque green valley.'

Locals had always been enthusiastic tourists, as schoolgirl Irmgard Hunt, who grew up in Berchtesgaden, remembered. Sunday outings took her past beautiful village churches and pilgrimage chapels that dotted the landscape. 'Every hamlet in the side valleys or on the plateaus had its own Catholic church, always next to at least one inn. If we were not too late or too tired, we would enter the coolness of these churches in the villages of Ramsau, Ettenberg, Oberau and Maria Gern and admire their painted ceilings, carved, gold-coloured altars, and statues of Mary, the saints and the apostles.'[13] Some tourists made a pilgrimage to the little village of Oberammergau for the *Passion Play*, portraying the sufferings and death of Jesus. In this typical Bavarian mountain village – enclosed by magnificent forests – almost every home had its picturesque individuality in the shape of colourful frescos, most of them dating from the eighteenth century. The village, with its 2,000 inhabitants, lies about 60 miles from Munich in the heart of the Ammer Mountains, the name given to one of the spurs of the Bavarian Alps, at an elevation of 2,745 feet.

Oberammergau's *Passion Play* gained notoriety especially in the United States and Britain during the 1920s. Christ was played by Anton Lang, a deeply pious potter, whilst the rest of the cast was cobbled together using locals. In a brochure promoting fully inclusive tours to the village, Cunard promised that locals would be a 'revelation of simplicity and naturalness to people that have to live in cities most of their lives':

> To stay in one of their spotlessly clean Old-World houses and enter into the life of the family is a unique and refreshing experience which adds to the interest of the whole occasion. The lucky ones will be the visitors who secure lodgings in the homes of the principal actors.[14]

Even today, eight decades after his death, Lang's well-tended grave in the Oberammergau cemetery remains a sacred spot.

Given such religious fare was sufficiently at odds with Nazi thinking, KdF propaganda described the play as a 'peasant drama ... inspired by the consecrating power of the soil'. According to local legend, even Hitler managed to sit through a five-hour performance. Paradoxically, the Nazis also promoted a diverse range of church ensembles and organists including the famous choir of St Thomas's Church in Leipzig, the 'Cathedral Sparrows' or boys' choir of Regensburg Cathedral, the organ of St Mary's Church at Lubeck and the organ at Passau Cathedral with its 17,000 pipes and 200 registers.[15]

Because of his other duties, Ley didn't spend a great deal of time offering advice to the KdF (which was, in fact, the only DAF department he directed personally), but a number of his disciples did play a major role in developing the organisation. Under the expert hand of Dr Bodo Lafferentz, the KdF's Travel, Hiking, and Relaxation unit ('Amt Reisen, Wandern und Urlaub') took 175,000 vacationers to Bavaria in its first year, a feat which accounted for around 80 percent of sales. Urbane and suave, Lafferentz was described as 'an extraordinarily intelligent opportunist, manager and expert at the adroit use of official connections'. He didn't conceive of his duties as setting up a transportation office or a pleasure organisation alone. 'Rather,' he once explained, 'we place considerable value on the ideas of promoting the ideals of the *Gemeinschaft* and the spirit of fellowship.'[16]

In Berlin, Lafferentz blew in and out of the DAF offices with all sorts of news and ideas; but when he needed approval for big budgets and grand plans, he turned to Ley. Together they promoted Berchtesgaden with such fervour that 'KdF vacation trip 44 Obersalzberg: In the beautiful Berchtesgadener Land' became a huge money spinner. The *Völkischer Beobachter* reported in September 1934 that the KdF had ferried 44,771 tourists to Upper Bavaria during the previous eight months.[17]

A seven-day trip including meals, accommodation and Berghof visit cost just RM28. A surviving brochure features page after page of information about local lakes, Rococo facades, churches, castles, gastronomy, the dialect and folklore, all peppered with stunning chromolithographic illustrations. The sale was well made. Historian and publicist Ernst Niekisch thought the effect of such materials couldn't be underestimated:

> The frippery, the hustle and bustle, the magic of travel, with which 'Strength through Joy' filled the worker's free time, and captivated him. 'Strength through Joy' is his substitute for democracy. Because he is allowed to stick his nose in all parts of the world at reduced prices, he should feel like a free man; he should carry his head higher and feel equal.[18]

6

A MIXED BUNCH

Before long the crush of KdF tourists became a common sight at resorts and beauty spots across Germany, bringing what one official diplomatically called 'negative effects'. Some complained of KdF groups causing excessive noise, littering and public drunkenness, sparking disgruntlement among residents and wealthier tourists on private vacations.

It is certainly true that there was no such thing as a 'typical KdF tourist', as the organisation itself was quick to point out. 'Whoever travels with Kraft durch Freude doesn't know his travel companions so well,' an official guidebook noted. 'One may come from a factory in the north, another from a bakery in the south. The third comes from a workshop, and the fourth was unemployed a few years ago.'[1]

Having heard interesting tales about the behaviour of KdF clientele, writer Bertram de Colonna booked a KdF vacation near the Czech frontier. But far from rowdy thrill seekers, his fellow travellers turned out to be 'comradely and helpful':

Many of the workmen I met on this trip surprised me by their knowledge of Europe. One could mention almost any part of Germany – if they had not been there, they had at least visited an adjacent part. From the Baltic to the Rhine, from the North Sea to the Polish border, they knew all the mountains and seaside resorts.[2]

The competing image, however, prominent in police reports and regional newspaper articles, was that even in a sea of tourists it was easy to spot KdF visitors, and not just from their sharp accents. They were the ones, locals complained, known for carousing, brawling and excessive boozing. On one occasion, a posse of 900 tipsy KdF passengers disembarked from a steamer in Koenigswinter where a fracas between a number of holiday trippers developed into a brawl at a flower festival. A few tourists – who were distinctly inebriated – fought with locals, insulted police officers and, more alarmingly, molested local girls. 'If the tour had not already given the followers large amounts of alcohol by issuing beer tokens during the outward journey, those extremely regrettable incidents could have certainly been avoided,' a local police source wrote scathingly.[3] Uncontrollable 'cliques' and sexual exploits amplified trouble and shocked respectable opinion. A well-known joke told how holidaymakers lost a lot of 'strength' through a lot of 'joy'. (The fact that many tourists were single contributed significantly to the lack of discipline and erotic excesses.)

Despite the huge press exposure, it is worth noting that KdF only took 10 per cent of the holiday traffic in 1934 as Germans continued to use traditional tour operators, offering a wider choice at all prices. Despite that, private travel agents were morbidly convinced that KdF was bent upon attracting wealthier customers for cheap thrills. This theme was echoed by the Baden State Tourism Association, which noticed well-heeled individuals taking advantage of the rock-bottom prices. 'KdF should definitely remain limited to the less fortunate, it must not be permitted to become a travel agency for all.'[4] Indeed, it was bitterly ironic that scores of 'normal paying guests' returned with the KdF to hotels and destinations they had previously frequented and spent less money.[5] Equally galling was when potential customers scooped up brochures from travel agents only to book a cheaper trip to the same destination. 'Many travellers collect information on rail times and catalogues from the travel agency,' *Der Fremdenverkehr* reported, 'yet then take a journey with KdF.'[6] Hermann Esser paid scant heed to this industry bickering and in later years slapped down attempts to drive traffic away from the KdF:

> Travellers who are not able to travel with travel agencies due to their income are taken care of by the German Labour Front through KdF. According to the Reich Tourism Association, it is not the task of the travel agencies to compete with KdF through the arrangement of equally cheap travel. I therefore urge the state tourism associations to point out to their members that contractual agreements with travel agencies, whose price offerings are the same as KdF or actually lie beneath them, are to be avoided in all circumstances.[7]

Although delegates simply nodded in acquiescence, the scene on the ground was much livelier given many hotels ended up serving both private guests and KdF groups. In one case, an argument erupted when an innkeeper – showing absolutely no tact – brewed coffee in different ways, so that his 'good coffee' served to commercial guests clearly stood out from the cheap slop offered to his KdF groups. Also, it wasn't unusual for private tourists, offended by the sound of lower-class accents, to make condescending remarks. In some cases, hotels assured well-heeled regulars by sending notes asserting that 'there are no KdF groups here'.[8] In response, KdF holidaymakers were quick to direct scorn upon rude hotel staff and innkeepers, especially Berliners, who were known for their harsh, sharp tongues.

On the other hand, many undeveloped towns welcomed KdF groups with genuine warmth. Despite a shortage of beds, the residents of Chiemgau and Grassau, east of Salzburg, gladly opened their homes.[9] According to the *Achentaler Nachrichten*, enough beds were found and, although it was a no-frills situation, there was a satisfactory standard of hygiene: running cold water in the room or hallway, a shared toilet, and hot water on request.[10] There is little doubt that the sudden influx of KdF visitors quickly became a vital lifeblood for many tiny communities.

The town of Rothenburg – the most German of all German towns in Bavaria's Franconia region – was also chosen as KdF destination given its Gothic and Renaissance architecture, the perfect specimen of a medieval city encircled by a covered wall pierced by a number of gateways surmounted by towers. With no buildings newer than the seventeenth century within its walls, Rothenburg to the KdF was 'a unique concept ... it is an everlasting witness to the glorious German history of the Middle Ages, a shining monument to German community in olden times'.[11] Although it remained popular with foreign visitors (especially Thomas Cook tour parties and independent coach tours), KdF virtually overran the town and even occupied the main tourist office. At the behest of Goebbels, the *Völkischer Beobachter* helped to drum up interest with a series of poetic features:

> Only those who really know Rothenburg are able to see how German forest and German meadow, German life and German art, are inseparably interwoven with each other. Whoever steps out of the metropolitan desire and struggle, out of the daily hustle and bustle, and in the peaceful quiet life inside Rothenburg's walls, would believe to being a fairy tale of a long-gone golden age resurrected a fulfilment of all longings for calm and happiness.[12]

Writing in similar vein, British journalist H. A. J. Lamb (along with a mix of day trippers on a Cook's tour) was enamoured of Rothenberg's quaint signs, picturesque fountains and disguising of anything likely to create a jarring note, but he gave a slightly earthier review:

> Telegraph wires are concealed as much as possible and many of the tradespeople rely on some queer picture to advertise their wares. The butcher's shop with its oddly-painted pigs is far more attractive than one with a window full of gory corpses and strings

of sausages. The ox-cart ambling through the streets strikes perfect harmony and it is not until the hooting of the motor-bus, laden with tourists doing a *Rundfahrt*, to the accompaniment of a guttural voiced guide, is the picture destroyed.[13]

In its quest to open new destinations, KdF allowed many communities to thrive in isolated areas such as Eifel, a remote region on the border of Belgium 'usually neglected by normal tourist traffic'. 'It is clear the KdF tours are of considerable economic importance especially for the border districts,' the organisation beamed, 'just as they are proving to be a factor of steadily increasing importance in the entire life of the German people.'

Despite the widening choice of destinations and bargain prices, not all KdF excursionists were entirely satisfied. Those expecting the comfort of a hotel or pension were directed to the small print (included in every brochure) stipulating 'specific places of accommodation do not exist' – meaning if hotels were full, guides would 'distribute' visitors among local landlords and residents.[14]

Everybody, though, seemed to enjoy the evenings when groups fresh from jaunts to the area's beauty spots would return to an old-fashioned *Heimat-Abend* (home evening). Seated at long tables with large ceramic beer mugs, they were first subjected to a welcome speech from a local official. 'Afterwards followed local dances and songs', according to a British student who joined a KdF jaunt to Upper Bavaria:

> The performers were dressed in Bavarian costume. The men had brightly-decorated shirts and embroidered leather shorts. The women wear blouses with decorated bodices over them and very wide, brightly coloured skirts. The songs are sung in the Bavarian dialect, which is as intelligible to a North German as really broad Scots is to a Cockney. As well as singing there was some very good yodelling – a very different variety from that heard in Britain.
>
> A boy played a Bavarian song very cleverly on cow-bells, accompanied by harp. There was also a quartet consisting of the curious combination of a violin, a double-bass, clarinet, and a

piano-accordion. During the intervals the village brass band played marches and popular songs in which the whole audience joined.[15]

After the evening concerts, a space was usually cleared for dancing. At the end of the entertainment, the National Anthem, 'Deutschland Uber Alles', and the national socialist song 'Die Fahne Hoch' were sung with great fervour.

7

TRAMPLE ON THE HILLS

All through the year, long before the word 'hiking' was applied to serious walking, thousands of people enjoyed treading among buttercups. With the help of the Reich Mountain and Hiking Association, the KdF, too, began extolling the pleasures of a long tramp over the hills or along country roads. 'Never before have facilities been so good for those who intend to let their feet take them on their holiday,' the KdF boasted as they created well-marked tracks, improved trails and loaned-out hob-nailed boots, rucksacks and maps. 'The man who works in a plant or under the earth gets in contact with the greatness of nature, this mighty power, which solves every riddle of the world,' beamed Karl Busch in the DAF publication *Unter dem Sonnenrad*. 'Once in the great outdoors, people find themselves again, they see again their deep roots, which connect each child of the earth inseparably to the course of the world.'

Pamphlets advised that wonderful meals could be made on a paraffin stove and suggested hikers take an enamelled mug, plate, cutlery and a bottle of iodine for treating blisters (cut the blister and apply a little iodine and your blister will trouble you no more). Numerous individual hikers, alone or in couples, also ambled along the mountain foothills on Sundays or during their holidays. The Wandervögel movement – intended to promote association between boys and girls of the various classes of society – enjoyed considerable influence in the promotion of rambling.

To encourage hiking, infrastructure projects were undertaken by local councils, bus companies and 'beautification associations' to clear lakeside beaches, construct promenades and map new trails. Even today, dozens of youth hostels and other shelters which sprang up during the 1930s remain dotted across Bavaria. Most prominent were Young People's Hostels, where older hikers were allowed to stay on condition they did not deprive teenagers of beds:

> Adults appreciate this form of accommodation, more especially the women, who are not annoyed by the fumes of stale tobacco and beer nor by the more unpleasant attendant phenomena provided by slightly tipsy or drunken clients. For smoking and alcohol are strictly forbidden in all these establishments at the insistence of the youth movement itself, which has participated so largely in the organization of the Young People's Hostels.[1]

Author F. S. Smythe, one of the most distinguished British mountaineers, recommended his readers avoid hotels and hostels, and put up for the night in 'some old post-inn':

> The traveller may have to sit on a wooden bench, but the wine is likely to be reasonable and the cooking good, the bed comfortable and the company excellent. He who travels, thus is no mere room number, he is a guest. He not only travels in the country, but enters into the spirit of the country.[2]

By the mid-1930s, KdF cooed that the idea of hiking in Germany was constantly gaining more adherents among workers. 'There is no doubt that a considerable further development in this sphere of the work of the National-Socialist Community "Kraft durch Freude" is to be expected in the course of the next few years.'[3]

One poetic guidebook paints a luscious picture of side valleys cutting their way into the mountains from Oberstdorf 'leading the hiker who is fond of nature into the heart of the Alpine world almost without any climbing, while the eye is surprised by constantly fresh and delightful pictures'.[4] Here, less practised climbers had a crack at scaling giants rising to 8,850 feet where green meadows, thickets and woods extend up as far as the snow-covered peaks. The longest funicular railway in the world (6,330 feet above sea level) ran up the Nebelhorn, making the peak accessible even to those who didn't want to climb on foot.

To encourage a love for the great outdoors among the public, particularly young people, films and books recounted the exploits German climbers shimmying up white walls of ice in the Alps or at Nanga Parbat, the fourth-highest peak in the world at 26,620 feet. Just as Everest was considered the 'hunting ground' of the British, Nanga Parbat became the special preserve of the Germans, referred to as the Himalayan 'mountain of death' because of the number of climbers who had lost their lives trying to scale it. A 1932 expedition managed to reach 23,000 feet, but blizzards and illness forced the majority of the party to abandon the climb and return to base. Another attempt in 1934 – bathed in the full glow of Goebbels' publicity – ended in disaster when nine climbers were killed after reaching 25,600 feet.

Although the KdF brand of hiking and climbing was hardly taxing by comparison, Bertram de Colonna's group at Riesengebirge on the Czech frontier did manage to ascend the Schneekoppe, a peak of 5,275 feet, just over 1,700 feet higher than Snowden.

> Here and there are mountain huts called *Bauden* where light refreshment is offered and a man in Tyrol costume plays a zither. The mountainside is dense with pine trees, while mountain sheep and other game abound. But we saw nothing of the latter, the animals no doubt disappearing into the thick woods on our approach.[5]

Like at other resorts, de Colonna spent the evenings with locals – dressed in traditional folk costumes – dancing and singing. 'We also sang songs in Silesian dialect but we had to be given the text beforehand otherwise even the Berliners wouldn't have managed it.'[6]

There is a wonderful account from a Scottish teenager who was lucky enough to join a KdF winter excursion by charabanc and alpine railway to the 5,970-foot Wendelstein, where his fellow travellers were all busy learning to ski. 'As it was snowing and very cold when the bus started, an anti-freezing mixture – consisting of salt and glycerine – was handed round to each passenger with which to clean the windows. Few bus companies are as thoughtful this for their passengers.' Similarly, an English tourist took a trip during the summer months in a large 100-horsepower Audi along with a honeymoon couple and a small group of German pensioners:

> We went to Mittenwald, stopping en route at a lakeside hotel at Walchensee for coffee. What a beautiful lake, it was absolutely still and was deep, deep green. With the high hills rising above all around it, it was truly magnificent and I think we may spend a holiday there. The route was beyond description: it has to be seen to be believed. Vast quantities of snow on the very majestic mountains to which we were quite close: and yet the heat was terrific – the leather of the car was like fire. The chauffer had to open the sides of the bonnet and he drove all day like that. Thank goodness it was an open car!7

According to the contemporary travel company MER's Automobile Travel Office, the picturesque and rugged beauty of Germany was made to be explored by car. With the promise of fresh air and sunlight, the Fröhlich family embarked on a ten-day road trip from Berlin down to the Rhineland, covering 1,200 miles in an Opel. 'It was a whirlwind tour,' Peter Fröhlich recounted. 'My father drove, my mother was the privileged passenger, and I was the historian.' From Berlin the family headed south-west through Wittenberg, then on to Leipzig and into Weimar, the city of Goethe and Schiller. Like most tourists, at Wartburg the family visited Luther's workroom, where he secretly translated the Bible into German.

> As we walked around the castle, we came upon the room where Luther had worked and where, legend tells us, he had thrown an

inkwell at the devil. There was a hole in the plaster at one wall about two feet long and wide and several inches deep, with touches of ink at its edges, which, the guide slyly confessed, he and his colleagues regularly renewed to make the visitors' impressions all the more memorable.[8]

The family encountered their first – and, astonishingly, only – show of anti-Semitism in a hamlet called Hahn. 'We were confronted with a large hand-lettered poster proclaiming to anyone who cared to know that Hahn was, and would remain, "clean" of Jews – *Hahn ist und bleibt judenrein*.'[9]

As expected, Hitler's massive boycott of Austria gave domestic tourism a much-needed shot in the arm. Carl Degener – the first German tour operator to offer 'trips for the little man' – abandoned Salzburg for the largely impoverished Bavarian village of Ruhpolding to where he packed off 700 tourists on a chartered Reichsbahn train.[10] More destinations including the steamboat excursions on the Rhine, seaside resorts like Straslund and the lush greenery of the Harz Mountains also featured in KdF brochures.

However, the antics of Austrian Nazis continued unabated as they continued to conduct acts of terrorism to discourage foreign visitors. 'Apparently, they now think that terrorist tactics will drive away the new source of revenue and bring Dr Dollfuss to his knees,' *The Truth* glumly observed. 'German psychology is obviously no better than it was in 1914.'[11] When Dollfuss was assassinated by Viennese Nazis on 25 July in a bungled coup attempt, the British public had little reason to restrain their hostility to Nazi Germany. 'I have been in Austria since June,' wrote a visitor from Scotland, struck by the emptiness of the hotels. 'Even at first, I could see, as every observant tourist must have seen, that Austria was not happy. Some of the hotel proprietors made extra efforts; some lost heart.'

Robert Ley's prolific fountain of ideas ensured that 1934 was a year of milestones for the KdF. From March, the organization's beneficence to blue- and white-collar workers also extended to offering cruises to England, Heligoland, the Isle of Wight and

Norway. Bodo Lafferentz cut a deal with Norddeutscher Lloyd and the Hamburg Süd to run the excursions at discount charter rates – KdF then shoehorned three times the capacity of passengers on board in an attempt to break even. To begin with, single cruises were squeezed in between the regular services upon which the vessel was engaged.

Although there were adventures to be had, sights to be seen and new friends to be made, not everything during those first trips won unqualified praise. In fact, many passengers were left distinctly unimpressed, especially those onboard the steamer *Stuttgart*. Not long into the jaunt it became clear that hot and cold water was only available in the first-class cabins whilst 'C-Deck' had no running water at all. To make matters worse, cramped sleeping quarters on *Der Deutsche* meant occupants of four-bed cabins wrestled to get dressed, forcing roommates to either scrunch up in bed or wait in the corridor.[12] On the *Oceana* – a vessel notorious for poor ventilation and plumbing – many cabins were occupied by six people, with some placed directly next to the engines, exposing occupants to the smell of diesel and exhaust gas.[13] Remarkably, despite the hiccups, all-inclusive cruises to Norway enjoyed phenomenal popularity as the *Guardian*'s correspondent discovered when he boarded a KdF steamer for a cruise around the fjords. 'It was chock-full from bow to stern,' he reported. 'The *S.S. Berlin* left the quay at Bremerhaven with the band playing amid scenes as lively as at any of its regular departures far Halifax and New York.'[14]

Priced at RM50, the trips were considered a bargain by the better-earning sections of the workforce.[15] 'Holidaymakers, not one in a hundred of whom had ever set foot in a liner before and many of whom had never seen one, prepared to settle down to their thrilling experience,' the *Guardian* reporter explained. 'They were given the complete run of the ship, with no barriers between the affluence of the first-class quarters, with their spacious dining-rooms, social hall, smoking rooms, verandas, and generous deck space'.[16] Thankfully, the view of various fjords from the deck was breathtaking as it was the closest passengers were able to get to land, as shore excursions were forbidden.[17]

To compensate, a specially produced KdF guidebook, *Norwegen Kleiner Schiffs-Reiseführer für KdF*, listed the passing attractions such as the Jaderen light tower and the medieval stone church in the village of Avaldsnes on the northern part of the island of Karmøy. Everyone noticed the climate was much milder than they had imagined, and at times too hot, especially in the more sheltered parts of the Hardanger Fjord, where passengers on the observation deck had a good view of fruit trees laden with cherries, pears and apples.

According to the itinerary, the ships sailed off the Norwegian coast on a course similar to that taken by Kaiser Wilhelm II's yacht *Hohenzollern*: 'Under Adolf Hitler, we are all emperors' was said to be a popular reaction.[18] Needless to say, thousands of postcards flooded home sharing different experiences from the invigorating 'Nordic' air, marvelling at daylight at midnight and the constant change of magnificent scenery.

Fjords were not enough to divert the gaze of security officers disguised as tourists who were busy keeping tabs on conversations and the mood onboard.[19] On the early cruises, DAF operatives monitored passengers, but they were eventually replaced by the Gestapo.[20] While most holidaymakers were not interested in politics,[21] disquieting reports of fights between passengers scuppered attempts to forge a *Volksgemeinschaft* atmosphere. This was especially upsetting given KdF excursion planners tried to integrate groups from different regions in the hope of eradicating the local differences.[22] Gestapo files are filled with details of culture clashes and tempers unfurled. On one cruise, four drunken Westphalians kicked off an argument with a group of Silesians in the smoking room of a KdF ship. As the sober Silesians tried to appease their tormentors, they were subjected to a tirade laced with bigoted language and dubbed 'Polaks' and 'Polish pigs'. The situation remained highly volatile when the Westphalians attempted to storm the Silesians' cabin later that night.[23] Another agent jotted down details of how Silesians and Bavarians would not sit at the same table and relations between Württemberg residents and Berliners was frosty. Furthermore, an agent noted, with a few exceptions, no engagement between people from Saalpfälz and Saxony emerged. A whole page was devoted to describing how a German-Austrian lady slapped an East Prussian woman because she made a sarcastic remark about the Austrian effort at a gymnastics class.[24]

Such close contact with fellow passengers proved difficult for many travellers, especially those prone to anxiety or claustrophobia. Journalist and author Bella Fromm recounted how her laundress took part in a KdF trip. 'Certainly, it was nice to see Norway,' she gushed, 'but I didn't have the feeling of rest.' In fact, she complained the entire journey provided no pleasant sense of leisure or forgetfulness.

> Not a moment to rest. Never alone. There is always someone around to monitor what you say and do. You don't get a chance to talk to a foreigner, you can't get a newspaper. And they never stop tossing in their propaganda maple. The journey was also quite exhausting. We were crammed into a third-class compartment. No, I like to travel alone.[25]

It wasn't all smooth sailing either. The KdF cruise ship *Dresden* was caught in a storm while sailing off the coast of Norway and struck a rock near Stavanger and sank. However, the fact that two women lost their lives didn't dampen enthusiasm and Lafferentz pressed ahead excitedly with his plans to expand the entire cruising department.[26]

The KdF cruises, in part, were very low-budget copies of existing Hamburg Süd trips which enticed 'young and old, manual and intellectual workers looking beyond the borders of Germany for the first time'. Their Monte class of ships were described as an embodiment of relaxation with comfortable cabins and airy, spacious dormitories; hot and cold water, warm sea baths (which alone do wonders for the nerves), bright dining rooms, writing and reading rooms, a library, music, dancing, plentiful food, shore excursions, and, according to the brochures, 'the assurance the entire ship's personnel was available to offer advice and assistance for the well-being of each and every passenger'.

In the December issue of the *Hamburg Süd Zeitschrift*, the company 'urgently advertised' special offers in an article entitled 'Sea voyages for everyone', which promised a practical basis on which the public, even those with a low income, could calculate and plan a trip. 'Travel on German ships is travel on German soil and benefits the German economy,' the company explained, before launching into a poetic description of the trips on offer.

> Experience mountain landscape in the middle of the ocean, and then return to the African shore to Casablanca. We are in close proximity to the mystery of the 'black continent', the glow of the desert, a breath from millennia-old history wafts around us. We can view sublime treasures at the sites of old Spanish horticultural art in the Alkazar gardens of Seville, then Lisbon and the Portuguese Riviera. At the end of June, Europe's southern peninsulas Spain, Italy and Greece open their most beautiful places: the Dalmatian shore, Palma de Mallorca, the Alhambra near Granada, to name just a few. In July and August, however, the Monte Rosa sets course north to the roaring waterfalls of Norway, to its fjords, and to the bright nights of the Arctic Circle, to the pristine ice world of Svalbard. Then the Monte Pascoal also steams to the beautiful fjords, but first to the coasts of Scotland, Ireland, and Copenhagen, and then in August and September seven trips to London, which have become a tradition. Sea voyages for everyone! Pleasure, recreation and tourist trips – everyone can plan it however he wants. Enrich one's knowledge and expand one's horizons, indulge the nerves with rest and relaxation, or, what is most beneficial for the body and mind, one of the two make a healthy mixture. The choice is wide enough. The colourful coasts of the morning and the west call, the colourful bazaars with a southern mixture of peoples, the British Isles and the land of the midnight sun call. The gates open to strange cities and to strange people.

The addition of pleasure cruises helped KdF expand at a rapid pace. In a conference of the Tourist Traffic Association held in Heidelberg, Ley forecast changes in the tourist industry which, he said, 'had to be subordinated to the great idea of KdF. National Socialism had replaced exclusiveness by the community.'[27]

However, he was quick to add that KdF was not intended to compete in any way with private tourist enterprises, but, on the contrary, was to 'strengthen it'. Hermann Esser, who was by then head of the Tourist Traffic Association, declared that the number of foreign visitors to Germany had increased in 1935 compared with 1934. 'It is probable that a large part of the increase (apart from the foreigners) is through the "Strength through Joy" holiday-makers.'[28]

For their part, private tourism concerns continued to be proactive. In an effort to further promote travel to suit 'every pocket', the head of the Hotel Proprietors' Association announced details of a scheme for fixed prices in hotels and the introduction of hotel vouchers. All hotels would be classed, according to the scheme, in seven price categories and vouchers would be available in tourist agencies, enabling foreign visitors to calculate in advance the cost of their holidays.

8

PRORA

Up at the Berghof, the public-spirited Hitler began to tire of tourists gawping and sought a little seclusion by fencing off his residence.¹ With the click of his fingers, the area was designated a 'Führer Protection Zone', meaning the public were forbidden from approaching and taking snaps, ending a great holiday tradition. Notoriously lazy, Hitler decreed Berchtesgaden the second seat of government, meaning he could run the country from the comfort of his adjustable recliner. 'Comment about the time the Reich's Chancellor spends at his mountain home, far from his three chancelleries and Reich ministries has been widespread,' *The New York Times* noted. 'Hitler's absences from Berlin, as a matter of fact, are of such long duration that his presence at the seat of government has become an event.'²

In the Nazi press, Hans Lammers, chief of the Reich's Chancellery, quoted Hitler as expressing how 'absolutely necessary' it was for him, 'as the one who guides the destinies of the German nation', to occasionally escape from the storm of questions, affairs of state, receptions and conferences and nerve-racking turmoil of Berlin to find repose and new strength in the 'pure and majestic' mountain scenery.

The Berghof in Obersalzberg is the place where the Führer, with the view of the mountain peak, soaring above everything petty and hurried and under God's starry sky at night, thinks out the decisive problems of the future of the German people and attains to that inner clarity which gives him the strength for his great decisions.

At these times too important affairs of state often demand rapid decisions, and thus even during his stays in Berchtesgaden the Führer cannot dispense with the assistance of the head of the Reich Chancellery. It was thus the Führer's wish that the head of the Reich Chancellery and those members of his staff whom he needed most should at these times also share the rest and the source of strength which the glorious scenery of Berchtesgaden has to offer. The new building of the Reich Chancellery in Berchtesgaden was erected for this purpose. As in former years, I shall continue in the future, together with some few members of my staff, to set up my official and private quarters there at such times as the Führer makes a long stay at the Berghof. As a rule this is the time from the middle of July till about the end of October, and a few weeks around the turn of the year.[3]

Hitler's secretary, Christa Schroeder, sighed that from then on Berghof life was excluded 'from everyday civilian and normal existence'.[4] A kitchen hand remembered how at 'every guard post we all had to go through the gates. By then the local farmers and peasants were long gone. Everything was bought up and levelled.'[5] Nazi voices even began to intrude on peaceful excursions into the countryside, recalled Irmgard Hunt, who grew up just steps from the Berghof. 'On returning from a boating trip on the Konigsee, our famed fjord-like lake, we ended a perfect day in the garden of an inn. As we waited for coffee, cake and hot chocolate, a voice began to blare from the radio out the window of the inn. Vati got up to listen to Dr Goebbels's speech – I don't know what is was about and the peace of the afternoon was shattered.'[6]

Despite increased security, many 'pilgrims' continued to gaze at the Berghof from afar. British journalist Leonard Mosley was greatly excited to spot Hitler during a ramble above Berchtesgaden. 'Sometimes he drives into the village with a few of his guests, with Doctor and Frau Goebbels, or Frau Göring and Frau von Ribbentrop, for instance, or with one or two of his foreign guests, like Miss Unity Mitford or the American dancer Miss Miriam Verne.'

Robert Ley arrived at the Berghof that summer clutching crudely drawn plans for a very different vacation experience. Fascinated by new British holiday camps, which were very much in vogue, he excitedly told the Führer about his vision for the world's largest resort amid the sand dunes at Prora on the Baltic island of Rügen. Whatever Hitler might have thought about this revolutionary concept, he put up the appearance of having endorsed it wholeheartedly despite functionality being placed above architecture.

With that blessing, architect Clemens Klotz – a lofty, almost aristocratic character – set to work. 'When the visitor arrives at the resort,' Ley told Klotz, 'he must forget the past immediately. I want to construct it in such a way that he enters into a bustle of music, dance and theatre that takes his breath away so that he forgets himself.'[7] Stunned by the proposed size of the project, 12,000 people gathered to witness the ground-breaking in May 1936, when, resplendent in a seaweed-green uniform and silk gloves, Ley bragged that 'this huge facility would be unique in the world'[8] and was the first leap toward new resorts at Kolberg in East Prussia and at Timmendorf Beach:[9]

> Up until now you needed seven days just to get adjusted to vacation time and to get in touch with other people. And during the last seven days you already had to get used again to the worries of everyday life. That must be stopped. Starting with the first hour, the vacationer must be submerged in an intoxicating environment [and it must last] up to the very last second, when he climbs back onto his train to go home. This is also the wish of the Führer, and so we want to construct this beach resort with these leisure principles in mind: a theater, a movie, evening shows, music, dance, locales and so on.[10]

The key to enjoying regimented cheerfulness was community spirit. Day-to-day activities would be strictly organised, whereby mealtimes, the itinerary and even bathing suits (provided by the KdF) would have been uniform for all vacationers. Each day would start at 07.00 with a roll-call accompanied by stirring brass over the loudspeaker system. Occasionally, coaches would run inland to tour surrounding beauty spots.

'These holiday places, where hundreds of thousands of people could be gathered together, were designed to serve the basic concept of Lebensraum in its internal dimension through control and discipline even during leisure time and in its external dimension by strengthening the nerves and preparing physically for the war that was planned,' says Jurgen Rostock, who wrote a study of the resort in the 1990s. At Prora – which would operate from early spring to late autumn – Nazi planners envisioned a main complex of 10,000 rooms, along with theatres, meeting halls, sports facilities, parade grounds, swimming pools and myriad other draws. With 3,000 people expected to check in and out of the complex daily, it was the perfect example of Robert Ley's megalomania. Over time, the plans became even more grand. A vast public area was to be created in the centre of the complex along with a marble-lobbied reception, and on the personal order of the Führer a hulking concert hall with frescoed ceilings designed by architect Erich Putlitz would accommodate 20,000 people. However, in the event, plans changed and the idea was abandoned.

After months of fevered activity, the cost was pushed higher by the addition of a waterworks, an electrical substation, warehousing, a small farm for fresh produce and a 300-room workers' apartment building. A dock for passenger ships was also planned, as it was assumed that some vacationers would arrive via sea, unload at the pier and register at the reception.

By the summer of 1936, Prora had turned into a roaring construction site where 9,000 labourers ploughed up a 7-kilometre strip of coast. Slowly, the shell of city rose from the sands. At the same time, Ley's dream of building a camp at Kolberg was abandoned after district leader Anton Gerriets resolutely opposed the idea of 'cheap flask and sandwich' tourists swarming into town.[11] There were also complaints that the camp would adversely affect smaller hotels, boarding houses and lodging houses. Such ill-thought-out plans led to bad feeling. Looking back on the situation, Albert Speer thought Ley was unable to communicate his wishes. 'Without doubt, Ley was an idealist at heart, who did all he could to improve the position of the worker,' Speer conceded. 'His ideas were confused and he was anything but a planner. He completely lost his perspective in anything that he undertook.'[12] Speer remembered Ley's nature often drove his subordinates to distraction or to despair:

> His desire to improve the lot of the workers had been secondary to his ambition to immortalise himself creating great schemes. Ley had no idea of financial matters and his own people were horrified by his opinions and methods.
>
> Although he launched many schemes which might ultimately have benefited the workers, he never realised that it was the execution of these schemes which required by far the greatest effort. Before carrying out one idea, he would already take up a new one and start promoting it. He thought up something new every other month and would lose interest in his earlier projects. This applies to Strength through Joy, his housing programmes, and all his other schemes.[13]

Alfred Rosenberg went further. 'Everything that was concerned with paid vacations, the office of Travelling and Hiking, the modernisation of industrial buildings, the providing of cultural goods, and so on, represented the beginning of social theory being translated into practice,' he recorded in his memoirs.[14] 'But Ley placed two obstacles in his own path: organisational schematization and gigantomania.'

By 1938, construction costs at Prora had reached RM237.5 million but the resort was, at least, partially completed. An uninspiring array of concrete apartment blocks – stretching a truly colossal 2.5 miles – arched along the beachfront, separated by a wooded dune typical of the Baltic states. Plumbing, heating and windows had still to be installed, as did the modest furnishings of two comfortable beds (with enough blankets to protect against the freezing breezes blowing in from the Baltic Sea), a writing desk, a cupboard and a wash basin. All guest rooms were also to have speakers installed. White-tiled toilets and showers in the stairwells on the landward side had a surgical cleanliness. Towels would be provided, and each room was to be cleaned and the bed made every morning. Party officials touted that a weekly vacation would cost RM20. From his airy office, Ley planned everything to the smallest detail. A final touch came with plans for a special railway ending at the foot of the resort.

Across Germany, the progress of the project could be heard in the unrelenting thrum in the press and the *Deutsche Wochenschau* weekly newsreel. Already incensed by the Prora project, Alfred Rosenberg gave a chilly response:

> Ley went completely haywire when he began constructing – on the island of Rügen, of all places! – A spa for twenty thousand. Giessler (one of Hitler's favourite architects) complained bitterly when, in my consternation, I questioned him. I told him that in attempting to give workers and employees a short respite from the pressure of the city, Ley was now driving them into a still worse crush of people. On Rügen, no less, where this noisy horde of twenty thousand would spill over into all the other spas. Giessler pointed out the technical impossibilities. The new spa, he said, would actually have to put up its own slaughterhouse. Since water wasn't available in sufficient quantities on the island itself, a huge pipeline to the mainland would also have to be laid, and so on. But Ley kept on proudly publishing pictures of the vast halls, the dance pavilion, and so on. Here a sound social idea became utter nonsense in reality.

9

LURING THE BRITISH

In an increasingly familiar pattern, Robert Ley's analysis of the Travel, Hiking and Holiday Department's achievements veered into the grandiose:

> Thus the total number of Kraft durch Freude travellers in the last three year, was considerably greater than the total population of Scandinavia, taking Norway and Sweden together. If the eleven million Kraft Durch Freude travellers joined hands the line would stretch from Berlin to Tokyo. In the course of their cruises, our ships have already covered twice the distance from the earth to the moon. The total distance covered by the Kraft durch Freude trains in 1936 was 1,350,000 miles, or fifty-four times the circumference of the earth. One of the most popular travel districts is the Rhine whose banks are crowned with numerous castles. Every German worker is now able to spend his holiday on the Rhine; no less than 400,000 of our fellow countrymen from all parts of Germany were there in the course of this year alone, and made unforgettable trips on this German river in the finest steamers.[1]

The year 1935 was certainly a highpoint for both foreign and domestic tourism. For the British, the siren voice of Germany continued to call persuasively and successfully. Travel writer

C. Wye-Kendall thought the German a 'past master in the art of making people welcome for which he has a special word: *gastfreundschaft*'.

> Now of course one does not go to Germany to be merely flattered and petted and well-fed. One goes there to feast the eyes as well as the body. Here, again, Fritz provides sumptuous fare; or rather nature does with his assistance.

Anticipating a bumper season in 1935, the German Embassy in London sent a circular warning they were 'literally overflowing' with travel inquiries during July. The Reichsbahn geared up for an unusually large influx of English travellers, as did the Norddeutscher Lloyd and Hapag shipping lines, which, the circular noted, 'had completely sold out on the routes from London to Hamburg and Bremen'. Local air travel and planned car journeys also exceeded anything previously experienced:

> It is, of course, urgently in our interest that these English citizens streaming to Germany return from their trip with favourable impressions ... How much it is in the German interest that travellers keep their new preference for Germany and not revert to their previous preference for France. I am also convinced that favourable travel impressions of this kind will have the best possible effect on the further shaping of the British mood towards Germany.[2]

Berlin agreed with this assessment. In a confidential memo, the Propaganda Ministry instructed district administrators to advise all mayors and community leaders of the Führer's 'express wish' that foreign travellers, especially the English, would be shown every courtesy during their holidays.[3]

During the whirlwind of preparations, curbs on tacky souvenirs, including 'silly hats', crass postcards and whistles were introduced as the Reich Chamber of Fine Arts believed such items 'defaced the landscape'. In St Goarshausen, on the eastern shore of the Rhine, the mayor mustered business owners, who, without exception, agreed to sell only 'tastefully perfect' souvenirs.

Despite the delicate subject matter, the issue of the 'Heil Hitler' greeting was also discussed by the President of the Reich Committee on Foreign Tourism. Guidelines laid down how the greeting should be used in both oral and written communication: Letters to Germans in foreign countries should be signed 'Heil Hitler' and to foreigners with 'respectfully'. When speaking to foreigners, they should always be greeted with 'Heil Hitler', with one exception if a foreigner greets in the language of his country. Then it was recommended, 'for reasons of international courtesy', to return the greeting in this language 'as far as the individual employee in the tourism department is able to do so'.[4] The greeting was the subject of some mirth (and occasional discomfort) among British and American holidaymakers, as a journalist from the *Penistone, Stocksbridge and Hoyland Express* found out during his Bavarian holiday:

> About this 'Heil Hitler' business. There is an impression that foreigners who do not acknowledge the salute in public places are subjected to incivility. I can state definitely that such is not the case. Not once during our stay in Germany did we perform the ritual, and on no occasion were we challenged or accorded 'black looks', though there were occasions when we must necessarily have appeared conspicuous in keeping our hands down. We felt it was not incumbent upon us to observe this ceremonial. There was, however, just one occasion when our refusal to acknowledge the national greeting might have appeared a trifle churlish. We had been out to a village where world-famous wines are produced. Having been conducted into the 'cellars cool', we returned to the village inn, where the landlord, who also was the burgermeister, received us into friendly company and gave us a jolly time. He was 'hundred per cent Hitler'. At last the time came to catch our train back to town. The burgermeister (now red-faced and jolly) stood forth. 'Before you go,' he said, 'let's all "Heil Hitler".' Such a call was not to be resisted. The company rose as one man to offer the greeting. The two of us declined it, but uttered a respectful

'Good-night, and thank you.' Honestly, we felt just a trifle shame-faced as we backed out of the door. However, our good friends at the hostelry showed not the slightest displeasure or resentment.[5]

Professor Alexander Gray of Aberdeen University thought the greeting was already beginning to peter out in the Moselle Valley, where he spent a summer vacation. 'Last year it was "Heil Hitler" everywhere, with most effective formula, clicking heels, holding the hand out rigidly, and shouting out in a voice that showed they were not ashamed of themselves. This year they made an apologetic sign with the hand that might be anything.'[6]

Throughout 1935, Thomas Cook promoted fortnightly departures crisscrossing through an ever-changing panorama of scenery: 'Every year, every seat on Cook's Grand Tour of Germany was sold in less than a month after the first announcement,' the company boasted. '2,000 seats gone in less than four weeks! 2,200 miles of travel, good hotels, sight-seeing at all places – 15 days for £23, which covers sightseeing and all necessary expenses.'[7] For those looking for cheaper options, operators like Glenton Coach Tours offered seven-day breaks priced at £8 inclusive. The obvious desire to travel to Germany prompted author Sydney A. Clark to write *Germany on Ten Pounds*, which asserted that with a little care and forethought everybody could enjoy Germany cheaply and provided a 'few secrets that will save you trouble and money':

SIX MARKS A DAY

At the present rate of exchange your £10 will bring you in the region of 120 marks. Half we allot to meals and hotels and the rest to travelling. This should give us ten days in Germany. Germany is one of the cleanest countries in the world, and so the traveller need have no fear of humble hotels and lodging-houses. Two marks or two and a half at the most, will find a good night's lodging in any German city except Berlin. Six marks a day should be our allowance for room and meals. In general, hostelries marked 'Pension' are cheaper, than those marked 'Hotel' – and in Germany a pension does not mean a place where you must stay five days and must take meals. Better still is the sign 'Logis' which merely means lodging, and in many of these places you will get a palatial room for one and a half marks.

BEWILDERING MENU

A word about food. Many restaurants in every city offer a meal for one mark or less, and these are where we must eat during the day. The German menu is at first a trifle bewildering, and so it is necessary to know a few of the German words. *Schwein* means pig, and combinations of the word mean pork in some form. Similarly, *Kalb* means calf (*Kalbsbraten* – roast veal), *Rind* means beef, *Schinken* means ham, and *Huhn* means chicken. Now we are ready to be off.

For British motorists, the excitingly new autobahn network inspired wanderlust. 'Norway and Sweden are both very popular, but many people are going to Germany,' an official of the Automobile Association explained. 'People have heard so much of Germany that they want to see conditions themselves, and those who have already been are satisfied and delighted with their experiences.'[8] Just days after the Nazi takeover, Hitler enthusiastically embraced an ambitious autobahn construction project, appointing Fritz Todt, the Inspector General of German Road Construction, to lead it. Since then, motorways had been ruthlessly driven through the countryside, meaning insuperable difficulties had to be overcome. In some areas – notably Saxony and Bavaria – countless valleys were bridged and tunnels burrowed, but nothing, it seems, daunted engineers.

To shorten his own journey to Berchtesgaden, Hitler pushed for the speedy completion of the Munich–Salzburg autobahn, which cut through lush forest, farmland and majestic snow-capped mountains. Taking pains not to destroy scenic beauty on any stretch of the project, the Führer oversaw plans for a service area on the banks of Lake Chiemsee including a hotel and a restaurant designed in rustic Bavarian style, along with a terrace and jetty for swimmers. (The Autobahn development company GezuVoR claimed Hitler was the originator of the entire route.) Although plans for motorways had already been worked out in the 1920s, Hitler adopted the guise of inventor of the autobahn, a myth expanded by Goebbels, Todt and the poet Herybert Menzel, who claimed that whilst in prison in 1923 Hitler had 'opened the map of our fatherland on his knees' and personally devised the whole network.

Travel brochures also sought to portray Hitler as 'architect of the Reich' and an enthusiastic admirer of architecture. The Reichsbahnzentrale's *Welcome to Germany* pamphlet went further, describing him as having given 'Germany an architectural style of its own', a simple and monumental grandeur already recognised in Munich, Nuremburg and Berlin. 'They are true buildings of community ... new German architecture is a service to the entire nation and many of these gigantic buildings have been erected by State contracts as indestructible evidence of the new German will to reconstruction.'[9]

For the cameras, at least, Hitler styled himself as the first construction worker. Clutching a spade, he personally broke the ground of the Frankfurt motorway in September 1933, an occasion Fritz Todt later mythologised:

> The guests of honour here were given somewhat short shrift since the real guests of honour were the workers themselves. The Führer spoke these words: 'Today we stand at the beginning of a mighty task. Its significance will not only be for the German traffic system, but in the broadest sense in later decades, its greatest worth will be seen in the German economy itself. In decades to come people will see that communication will be dependent upon these new great highways that we will build throughout the whole of Germany ... I know that this festive day makes us forget that the time will come when rain, frost and snow will make work for the individual worker sour and difficult. But it is imperative that the work be done. No one helps us if we do not help ourselves.'

Commenting on Hitler's efforts to get stuck in, *Die Strasse*, a Nazi building journal, opined that Hitler's shovelling was 'not a symbolic ground-breaking ceremony, it was real earthwork' and highlighted 'the first drops of sweat' from the Führer's brow (he filled a whole wheelbarrow with mud).

By the mid-1930s, over 120,000 workers were directly employed in construction, as well as an additional 270,000 in the supply chain for construction equipment, steel, concrete and maintenance equipment. In rural areas, new camps to house the workers were built near construction sites. In an effort to keep road workers entertained, a KdF travelling theatre company burst into life at a barracks of 150 men in Frankfurt an der Oder during the winter of 1935. Full of noble purpose, this Reichsautobahnbuhne ensemble presented a wide range of drama, variety and vaudeville. In one of the first shows, actors raised the curtain on *Krach um Jolanthe*, a lowbrow comedy about the excitement in the country when a sheriff tries to collect a tax on a prize pig. 'Stormy applause and resounding laughter alternate with expectant silence,' wrote H. Bauer in *Arbeitertum* in a double-paged feature plastered with photos of contented labourers lapping up the performance. In a postscript, Bauer wished the road workers 'accomplish their great task – the men of the streets of Adolf Hitler give new strength through true joy'.

Travelling in a red coach (the KdF Theatre-Wagen), the ensemble motored on to Bad Württemberg and Bavaria and all stops between.[10] The theatre performances were followed up by the KdF's Sonderaction fur Reichsautobahnen, which provided books, film shows and sports courses to road workers at 600 camps across Germany. 'A far-reaching system of libraries brought good books to people in even in the most remote corners of Germany,' the KdF boasted. By 1936, about 200 travelling libraries of 250 volumes apiece were at the disposal of the autobahn workers, training ships and local offices of the DAF.[11]

The sheer number of official events during the autobahn construction project was mind-boggling. Celebrations honoured almost every completed stretch of road, viaduct, service station or bridge. The project was marketed everywhere – in paintings, highway poetry, novels, board games and images on postage stamps. Jewish diarist Victor Klemperer – a former professor, forcibly retired by the Nazis, and swindled of most of his pension – found himself on the new autobahn from Wilsdruff to Dresden, less than an hour after it was opened.

> There were still flags and flowers from the ceremony in the morning, a mass of cars moved slowly forward at a sightseeing pace, only occasionally did anyone attempt a greater speed. This straight road, consisting of four broad lanes, each direction separated by a strip of grass, is magnificent. And bridges for people to cross over it. Spectators crowded onto these bridges and the sides of the road. A procession. And a glorious view as we were driving straight toward the Elbe and the Lössnitz Hills in the evening sun. We drove the whole stretch and back again (two times 7½ miles), and twice I risked a speed of 50 mph. A great pleasure, but what a luxury, and how much sand in the eyes of the people.[12]

The reverend James Duncan was one of the first foreign tourists to rush along the new road 'like the wind at eighty miles an hour'. 'When finished, these highways will rank among the best in the world,' he marvelled. 'Wide enough to permit one-way traffic in either direction, the surface is hard and smooth. It is forbidden to pedestrians, and with minimum risk of accident there is little need for the usual police and signal precautions.'[13] Nora Waln described the autobahns as things of beauty, exciting in their charm:

> They are not ugly scars across their land ... Then one comes on them – silver ribbons. No telegraph poles, advertisements, rows of refreshment stands, gasoline stations, or ugly houses line their banks. Grass strips separate the two ways of traffic, and these often divide round hills to meet and run side by side again. The roadsides are planted with shrubs and trees natural to the district; the bridges harmonise with the valleys they transverse.[14]

Although the autobahns formed the first limited-access, high-speed road network in the world, traffic was generally thin, except for peaks at Easter and Whit Monday. Professor Alexander Gray was astounded to clock only six cars on the road during an entire Sunday during a daytrip to the Moselle Valley. 'There were

Luring the British

also no bus services, whereas at a corresponding place in this country, there would twenty-minute bus services.'[15]

Hitler – himself a motor enthusiast – was determined to pull the country from the Old World by making 4 million Germans car owners by developing a new Volkswagen, or 'people's car', designed to his personal specifications. This was no mean feat given there were only 1.1 million cars in Germany at the time, equating to 1.6 cars per 100 inhabitants, lagging far behind the UK, France and USA.[16] Although compact, the people's car would have a top speed of 50 mph and clock at least 40 miles to the gallon, but affordability was the key considering the scale of the plan. With that in mind, Hitler demanded the price for the vehicle must be capped at RM1,000, well below the production cost.

After a year at the drawing board, a black, two-door prototype was completed in 1935 by designer Ferdinand Porsche, a slim and serious man who imbued the model with comfort, convenience and style. To gauge ideas for cheap production, he visited the Ford Motor plant in Detroit to discover first-hand how assembly lines worked. Understandably given the slim profit margins, private industry expressed scant interest in the project; Robert Ley, however, was very much interested, which Hitler saw as a deeply significant development. 'Originally the project was to be taken on as a joint scheme by the automobile industry,' Albert Speer recalled. 'They wasted a lot of time without getting anywhere, until Hitler finally became very impatient. The project was then taken over by Ley in his typical manner, without giving any thought to the financial problem.' The comment isn't entirely fair, as Ley saw his immediate task clearly: the KdF would oversee the initial capitalisation make a 'cast iron promise' to the people of Germany that for just 5 Reichsmarks per week – paid to the KdF – every family could fulfil the dream of car ownership by 1941.

There was no upper limit to the deposits, and larger down payments could also be made. However, the purchase of a KdF-Wagen for cash, without entry into the stamp-collection system, was forbidden. The car would be insured for a period of two years on delivery. Colours available for the first batches were dark blue or grey (customers had no choice).

Unsurprisingly, the offer – backed by a huge advertising campaign – brought in cash from all directions, and by the end of the decade over RM280 million had been collected for future car deliveries, with at least 300,000 people having made the full down payment. Soon after, a vast ultramodern complex at Wolfsburg – known as the Stadt des Kraft durch Freude-wagens ('town of the Strength Through Joy cars') – was built on a barren stretch of riverside and quickly became one of the biggest industrial sites in Europe. At the ground-breaking, Ley promised Germans would race toward new frontiers, powered by a seemingly limitless number of home-built cars. Fuelling a future vision for a new motoring class and nationwide driving holidays, the public were promised no fewer than 1.5 million cars would be roll off the assembly line in 1946 when full production capacity was reached.

During the development stage, the new 'people's car' could be seen whizzing smoothly along the famed Avus in Berlin – the site of the German Grand Prix of 1926 – which held the record as the fastest racetrack in the world. The course featured prominently in *Beautiful Berlin*, a brochure published in German, English and French. The blurb – which describes Berlin as a city 'set in emeralds' – is so enthusiastic that it came very close to self-parody:

> It is a city of order, cleanliness and hospitality. Within the first year of Adolf Hitler's dispensation, more than a million visitors came to see the historical and cultural sights, the lakes, woods and richly-varied surroundings of the largest city on the Continent. These pages contain only a selection out of the ample treasury of well-known buildings, pictures of the metropolis and landscapes of interest to visitors, an invitation for those who are as yet not acquainted with Berlin, a souvenir for those who already know and love Germany's Capital City.[17]

Prior to the arrival of the Nazi administration, Berlin thrived as Europe's epicentre of gay tourism with over 150 entertainment venues catering for the homosexual and lesbian scene alone.

Luring the British

'Berlin meant boys,' wrote Christopher Isherwood, the British writer who arrived in the city to devour the nightlife. Paris, he opined, monopolised the 'straight girl' market, while Berlin offered visitors a host of alternatives, undisturbed by the police. Soon after the First World War, an extensive gay community took shape in the streets, pubs, saloons and nightclubs of Berlin. Gay writers, actors and journalists produced distinctive literature which was widely available and included the magazines *Die Freundschaft* (Friendship), *Die Freundin* (The Girlfriends), *Frauenliebe* (Women's Love), and *Das dritte Geschlecht* (The Third Sex) for transvestites and transsexuals.

Thomas Cuthbert Worsley, the well-known British theatre critic, was astounded to hear about the delights Germany could offer a gay man. 'How shallow my sophistication may be judged from my surprise, my positive disbelief, when a junior colleague who knew of my inclinations told me there were places in Germany where boys offered their services for a modest sum,' he recounted. 'Male tarts? Were there really such things? Was it conceivable?'

Indeed, it was. Americans, British, Scandinavians and Russians lapped up Berlin's sex culture at venues like Gertrude Stein's saloon, Kliest Diele and Cosy Corner – notorious for opportunistic sex and male prostitution. Public cross-dressing and riotous (and in some cases seedy) nightlife, filled with transvestites, hustlers and exhibitionists, also attracted the curious onlooker. At the Resi nightclub near the Berlin Zoo, a venue popular with foreign visitors, customers could call each other on special pneumatic tabletop telephones. The only rule, according to Marlene Dietrich's biographer, Charles Higham, was that 'if a man beckoned a pretty girl, she must prove when she came to his table that she really had breasts. Often, the unwary male could find himself caressing the leg of a well-known athlete dressed in convincing drag!'[18]

During the height of hyperinflation in the mid-1920s, Klaus Mann had his first unforgettable encounter with male prostitutes on the corner of Kurfürstendamm. 'Some of them looked like fierce Amazons, strutting in high boots made of green, glossy leather,' he recalled with a hoot.

Holidays with Hitler

One of them brandished a supple cane and leered at me as I passed by. 'Good evening, madam,' I said. So, she whispered into my ear: 'Want to be my slave? Costs only six billion and a cigarette. A bargain.'

There were cheaper options. For those seeking brief, intimate encounters, the Tiergarten, public swimming baths and rail terminals provided places for a 'quickie'. Public urinals, known as 'Café Achteck' (Octagon) due to their unusual shape, became a common hook-up point. Djuna Barnes, the American illustrator and writer, enjoyed an unforgettable holiday in a 'flourishing gay world' but made some sobering observations:

> It was very nice, things so cheap for us that you felt almost ashamed to be there. Full of buggers from America who bought boys cheap.

In 1928, a lesbian travel guide recommended twelve venues, all located in the hotspot of Schöneberg, including the popular dance bar Dorian Gray – a favourite haunt of Marlene Dietrich. There was also the legendary Eldorado, famed for its stunning female impersonators, drag balls and nightly dance parties, which achieved fame far beyond the borders of Germany.

However, in 1933, the Nazis declared war on homosexuals under a new policy of 'national moral renewal'. The degree to which gay men had to fear arrest remains almost impossible to understand today. By March, fourteen bars were closed as the Nazis sought to destroy the organisational structure of the gay scene by banning gay newspapers and surveillance of gay meetings. As police sallied forth into battle, the owner of the Eldorado pre-empted pressure and closed down. (Ironically, the building was afterwards used as a Nazi election campaign centre.) Berlin residents were also encouraged to report homosexual activity to the authorities. 'Hediwig R', a Berlin housewife, lost no time in contacting the local Gestapo to outline details of her 'suspicious' neighbour:

We've been living in the house for 12 years and he has never once been out with a girl (...) Of course I can't claim anything, but it seems suspicious to me. What are those lads doing at his place? But I'd like to ask you not to mention my name.[19]

Not surprisingly, some gay men were already beginning to plan their escapes from Germany. One of them was Paul Wendel, a well-known singer on the Berlin cabaret circuit. Because of his sexuality, Wendel had been subjected to a stage ban and fled to Vienna in 1933 and then moved onto Prague in 1938. There, he was arrested during the Nazi takeover and in 1939, after internment at various locations, transferred to Sachsenhausen concentration camp as a 'homosexual' in May 1940, whereupon he was sent to the isolation section. Soon after Wendel was found hanged; he was one of many prisoners murdered by local guards on the orders of the camp leaders.[20]

In *Goodbye to Berlin*, Christopher Isherwood wrote of the city as having two centres – one of expensive hotels, pubs, cinemas and shops round the Kaiser Wilhelm Memorial Church, 'a sparkling nucleus of light, like a sham diamond, in the shabby twilight of the town', and the other the 'self-conscious civic centre of buildings round the Unter den Linden'. But the real heart of Berlin, Isherwood thought, was the Tiergarten, 'a small damp black wood' where peasant boys 'cower on benches, to starve and freeze'.

For most people, however, the Tiergarten's sleepy rhythm made it a place for leisure set in acres of flowerbeds, lakes and oak trees dense enough to keep perpetual twilight on the paths below. Thousands ate Sunday and holiday lunches on the velvet lawns, which even today remain among the largest urban gardens in Germany, rich in animal life; brush rabbit, squirrel, grey fox, rats, mice and moles are all common. Robert Walser, the Swiss-born author known for 'prose pieces' that became his hallmark, thought the Tiergarten was like a painted picture or agreeable kiss. 'What's the crowd like here?' he pondered in his novel *Berlin Stories*. 'Well, it's a mixed bag, all sorts of people tumbled in together, the elegant and the simple, the proud and the humble, the gay and the grim. What resident of Berlin could fail to adore it?'

Nature lovers could also take the subway to Dahlem, where within the confines of the Botanischer Garten more than 10,000 kinds of plants and flowers blossomed. For 50 pfennig, day-trippers could see carnivorous plants, a cactus pavilion, giant white water lilies, a perfumed garden, and tropical plants like the giant bamboo. The botanical garden achieved some extraordinary feats, among them discovering the horticultural curiosity of growing cactus in glass bottles, setting off a domestic 'cactus craze' in Britain during the Edwardian era.

During the long dry summers, most visitors found time for a splash at Wannsee beach in the forests west of the capital. Offering fresh air and nature, it served a release valve for all of Berlin. When the steel-jawed turnstile bell sounded at nine o'clock the waterfront suddenly sprang to life; old men peddled hot sausages, candy and fruits from pushcarts as a river of humanity splashed in the largest inland lido in Europe. 'There they sit in family groups,' a British visitor prissily observed, 'with no more than a few bathing slips between them, burning themselves to the semblance of Indians, each with a sandwich in one hand and a glass of beer or lemonade in the other.'

A year after Wannsee opened in 1907, engineers displayed boundless ingenuity by installing over 200 tons of white Baltic sand and seashells from Lubeck onto its shore. At the same time, a fence was built around the beach to protect bathers from the eyes of curious (or indignant) onlookers. In the beginning, supporters argued there was nothing immoral or indecent about sunbathing; on the contrary, they said, it promoted cleanliness, purity and health. However, 'Police Ordinance Concerning the Wannsee Swimming Pool', dated 24 July 1909, stated men must wear long trunks while women bore the lion's share of physical restrictions by being required to cover their shoulders, chest, body and legs up to the knee. Despite such square-toed attitudes, over a million guests thronged into Wannsee annually by the mid-1930s to enjoy the new promenade, shops and restaurants. As time went on, bathers grew more liberated and ignored regulations, despite a campaign of anonymous letters to councillors. 'Berlin's great open-air swimming bath just about took away my breath,' were the words of an astonished British columnist after the exposure to beer and raw flesh. He went on:

> I had read about it; but nothing I had read made any impression upon me comparable with the impression made by the bath itself. I found it difficult to realise that it was actual and usual. On a Sunday or holiday, when the weather is fine, the crowds in the trains remind me of a crush in the London tube on a Cup-tie day. Bathing takes place on the sands of a beach about half a mile long. It is a remarkable stretch of sand to find on the side of a lake.
>
> There is an upper and a lower promenade, and they must be about a quarter of a mile long. You step from the lower promenade right on to the beach. Everybody mingles on the lower promenade – girls in red, blue, and other fancy bathing costumes, a few wearing dressing gowns; girls in yellow pyjamas selling chocolate; men in pants or bathing costumes, mostly only in pants; spectators like me merely looking on.[21]

Over time, rowdy young men lowered the already tarnished tone as they displayed their political views, in some cases by sewing badges on their bathing trunks. As day merged into night, ideological disputes often turned into fistfights and, in 1933, the Nazis succeeded in discrediting lido manager Hermann Clajus, a known anti-fascist who, distraught at the possibility of losing his dream job for his views, committed suicide when dismissal loomed.[22]

However, with so many Germans finding the summer heat almost intolerable (temperatures can reach above 35°C) similar inland lidos sprang up from Bavaria to the Baltic. Cologne municipality was especially proud of its fully tiled effort, which boasted a sundeck overlooking the Rhine. Clad in summer whites, student John F. Kennedy, the future US President who once opined that 'fascism was right for Germany', was certainly impressed during his Rhineland sojourn:

> Very beautiful, because there are many castles along the route .... The towns are all charming, which shows that the Nordic races appear to be definitely superior to their Latin counterparts. The

Holidays with Hitler

Germans are really too good – that's why people conspire against them – they do it to protect themselves.

So far as is known, local authorities complied with earlier directives to aggressively ensure tourists left with a positive image. A Cologne municipal report specifically urged 'understanding between foreign guests and our national comrades' while simultaneously encouraging school kids, Hitler Youth members, SA and SS men to pose for photos with holidaymakers.[23]

However, despite their best efforts, some aspects of life proved unpalatable for guests, including 'Mrs Jackson' of Golders Green. During her Cologne vacation, she was horrified to spot 'great banners' urging citizens to boycott Jewish shops. 'That seemed very cruel; in fact, this Jewish persecution is one aspect which annoys us,' she recorded, adding she had not encountered a single Jew during her holiday.[24] 'Now there's no use saying that we just didn't happen to notice them,' she explained, 'we were actively looking for them – and it's no use saying we don't know a Jew when we see one! But the fact remains we saw none.' Thankfully, there were some cheerier moments, such as an encounter with a group girls from Bund Deutscher Madel (the girls' wing of the Hitler Youth) during a Rhine river cruise: 'Soon we had made friends with a big crowd of Rhinelanders,' Jackson recounted. 'How very pleased they were to talk in English with people! The atmosphere was so jolly, everybody was singing and laughing and a great deal of conviviality all around.'[25]

That same summer, reporter, John Feardon toured Hamburg where he spied a converted galleon serving as a hostel for Scouts and Bund Deutscher Madel members. 'They hike and cycle from all parts of the country to this holiday ship and the cost is only two shillings a week.' Although his reports were largely positive, Feardon was 'naturally warned not to say in public anything derogatory about Herr Hitler'.[26] The Revd Lionel G. Meade was not shy in speaking out; on returning from Bavaria he lamented that the 'total absence' of spiritual life among Germans was hideous. 'Here was a complete lack of any sense the need of prayer,' he grumbled. 'The sole preparation of the maintenance of peace was drilling and the piling of armaments.'[27]

Likewise, J. G. Burnett, a correspondent to the *Aberdeen Press and Journal*, endured a difficult vacation in Garmisch. 'One rainy evening,' he grimly noted, the film *Victims of the Past* – a type of cinematic brainwashing for the local population – was screened to tourists. 'Its subject,' he winced, 'was the problem of hereditary disease, for which special methods of segregation and sterilisation are being adopted.'[28] (It was not uncommon for Nazi race theories to be propagandised in motion pictures.)

10

SOARING ABOVE: AVIATION

Small-time actress Emmy Sonnemann's encounters with the German public culminated in her engagement to Hermann Göring. Having bid farewell to the theatre, she set wheels in motion for a majestic wedding to be held in the summer of 1935. However, unexpectedly and in contradiction of Nazi policy, the couple arranged a Lutheran ceremony officiated by Reich Bishop Muller, an unusual move given that Nazi attacks on the Christian faith and ecclesiastical institutions had become par for the course.

Since taking power, as well as attempting to popularise pagan rituals Hitler had steadily increased his grip upon religious institutions by outlawing Jehovah's Witnesses and the Baha'i faith, while the fate of Judaism needs no explanation. Clergy, nuns, and lay leaders were targeted, with thousands of arrests over the ensuing years. Martin Bormann, Hitler's bull-necked personal secretary, was rabidly anti-Christian, as indeed was Alfred Rosenberg, the chief exponent of Nazi doctrine.

Although Göring's increasing girth reduced his capacity to endure strenuous engagements, he revelled in what was dubbed 'Berlin's most brilliant social event since the war'. His wedding day saw 33,000 people given a holiday to form a 'guard of honour' outside the Berlin Cathedral. Inside, the altar was bathed with magnificent gold floodlighting, young birch trees and banks of azaleas, transforming the cathedral into a spring garden. A British correspondent, concealed behind an artificial hedge, described the scene:

> The bride, who carried a red bouquet, wore a white dress with a long train, which was held by two small boys of the Hitler Youth. As General Göring led his bride towards the altar, a dozen arc lamps made a dazzling patch of light, women pressed forward, stood on pews, and craned their necks to catch a glimpse of the couple. Herr Hitler (the best man) and the rest of the Cabinet occupied the front row. When Reich Bishop Mueller asked, 'Do you take this woman to be your lawful wedded wife?' the response, the single word 'Ja,' spoken with military abruptness, was heard all over the Cathedral.

At the peak of the celebration, a crack air force squadron of Richthofen fighters circled overhead as the newlyweds, beaming from the back seat of a cabriolet, passed lines of medal-bedecked air force officers to the reception at the Kaiserhof Hotel banqueting hall. Placed under a forest of pink tulips and red azaleas, the 300 guests sat down to sumptuous meal of pâté de foie gras, roast chicken, ice cream and champagne. Goebbels demonstrated that in real life he was not at all ethereal or detached from everyday reality. Sitting behind a mountain of food he privately scowled, '7 courses ... uplifting sight for the hungry. Best forget it.'[1]

In the following months, Göring became an exhausted giant as he focused on developing the Luftwaffe and civil aviation, the latter of which was experiencing a shift to tourism traffic. In certain respects, by the time the Nazis took power, Germany was already leading the world in the development of regular air services. Certainly, vintage timetables reveal Lufthansa, Imperial Airlines and KLM were busily developing new tourist routes crisscrossing the continent from Helsinki in the north to Lisbon near the tip of Africa.

Using a modern fleet of Junkers turboprops capable of carrying twenty passengers, Lufthansa also connected America, Asia and Africa with a regular scheduled service. As aviation grew in size and importance, passage could be booked through the Reichsbahnzentrale, which operated dozens of offices spanning from Budapest to Havana.² One of the earliest directives from the Nazi government was that all German airplanes and airships would bear black, white, and red stripes on the starboard side and a swastika on the port side.

With the proliferation of passenger air services and additional carriers, the proportion of tourists coming and going by plane was steadily increasing. By 1935, Tempelhof Airport was earmarked to become an architectural advertisement for the thrill of air travel.³ A new 1.2-kilometre crescent-shaped terminal morphed into the largest building in Europe, a glorious entryway into the new Germania in the heart of Berlin. The plans, it was rumoured, all arose from a remark made by Hitler when he landed at the airstrip in January 1934 and reportedly barked, 'This aerodrome is much too small. It is not good enough that 80 passenger planes should have to remain in the open air overnight.'⁴ Still a shrine for architecture buffs, the limestone building was an amazing feat of technological improvisation and served British Airways, Swedish Airlines, Air France, Sabena, Belgian Airlines, Czechoslovakian Airlines, and the Danske Luftfartselskab.

During a tour of the new airport, Atlantic flight pioneer Charles Lindbergh expressed enthusiasm for 'this magnificent structure'. It was one of his many complimentary comments about German aviation which saw him courted by Göring, Hitler and other members of the Nazi elite. He often took long vacations in Germany, always finding time to inspect Luftwaffe detachments, Lufthansa operations and airplane factories. This solid support earned Lindbergh the Order of Merit of the German Eagle, a decoration designed for citizens of foreign countries who rendered services to Germany. (Henry Ford was another grateful recipient.) Lindbergh's wife Anne even penned the booklet *The Wave of the Future*, which declared fascism to be the inevitable way forward; she had also written a letter praising Hitler in unequivocal terms.

Soaring Above: Aviation

The head of Lufthansa, Martin Gustav Wilhelm Wronsky, a monocled gentleman with unmistakably diplomatic comportment, wasn't far wrong when he claimed Berlin would become the 'Clapham Junction of the air' and the centre of Europe's air traffic. Over time, he earned his spurs by running fifty-four routes, connecting fifteen foreign and fifty-seven domestic airports, including services to London, Malmo, Copenhagen, Moscow, Prague, Vienna and Budapest. There were two direct links between London and Berlin in each direction daily and, for the first time, a direct connection between Berlin and Madrid was established, leaving Berlin at 7 a.m. and reaching Madrid at 5.25 p.m. having covered more than 1,300 miles. Always on the cutting edge, a unique Lufthansa innovation appreciated by businessmen allowed for private telegrams to be transmitted from the aeroplane to the ground station for any destination in Europe when the aircraft was over Austria, Belgium, Czechoslovakia, France, Germany, Holland, Hungary, Sweden or Switzerland. Telegrams were tapped out 'as and when the necessary wireless communication in connection with the navigation of the aeroplane permits'.[5] To keep travellers entertained, the airline launched a stylish in-flight magazine, *Ikarus*, featuring an 'aerial guidebook' giving passengers the opportunity to identify landscapes and landmarks during their journey (from 1935 onwards, photography from the plane was strictly forbidden). American author Jean Merril Du Cane described Lufthansa as the nation's glamour carrier:

> '*Bitte schlagen Sie diesen Flugplan* ... Look at this air-map...This is Wilhelmshaven, where we cross the coast. Here's Hanover ... and in just another 20 minutes well be flying over Berlin by night.' The steward of the giant Nazi airliner was justly proud of his ship. A big Fokker-Wulf-Condor, it was faster than anything on Imperial Airways, French or Dutch airlines. It could cruise at over 200 miles an hour, while we dined in comfort by night on Frankfurters and sauerkraut kept hot in electric ovens and sipped Moselle wine cooled in the airliner's refrigerator.[6]

Cologne earned a permanent place on the air network and experienced a dramatic expansion in tourism. Although some miles outside the town, the attractive settings of Cologne airport saw it (and many others) become a popular rendezvous point among the townspeople. The restaurant was regarded in the nature of a club and became a focal point for large weekend gatherings where customers watched the airstrip and dined with friends. A special treat was the lunchtime arrival and departure of the Imperial Airways daily flight from Croydon, which touched down in Cologne at 2.25 p.m. (a shuttle bus had passengers installed at the Dome Hotel by 2.55 p.m.).[7] In September 1935, a new record for the Croydon–Cologne route was set when an Imperial Airways de Havilland covered the distance in just 1 hour 32 minutes.

◆ ❖ ◆

Of all the Nazi tourism imagery, none is more arresting than the *Hindenburg* airship docking at its lakeside base in Friedrichshafen. 'A marvellous, a glorious sight!' gushed one American passenger on catching his first glimpse of the silver craft. A point of pride and propaganda for the regime, it was described as Germany's 'Grand Hotel' of the air with accommodation for fifty passengers and two promenade decks.

Composed of durable aluminium alloy filled with highly flammable hydrogen, the *Hindenburg*'s regular USA service saw ten flights each way between May and October. It could reach cruising speeds of 122 km/h and a maximum speed of 135 km/h, with an average journey time from Frankfurt to Lakehurst of 63 hours 42 minutes (and the return leg in 51 hours). Although there wasn't any evidence to indicate the airship created a new market, its state-of-the-art ultra-luxury flights became the preserve of the elite given a single journey cost RM1,000. Dan Grossman, a historian of the *Hindenburg* and other dirigibles, says that while ocean liners were always going to carry a larger number of passengers and freight, for the obvious reason of their size airships were seen as a threat to skim off some of the most affluent passengers, not only because they cut the transatlantic travel time in half but because airship passengers did not experience seasickness, which was still a major concern during that era. 'Airships also had the potential to take a significant per cent of much of the business mail carried overseas.'[8]

The *Hindenburg* was the biggest commercial airship ever built, and, at the time, the most technologically advanced. It stretched 245 meters in length and 41.2 metres in diameter. In the starboard salon, passengers were able to relax with a drink and listen to Ernst Lehmann or other gifted passengers tickling the ivories after a sumptuous multi-course dinner. (This was the only form of live entertainment.) 'I went first into the lounge, a large room, along one side of which ran long windows of some transparent celluloid – like material,' wrote Sidney Rogerson, a British journalist. 'The room was carpeted, comfortable metal chairs were grouped round tables, and the walls – all of the thinnest fabric – were beautifully decorated.' The cabins on both sides of the ship were similar to first-class sleeping compartments on express trains, with wide beds, a dressing table and washing bowl with hot and cold water. 'These were exactly the same as one sees on board the average liner, one bunk above another,' Rogerson observed. 'The white tip-up basins in each cabin which looked so solid were made of celluloid.'

Rogerson also inspected the kitchen where joints of veal, lamb and beef were being put into refrigerators while cooks made jellies and prepared dinner. Menu cards show dishes included beef broth with marrow dumplings and Rhine salmon a la Graf Zeppelin. American passengers, unused to stodgy, starchy German cuisine, occasionally complained about the thick sauces and gravies smothering every dish. Those desiring a lighter meal were always offered the option of an omelette. At the bar, passengers could enjoy a selection of more than 200 fine wines and cocktails like the signature drink 'LZ-129', an iced mix of gin and orange named after the airship's moniker, LZ-129 *Hindenburg*.

Rogerson was amazed to discover the ship was centrally heated. 'The question of heating is an important one, for almost before you realise that you have left Europe, the ship is in the tropics.' It was comfortable, too; no single case of air sickness was recorded. For Rudolf van Wehrt, a passenger on its maiden flight to South America, it was an unforgettable journey. 'As darkness overtook us the lights were suddenly switched on. Over the much-feared Bay of Biscay we were met by rain swirls, and the head wind whistled in the fuselage.' He recalled the searchlights springing into life, and gazing down on the restless waves below. 'But in the bright and friendly decorated lounge we were oblivious to any threatenings from air or water. From time to time, however, we were made aware of outside turmoil by the thin shrieking of steamship sirens as we passed over battling vessels.' Even as the wind rose and a storm raged, Wehrt said the *Hindenburg* forged ahead without pitching or rolling. 'Indeed, she seemed oblivious to the anger of the elements, yet in the searchlight's path we sometimes caught glimpses of sea vessels being tossed about like corks and smothered time and again in a welter of green water and foam.'[9]

In the same charming article, Wehrt tracked the scene moment by moment from the observation promenades, which featured windows that could be opened in the air. 'During the voyage across the Southern Atlantic the *Hindenburg* behaved remarkably well. As we were coming along towards South America we were caught in a very severe storm that tested the airship as nothing else could. There was a turmoil of cloud and wind, but with engines speeded up the *Hindenburg* rose easily, and never for a moment deviated from her true course.'

That year, 1936, the *Hindenburg* set up a new record for the Atlantic crossing from east to west, making the journey in 52 hours 51 minutes – just over two days.

Banking on an increased flow of traffic, the *Hindenburg*'s timetable for 1937 provided for eighteen flights each way. But disaster struck on its first trip of the new season on 6 May 1937, when after three days crossing the Atlantic it approached Lakehurst in New Jersey during a storm. As it prepared to moor, a terrific burst of flame from its stern lit up the sky. Seconds later, the *Hindenburg* erupted in fire and its twisted steel frame fell 300 feet to the ground, killing thirty-six people out of the ninety-seven on board. In the following days, millions of radio listeners heard Herbert Morrison's eyewitness radio account in which he described the scene in vivid detail and exclaimed his famous line: 'Oh, the humanity!'

After extensive investigations, the tragedy was blamed on an electric spark igniting the hydrogen gas that kept it aloft. At the stroke of a pen, Hitler ended the Nazi airship programme.

11

THE LUCRATIVE OLYMPICS

The XI Olympiad was Nazi Germany's coming-out party, a show of its rising military and economic power and its re-emergence as a global power.[1] Amid the mounting drama in the early summer of 1936, when German troops occupied the Rhineland, Berlin pulled out all the stops to appeal to foreign tourists.

'I wish every American could have an opportunity to make a trip to Germany and form a clear picture of this beautiful and industrious country,' Grace Morrison-Poole, President of the Federation of US Women's Clubs, marvelled. 'I have learned to love and respect Germany and will carry back the truth to our country.'[2] Such quotes, designed to chip away at existing scepticism, were rolled out ad nauseam in official travel brochures prior to the Games. Dismissing the caution with which many people observed Germany, press baron William Randolph Hearst sent glowing praise to the 'America Speaks for Germany' section of a glossy Reichsbahn pamphlet:

> There are no towns in the world as picturesque as the ancient walled cities of Germany. They are among the most beautiful and instructive things to be seen in the world. I know of nothing which transports one so completely to another age, unless it is the perfectly preserved temples of ancient Egypt still standing in solemnity and solitude on the banks of the Nile.[3]

'The German people hope that visitors to the Games will return home with such accounts of their experiences as will be a most valuable advertisement for the country as holiday resort,' declared the *Belfast News-Letter*.⁴

To make Berlin as appealing as possible, police prepared to oust a number of people regarded as undesirable. First off was the removal of the Sinti and Roma population. On 10 July, less than a month before the opening ceremony, a top-secret memo was distributed to 520 Berlin police stations announcing details of the transfer of gypsies from the city to a 'resting place in Marzahn' on the outskirts. The opening paragraph stated:

> On one of the next few days at 4am, the words 'Gypsy Camp' will be the signal for police all over the city to surround all Gypsy encampments and transport the inhabitants with their vehicles to Marzahn.

The order adds details about the 'management and execution' of the action, the 'removal', the 'route' (main streets were to be avoided,) and surveillance of the camp. The gypsies were free to leave the camp, 'but only in an easterly direction and avoiding Berlin city limits'.⁵

As this was happening, police rounded up more than 2,000 prostitutes, barmaids and dancing girls and forcibly examined them for venereal disease (300 were treated). At the same time, all blatant forms anti-Semitic measures were paused and offensive notices painted over, especially in the vicinity of the Adlon Hotel, the bolthole of the elite which oozed privilege with its walnut panelling, gold bathroom fixtures and sumptuous furnishings. An Edwardian travel guide cemented the Adlon's reputation in the early part of the twentieth century by noting every bedroom was piped with hot and cold water which was always obtainable. It continued, 'A telephone is of course found in each room. A remarkable arrangement that secures prompt attendance.' Even more impressive was that all bedrooms were equipped with three ivory pushers on a bell handle – one labelled for the chambermaid, another for the waiter, and the third for the valet.

The cellar boasted a million bottles of fine wines, making the lobby bar the social centre of Berlin for well-groomed gentlemen and their ladies.

Reporting on the Olympic build-up from his suite at the Adlon, CBS's William Shirer growled that 'Hitler saw to it that the country was on its best behaviour; no persecution of the Jews. No action against unruly Catholics and Protestants. No savage attacks against the "decadent" Western democracies and "Jewish-dominated" America. All was, for the moment, sweetness and light.' He was not, however, a lone voice in his condemnation. Martha Graham, the leading figure in American dance, refused to let the wool be pulled over her eyes. She flatly refused an invitation from Goebbels to attend an international competition, run on the side lines of the Olympics. 'I would find it impossible to dance in Germany at the present time,' she explained. 'So many artists whom I respect and admire have been persecuted, have been deprived of the right to work for ridiculous and unsatisfactory reasons that I would find it impossible to identify myself by accepting the invitation with the regime that has made such things possible.'

While a raft of celebrities, royalty and nobility including IOC members, the King of Bulgaria, the Maharaja and Maharani of Baroda and the Crown Prince of Italy enjoyed the glamorous trappings of the Adlon and Kaiserhof, most provincials booked themselves into family pensions, guesthouses and the KdF 'Olympic Village' on Heer Strasse – 'built to enable every "national comrade" to participate in the Olympic Games' – where tourists were provided with beds under canvas, washing facilities and access to a beer hall.[6] Local reporters labelled it the 'second Olympic Village'; surviving plans show it provided a restaurant and beer-drinking accommodation for 24,000 people, whilst twelve electric kitchens spat out hot sausages every day from 5 a.m. till midnight. The equipment included a soup pot capable of cooking 500 quarts of soup at once. Reporter Albion Ross observed:

> In the main village, there are six halls; each with a cabaret stage on which simultaneous programmes will be kept going most of the afternoon and all evening. In the village are found a modern

The Lucrative Olympics

barber shop and a long series of wash and dressing rooms. Twenty to thirty special trains will arrive every morning with a total of 20,000 German workers who will spend the day visiting one sport event – a minor one – and will depart at night after spending the evening drinking beer and wine and listening to the cabaret programmes in the six halls in the 'Strength Through Joy Village.' Foreign visitors who want to join in the fun will be made more than welcome.[7]

'Really. I never knew there were so many Germans,' exclaimed sports writer John Macadam, who was impressed by the 'natural good manners' and discipline of the locals. 'They are here from Bavaria, from every quarter of the Rhineland, from Danzig. They flood the streets and overflow into the cafés.' In addition to regular tourists, a special 'Olympic camp' of the Hitler Youth was setup in Berlin's Grunewald to house 1,100 teenagers (forty each from the twenty-five regions). The *Westdeutscher Beobachter* described the camp as 'excellently organized, with a separate electricity supply and a private radio station'.[8] Over the coming three weeks, the Reichsbahn laid on over 100,000 special trains; 4.5 million admission tickets were sold, while the cost of the spectacle shot up to RM6.5 million.

However, the payoff was worthwhile and the public marvelled at the beautification of Berlin. Throughout the day, gondolas plied on the Spree River, while Viennese droshky carriages and French horse-drawn fiacres trotted between information kiosks at Stettiner Station, the Kaiser Wilhelm Memorial Church on Tauentzien-Strasse, Anhalter Station on Askanischer Platz, Friedrich-Strasse Station, Zoo Station, and the Reich Sport Field. Berliners with knowledge of foreign languages were posted to an information bureau at Columbus House on Potsdamer Platz next to the Reich Tourist and Travel Bureau:

> The officials who were engaged for this work were men and women who had travelled extensively in foreign countries and commanded several languages. Information in the majority of cases was requested in English, this being followed by French, Spanish,

Italian, occasionally Greek and in isolated cases less familiar tongues. In contrast to the telephone information office, few requests were received in the Northern or Slavic languages. Timetables, badges, Olympic bells and official guide books were also sold at this office.[9]

Tourism workers distributed the *Olympia Zeitung*, the official organ of the Games, published daily in four languages. Keenly aware of the potent power of language, heroic and glamorous words such as 'huge', 'majestic' and 'giant' were littered throughout each edition:

> The German genius of all arts and sciences [has] risen powerfully ... in order to ... conjure up the miracle of the Reichssportfeld and the Olympic village.[10]

The newspaper worked unrelentingly to create the narrative of youth, virility, national identity and 'one people' regardless of social status. Emotional terms with a positive connotation such as 'Community', 'Fatherland', '*Heimat*' and '*Kameradschaft*' appeared frequently. This was consistent with a flurry of instructions ordering 'every good German' to act as the perfect host to assist guests and, above all, to see that they enjoy themselves and are sufficiently impressed.[11] Every shop, however small, boasted some decoration, while railway carriages, engines, cars, carts and trams bore the badge of the Olympiad. The German Retail Merchants' Association took special measures in order to enable shopkeepers to cope with the influx of visitors. As early as the autumn of 1935, courses in salesmanship, languages and shop decoration were organised in every part of Germany likely to be visited by large groups of tourists. 'The local committees examined shop fronts, show-windows and shop interiors, and it could be noticed that as a result of suggestions and advice many unattractive metal signs disappeared,' claimed the official Olympic report.

> In order to prevent cheap or shoddy application of the Olympic rings, all decorations containing them had to be approved.

Decisions were made in hundreds of cases regarding decorative schemes, and advice was also given.[12]

British journalist K. L. Bailey wrote of the beautification campaign:

> Flags are everywhere. They hang from every window. They billow from the great poles that line the principal streets. For instance, the famous Unter den Linden is now one great length of bunting reminiscent of the streets of London during the Jubilee celebrations. There is also a pretty display of floral window-boxes – again by order of the Government – and many housewives taking lodgers have for some month's past been undergoing a course in foreign languages and even in foreign cooking. An information bureau has been set up to provide free guides, members of the students' organisation, for any visitor wishing to explore Berlin.[13]

The municipality placed gilded iron girders along the Unter den Linden boulevard splashed with tons of gold paint and topped with Swastika flags. 'At first, foreigners were sceptical of us because they thought all Germans were Nazis,' recalled Dorothea Günther, who made the best of a sticky assignment guiding British and Danish tourists. 'But they soon found out that National Socialism was not that strong. They could not have known that they were being presented with a friendly, open Germany that, however, had nothing to do with reality.' She remembered long discussions with her guests without ideology intervening. 'In the evenings we particularly liked going to the Zigeunerkeller on Kurfürstendamm because there was a special atmosphere there, fuelled by Hungarian wine. An unforgettable memory was the night when we danced and sang the "Lambeth Walk" with a group of English people on the Westkreuz S-Bahn platform.'[14]

Those with an interest in National Socialism couldn't resist the prospect of being served coffee by Hitler's half-brother Alois at his pretentious two-story eatery on Wittenbergplatz adjacent to the KaDeWe department store. The Alois Restaurant thrived on the afternoon coffee trade and inevitably became one of the most successful establishments for ordinary soldiers, sailors and airmen as well as SS hardliners and stormtroopers. By all accounts, Alois was a larger-than-life personality: 'He plays a concertina, is jovial, and speaks excellent English,' the *Aberdeen Journal* reported. When visitors expressed surprise at his fluent English, he replied, 'And why shouldn't I speak good English considering how many English girls I was in love with during my eight years in England as a waiter before the war?'

Kids also had great fun as they sought autographs from international athletes. 'Chinese, Japanese and Arabic names were particularly popular,' recalled Werner Viehs, then twelve years old. 'Everyone who visited us for the Olympics could see that our people and especially the workers were not doing badly. It was not easy to get the appropriate tickets. Father had received them at his company through the DAF.'[15]

In all, arrangements were made to host 80,000 spectators and 4,202 entrants from twenty-eight nations. This sporting dream came beautifully packaged across twenty-two venues including the Olympic Stadium – a vast structure flanked by 136 vast pillars – which lived up to its aspiration as a national landmark. Clad in Franconian limestone, the stadium was surrounded by a sports forum, hockey rink, equestrian stadium and an outdoor theatre with shelf-like seats.

To the right, a filtered swimming pool catered for 18,000 spectators, while to the front sat the great Mayfield parade ground, a grassy plateau capable of holding 250,000 people. Outside the stadium, perhaps the most surprising sight for locals was the freshly laid grass which was difficult to grow owing to the sandy nature of the soil; sod had to be shipped in and constantly watered. The entrance was dominated by two 35-metre towers, between which the Olympic rings were suspended. 'In the centre of the stadium complex was one huge restaurant where visitors could eat,' recalled American tourist Esther Wenzel. On the colonnade between the two floors of the stadium there were shops for all kinds of memorabilia, film, cameras, Olympic flags and pictures of Hitler and Berlin. 'These shops were sufficient; no other vendors were allowed. The Games were all about sports.

They were not a money-making business, as they are today.'[16] It was hardly surprising that Jews were forbidden to do any trading at the Games – only those recommended by the Nazi Party were awarded police permits to sell cigarettes, drinks and other refreshments to the crowds.

The Nazis staked everything on the Games, galvanizing the nation, spending millions to build facilities, and producing the kind of ceremonies that left spectators breathless. For detractors (and there were many of them) the event would be criticised for its hackneyed presentation of Germany as a land of athletes and Aryan heroes. By the start of 1936, tickets were already being snapped up from British tourist agencies and the German Railways Information Bureau on Regent Street, which offered special 'Travel Marks' giving tourists a 'reduction of expenditure in Germany'. Before the Games began the official exchange rate in London was RM12.4 marks to the pound, but for tourist travel purposes, 22 'Travel Marks' were given to the pound, allowing the German Central Bank to literally 'cash in' foreign exchange. The only downside was the 'Travel Marks' could only be used for personal expenses and travel in Germany, not for purchasing articles of commercial value. 'The Games were managed as a brilliant banking coup which, with the excitement about how far and fast athletes could run and jump and swim over and under things, no one seemed to notice,' an American financial reporter observed.[17]

While the well-heeled flew into Berlin's Tempelhof Airport with Lufthansa, KLM and other airlines, budget travellers, including Mr. G. Ramsbottom, principal at the Fleetwood Weight Lifting Club, made the journey by sea and rail:

> We travelled from Dover to Ostend in the Belgian steamer *Cote d'Argent*. After three hours at sea we sighted Ostend and the lights of its sea front looked like Blackpool Illuminations on a small scale. It took us an hour and a half to pass the Customs, and it was two o'clock when we entrained on the Belgian State Railway for our 15-hour journey to Berlin. The trains had wooden seats, and for the first time in our life we really appreciated third class

L.M.S. At 5.30am, we were awakened from more or less peaceful sleep at Aachen, on the German frontier, where our engine was changed for one of the German expresses. We had to wait about an hour there in which time all our English money was checked, and we were given receipts. Luckily for us, we had previously obtained 150 Reichmarks. At Aachen we gladly took the chance of getting rubber air-cushions, and the general inflating of them was an amusing sight, but they were worth it! For 500 miles we rode through an ever-changing landscape. Not an acre of land was wasted. Everywhere there were either trees or cultivation. Everybody seemed to be at work. It was twenty to six in the evening when we reached Berlin and we had a great welcome from the Germans or, Deutschlanders as they call themselves.[18]

Ramsbottom steamed into the imposing Anhalter Bahnhof, a fitting entrance to Berlin's government quarter. Built in the Neo-Renaissance style with Greppiner bricks, the station boasted a Main Concourse with iron trusses 110 feet high, spanning 200 feet across, making it the biggest in Continental Europe. Since the turn of the century, the station had morphed into an international hub serving arrivals and departures to Vienna, Rome, Basel, Athens and Constantinople.[19] By the early 1930s, trains left its six platforms every three to five minutes, with tens of thousands of people commuting into and out of the terminal. Staff frequently unrolled a long crimson carpet down the steps at the entrance to welcome historic figures including Ramsay MacDonald, Arturo Toscanini, Benito Mussolini, Vyacheslav Molotov, Japanese Foreign Minister Yosuke Matsuoka and countless other statesmen who made their grand entrance on the platforms of Anhalter.

12

LET THE GAMES BEGIN

On the final stages of its 2,000-mile journey to Berlin, the Olympic Flame crossed the German frontier on 31 July. By this point, all foreign athletes were snugly ensconced behind the head-high wire fence at the magnificent Olympic village in Elstal, 12 miles west of the main stadium. To justify the massive scale of the project – which included restaurants, sauna, infirmary, swimming pool, and a long line of hutted accommodation – authorities earmarked the village for future use as a military barracks.[1] The entire complex, around 540,000 m², was landscaped to hills and a lake. In order to bring this artificial nature to life, water birds were brought in from the Berlin Zoo and placed on the shore of the lake near a small Finnish sauna and terrace café. The large 'Hindenburg House', a two-story building of function rooms, contained an auditorium for concerts, dance, theatre and film performances – mostly organized by the KdF. (Several times a day, a military band played at various locations in the village.) The central point of the complex was the 'Dining House of Nations', with its thirty-eight kitchens and dining rooms. Long before daybreak, a stream of vans brought imports from around the world to be cooked by chefs from the Norddeutscher Lloyd. Imports included sacks of coffee from Brazil, ripening bananas from Central America, wines from

Portugal, bacon from Denmark, and tea, sugar, chocolate, fruits and vegetables from other world markets. Journalist Gerald Frankin thought it so outstanding that it deserved description:

> It stands in the midst of the Brandenburg woods, and the Berlin Zoo is supplying brilliantly-plumed parakeets, herons, and water birds to sport in the artificial lake in order to make overseas visitors feel at home. One notable feature will be the 'Hall of Nations,' where the various representatives of the countries will welcome their competitors. These are to be accommodated in compact bungalows, with bedrooms, and washing and shower equipment. At one end of the village are huge dining halls, and the competitors are to be allowed to bring their own chefs so that they will be able to have their national dishes.[2]

Passing a large crowd at the Brandenburg Gate on the afternoon of 1 August 1936, Hitler's motorcade roared towards to the stadium under the shadow of the huge *Hindenburg* hovering overhead. The excitement with which Hitler swept into the stadium gave his arrival the feeling of a coronation. M. J. Olivier of the *Yorkshire Post* found herself involuntarily raising her right hand 'and without a thought of politics, joining in "*Deutschland Über Alles*". At the same moment, Jane Turner sprang to her feet as the crowds turned towards Hitler with outstretched hands 'as if the whole stadium with its 100,000 people had been transformed into a gigantic spider's web'.[3] After countless salvos of applause, Greece led the march past with other nations following in alphabetical order. About half of them gave the Nazi salute: most of the others dipped their flags. The British marched past with eyes right in military fashion as Richard Strauss's Olympic hymn blared across the stadium.

For French Ambassador Andre Francois-Poncet, it was a dazzling sight. 'Hitler has forced himself on Europe as an extraordinary personality,' he commented admiringly. 'He not only spreads fear and loathing, but also arouses curiosity and wins sympathy. His reputation is growing.' On the face of it, the French diplomat thought the coming together of kings, princes and famous guests in Berlin was more focused on meeting the 'man who would be shaping the future' than watching sporting events.

During the first weekend, 2,000 distinguished German and foreign guests attended a special event at the opera,[4] where, from a cloistered perch, Hermann Göring told them it was a singular opportunity to 'give themselves up to the wonderful atmosphere of the eleventh Olympic Games'. He also splashed out on another party at his Reich Aviation Ministry where a mock medieval village in miniature constructed in the gardens became the epicentre of a gastronomic feast. 'The whole world is thrilled by the perfect organization, the absolute order and discipline, cultivated with extravagant generosity. It is, indeed, a grand picture,' Francois-Poncet proudly recorded.[5]

Such displays of extravagance were common, according to US chargé d'affaires Hugh R. Wilson, who thought Göring 'almost abnormal in the fatness of his figure built upon a powerful, rather short frame'. A man who clearly had a quickness of wit, Wilson garishly described how Göring's ability to handle great shows could 'strike envy in the hearts of any of our Hollywood directors':

> There was a huge orchestra from the opera, the best singers of Germany, the best dancers gathered together, supper and wines were of superlative quality. We were at Göring's table. He entered late amid a blare of trumpets, followed by a burst of music from the orchestra. A fat round figure in resplendent uniform with a striking, clean-shaven face, he strode into the room saluting and taking the salutes of everybody present.

Oddly enough, for all of Göring's flowery grandeur, it was Joseph Goebbels's gigantic fairyland party at Pfaueninsel, a small island near Wannsee, that grabbed the headlines. Everybody was left breathless at the thousands of delicate, butterfly-shaped lamps spread across the gardens for the lavish gathering, which ended with a huge firework display, reminding some guests of the artillery fire of the First World War. That comparison pleased Goebbels to no end.

In addition to the sporting fixtures and exclusive gatherings, the Games were accompanied by numerous theatre, opera and art exhibitions, some of which were considered highly suspect. A performance of *Hamlet* featuring leading actor Gustav Grundgen was singled out by Janet Flanner from the *New Yorker*. She thought the production at the Schauspielhaus was characterised by a degree of violence never before seen in the play. Grundgen's death scene, which was endlessly drawn out by marching soldiers, trumpets and a display of weapons, appeared to her almost a farce. 'Hamlet,' she opined, had been accorded a 'first class Party funeral'.

Meanwhile, on the sports tracks, the Games were filled with incredible athletic accomplishments. The black American athlete Jesse Owens, a man ambitious beyond belief, stole the show by winning victories in the 100 and 200 metres, the long jump and the sprint relay – a feat which ridiculed the 'superiority' of an Aryan race. 'White mankind should be ashamed,' Goebbels fumed in his diary before instructing his journalists to pay little attention to the enthusiasm Owen's antics were generating.[6]

Marianne Gartner was a ten-year-old schoolgirl when she took part in the Youth Pageant at the Games, then spent the next two weeks as a spectator with her father:

> Over the next two weeks I was introduced to competitive sports at their best. My father had organized tickets for the main athletic events and I was privileged to watch Jesse Owens set new world records, a Japanese come first in the marathon and Finnish runners triumph over the long distances. I set my teeth every time a high-jump favourite attempted to beat a new height and trembled with the three pole-vault finalists, who, in a three-hour battle, would not concede victory, not until, under searchlights and amid the bated breath of spectators, a last supreme effort secured for one contestant the gold medal.
>
> As I watched the athletes and shared the champions' euphoria and the losers' disappointment, I bit my nails, cheered, applauded or sighed in chorus with the crowd.
>
> There were many hilarious moments when laughter dispelled the tension. There was drama, when a member of the German women's relay team dropped her baton only seconds away from victory.

But then I was beginning to realise it was all part of the Games, and my father explained that it was the sort of thing that made them human. But the athletes' fighting spirit impressed me most, their battle for centimetres or tenths of seconds for which they had to tap their last physical reserves, and which struck a waiting chord inside me. For two weeks my father and I talked like experts about track records and the placing of individual competitors, we bent over our programmes and counted team points, we chewed an endless number of bockwursts splashed with mustard and sandwiched in crisp rolls. I was happy.

As the days rolled on, the public got used to seeing two familiar faces perched up in the VIP section surveying proceedings. Dr Karl Gebhardt, a well-known sports doctor and the senior physician, often sat with Leni Riefenstahl, the vain, pompous, egotistical self-advertiser with a talent for filmmaking. 'She wears long grey flannel trousers and a sort of jockey cap and attracts negative attention wherever she goes,' journalist Bella Fromm noted sarcastically. 'Once in a while she sits down next to the Führer, a frozen smile on her face such as one sees on the cover of illustrated magazines, her head illuminated by a halo of importance.' In contrast, the affable and charming Gebhardt made many new friends that August. However, less than a decade later, his career ended at the end of a rope after he was convicted of committing crimes against humanity by conducting medical experiments on women at Ravensbruck concentration camp, leaving some dead and others with permanent disabilities.

The main Olympic sideshow, however, was the World Congress for Leisure Time and Recreation in Hamburg and Berlin, with the finale being staged at the Olympic Stadium Reichssportfeld on 10 August. The event was called '*Musik and Tanz der Volker*' (Music and Dances of the Nations). A special introduction was written by KdF's Berlin Director Gunter Adam in the official programme:

> The World Congress for Leisure Time and Recreation has shown us the spirit of reconciliation and peace of all the men who – in

the different countries of the earth work at the wonderful Leisure-Time-Work for the benefit of their nations. The delegates and the guests of the World Congress believe more firmly than ever in the blessing of their work for mankind. They will return to their countries as apostles of joy, and with an ardent wish to help to keep up the peace of the world.

This night is given to music and dancing, two things wonderfully fit for uniting the nations. People who sing and dance will know neither hatred nor quarrel; they want to live in peace and harmony and to do their work undisturbed. May Joy, this magic power, unite the nations of this earth, may it lead them towards a happier future. Since always the good conquers the evil, joy and cheerfulness must get the better of hate, discordance and malice.

When the Games wrapped up, Germany was jubilant having secured eighty-nine medals and attracted 1.2 million visitors to Berlin, including 150,000 foreigners. However, before the bunting had been packed away many critics – some from within sporting circles – sharpened their knives. British athlete A. G. K. Brown poured out a series of anti-German sentiments by complaining the spectators were 'probably the most unpleasant' before which athletes had the 'misfortune' to compete. 'When the head of a State sets the example by applauding only competitors from his own nation, people may find it difficult to be well mannered.' In a three-column story, Brown also waspishly noted that he went to Berlin with the 'mistaken idea' that he was going to watch or take part in a sports meeting. 'Instead we were treated to piece of political propaganda.'[7] Likewise, E. H. Temme, a water polo international, was also leery of the Nazis. 'Not only am I going to retire but I shall call for an inquiry into many things which happened in Berlin,' he acidly announced, citing poor travelling facilities and laxities of administration.[8] In response, Berlin persisted in the view that it had been unjustly criticised and that personal grudges were to blame for everything. Interestingly, the official report on the Games is candid in listing individual police actions, such as the arrests of pickpockets and the 'struggle against the scourge of begging'. According to the report, police devoted 'greater attention' to prostitution. In this case, legal prosecution 'had temporarily been relegated to the background in favour of public health surveillance' with the result that 'the increased spread of venereal disease observable at previous Olympic Games did not occur in Berlin'.

Another police report tells of a man who repeatedly approached foreigners in restaurants and asked what they thought of Berlin, only to refute their enthusiastic impressions by remarking that 'he could show them another side, especially since he had been in a concentration camp'. The report goes on to say that after the location of the 'perpetrator' by the local police, the man – who had not yet been in a concentration camp – was sent to one for five years.

13

SPECIAL PRESENTATIONS

As memories of the Games faded, travel bureaus and KdF excursion organisers snapped to attention to promote several major exhibitions in 1937, sponsored by the Ministry of Propaganda. First off was the inauguration of the House of German Art and the Great German Art Exhibition, which opened with a parade depicting 'Two Thousand Years of German Culture', created by 4,435 sculptors, painters, musicians and artists. But by far the most popular event was the 'Degenerate Art' exhibition, which opened in both Munich and Berlin opposite the Reichstag to show 600 'degenerate' works by artists including Max Beckmann, Lovis Corinth, Otto Dix, George Grosz, Wassily Kandinsky and Paul Klee.

Hitler's war on degenerate art found enthusiastic acceptance among the public throughout the country, with some delighted to see the Nazis cleaning up galleries and suppressing the 'rubbish' which passed for art 'under one fancy name or another'. Hitler detested impressionists, post-impressionists, futurists, vorticists, and surrealist art which, he thought, distorted truth and perverted beauty. To enforce this view, the Ministry of National Education even sent out a press release declaring, 'We reject Rembrandt, the painter, from the Ghetto.' Applause for the exhibition also came from foreign shores. Commenting on Hitler's crusade, Britain's

Special Presentations

Daily Mirror asserted there was little doubt that a great deal of modernist art was not only 'unhealthy but stupidly incompetent. Much expensive rubbish masquerades under the name of modern art. It even gets bought for public galleries all over the world.'[1]

The director of the State Academy in Munich, from where the exhibition originated, said it was designed 'to open the eyes of Germans to the danger of world Bolshevism'.[2] Throughout the Berlin exhibition, each room bore a different motto. The first, for instance, read: 'The masterpieces decadent art praised beyond all bounds by Jews and hysterical drivellers, which were paid for by the taxes imposed on working Germans.' In all, 320 oil paintings, 40 plastics, and 200 drawings were displayed, which according to the catalogue gave an 'insight into the last horrible chapter of the cultural decline of the last decade before the great change'.

The exhibits were divided into nine groups: paintings which utterly disregard colour and form; paintings of a religious origin; paintings of political origin; paintings with political tendency; immoral paintings; paintings which show a Marxist and Bolshevik tendency to kill any race sense; paintings with an Idiotic ideal; paintings by Jews; and utter madness.

Remarkably, the show attracted more than 2 million visitors during its four-and-a-half-month run. The personal control which Hitler maintained over art even extended to the official artists of whose work he generally approved. One exiled artist, speaking under the promise of strict anonymity, claimed that Hitler sat on the selection committee for official exhibitions and often threw out pictures on unusual grounds. On one occasion, he rejected three pictures by well-known and officially approved artists because they were too dark, and he preferred to see pictures of the day, not the night. A torso was rejected because it was incomplete, and he would have nothing in the exhibition that was 'unfinished'. He also turned down a statue of a hyena, on the grounds that it was not a German animal.

Typically, the Nazis profited from the sale of 'degenerate art' to dealers abroad. A special bank account reserved for such sales took deposits of over RM1 million in foreign currency. At a sale of 125 pieces in Zurich, the *Times of London* reported that 'directors of art galleries from all parts of the world, international art dealers and numerous private purchasers' made their way to the unique event'. Van Gogh's *Self-Portrait* raised U$21,000, and Picasso's *Two Harlequins* sold for 80,000 Swiss francs.³ Rather than clog up storage space, Goebbels later approved a proposal to burn modernist artworks deemed unsellable. In all, 12,167 paintings, drawings and sketches were available for the bonfire.⁴

Encouraged by the response to the Degenerate Art exhibition, tourist agencies pushed the opening of The Eternal Jew, a traveling exhibition which first opened in the Deutsches Museum with the aim of spreading anti-Semitic caricatures of Jews. Staged in an area of 3,500 square metres, a defamatory image of Jews was created mainly with photos and paintings. The twenty rooms of the exhibition showed giant plaster casts of Jewish noses, ears and lips. One journalist noted: 'The exhibition consists of pictures, diagrams, and other material in no respect complimentary to the Jews.'⁵ Among those pilloried were Charlie Chaplin, of whom a life-size portrait was shown as a type of the 'Eternal Jew', alongside members of the Goldschmidt banking family and the tenor Richard Tauber. 'This exhibition is quite beyond description,' gasped Kenneth Lawson, a well-known Oxford tutor. 'If we were ever in any doubt about the essential and primitive beastliness of the extremists of the present regime, this performance must place the matter beyond any speculation.'

> With the most blatant misrepresentations of fact, the grossest libel and distortions of truth, a hoarse-voiced guide led us through a dozen chambers of horrors. Great names that have added lustre to German life and thought, from Heine to Thomas Mann, from Walter Hathenau to Max Reinhardt, were plastered up on the walls, together with the most fantastic 'information' about their life and work. There is no attempt to conceal what has been done and is still to be done. The Jew must be exterminated, because he is essentially and entirely immoral, decadent, cruel, and beastly. And that goes for Einstein, Gustav Mahler, the Zweigs, Bruno Walter, Elisabeth Bergner, and a hundred others whose pictures and 'biographies' are displayed.⁶

Special Presentations

In one room reserved for foreign journalists, a huge poster read 'How the English Press is directed by Jews', while another room showed a replica of a Masonic Lodge. Julius Streicher, the crackpot Jew baiter, in his opening speech at the Munich exhibition said that the Jew was a mongrel race mixed with the blood of 'Negroes, Mongols, and Nordic people'. 'They at all times were the destroyers of good,' he barked, before quoting passages from the writings of Jews, including many passages from Disraeli, in support of this statement. 'Bolshevism,' he continued, 'is the most brutal revelation of this Jewish desire to rule the world. The great doctor Adolf Hitler came in time to save our infected soul.'

More than 400,000 visitors were said to have been counted during the eight-week exhibition, which was, unsurprisingly, a must for school classes and KdF excursions.

14

HAMBURG

Great ocean liners with their flags fluttering were a common sight on the Elbe and in Hamburg's harbour, coming and going to Norway, Spain or, as they did on many weekends, up and down the German coast.

When the more powerful, ostentatious ships of Hapag dropped anchor in late 1937, crews were putting the final polish on the itinerary for a series of fourteen different leisure cruises 'over blue seas to sunny lands'. For RM1,460, the well-heeled could march up the covered gangways with their cartloads of matched luggage on cruises taking in Mexico, Florida, Cuba, the Antilles and New York. Tourist class wasn't much cheaper at RM1045. The itinerary ran thusly:

Dec 4:   Leave Hamburg
Dec 6:   Arrive and depart Southampton
Dec 6:   Arrive at Cherbourg, depart late evening
Dec 10:   Arrive at Funchal, Madeira. Day excursion, depart evening.
Dee 17:   Arrive at Port de France, Martinique. Depart late evening.
Dec 18:   Arrive at Grenada, British West Indies. Depart early evening.

Dec 19:   Arrive in Trinidad, motor coach tour of Port of Spain. Depart evening.
Dec 21.   Arrive at La Guaira, Venezuela. Depart late evening.
Dec 22:   Arrive at Curacao, Dutch West Indies. Tour of the capital, depart evening.
Dec 24:   Arrive at Cartagena, Columbia. Citybus tour. Depart evening.
Dec 25:   Arrive at Cristobal, city tour and Christmas lunch. Depart evening.
Dec 27:   Arrive at Kingston Jamaica. Depart evening.
Dec 29:   Arrive in Havana, Cuba. Tour and evening in the city.
Dec 30:   Depart Havana.
Dec 31:   Arrive in Miami. Tour and lunch at the Palm Beach.
Jan 1:   Sail for Hamburg

On arrival in Hamburg, passengers caught sight of the great wooden piers, where a string of waterfront pubs, inns, barbershops, kiosks and food stores served seafaring men and dockworkers. Then, as today, Hamburg was defined by its relationship with the Alster Lake in the heart of the metropolis and the Elbe, which brought ocean liners and cargo from the North Sea.

Despite its grotty reputation, many foreign arrivals enjoyed their brief stay in Hamburg, especially in the pretty Alster district which centred on the eponymous lake. 'I took a ride on a motorboat with some people we met on the steamer,' an American tourist recalled with a hoot in a postcard.[1] 'We went to the pavilion where we had afternoon coffee and cake served at tables along the edge of the lake. Hamburg is much larger and more beautiful a city than we had expected.'[2]

Hitler had dazzlingly ambitious plans for his largest port – a place he envisioned as the ocean gateway to the world of National Socialism. In his mind's eye, he mapped a new city featuring an American-style limestone skyscraper and a vast iron suspension bridge modelled on San Francisco's Golden Gate. What was more, Hamburg was to be filled with 'architectural must-sees', designed to impress international visitors. 'Hamburg has something American about it,' Hitler reportedly observed during a boat trip with Hamburg's mayor Carl Vincent Krogmann. He thought the 'capital of German shipping' should have a silhouette that impresses visitors at least as much as the New York skyline. 'That's where the skyscraper should go,' Hitler is said to have told Krogmann, pointing to Altona.

As the project gained traction, Konstanty Gutschow, a local designer and planner, was hired to head the redevelopment – which quickly took on a life of its own. Gutschow's architecture firm – which until Hitler's commission had only a handful of employees – grew to more than 150 staff, plus around 100 technical experts.

Gutschow's unexpected promotion meant he could travel to the USA to find inspiration for 'Elbhattan', modelled on the vertical lines of Manhattan's skyline. The pursuit of this vision would cost RM1.6 billion, with a planned completion date of 1965. In the meantime, the public were given an idea of what lay in store for the port, as a KdF holiday guide for Norwegian cruises noted:

> Since 1933, new life blooms from the ruins. The chimneys are smoking again, the shipyards are working, trade and shipping are increasing noticeably, and ships are once again spanning the entire globe. Gauleiter Karl Kaufmann is responsible to the Führer for the fate of Hamburg. The Führer has major tasks for Hamburg within the framework of the four-year plan that extends to all areas of life. The 'new' Hanseatic city will administer the trusteeship given to it by the Reich at Germany's gateway to the world, as it corresponds to the dignity and size of the megacity.[3]

Such ambitious plans meant consigning Hamburg's tatty image to history. Organised to coincide with the 1936 World Congress for Leisure and Recreation, councillors attempted to reverse the reputation of St Pauli – the equivalent of London's Soho – by curbing vice and running an aggressive press campaign to lure tourists. In a carefully managed media campaign, 'St. Slovenly', as the district was frequently dubbed, was re-badged as Hamburg's 'Anchor of Joy', which promised wholesome entertainment with an exotic allure. The *Deutsche Allgemeine Zeitung* explained that, although St Pauli harboured a few skeletons, the locals remained honourable folk.[4] In concert with the Reich Committee for Tourist Travel, Mayor Krogmann co-financed a glossy brochure aimed at foreign visitors and wrote the introduction:

> That Hamburg is Germany's largest port and the second largest town in the 'Reich' is a fact known not only to Germans, but to the whole world. What, unfortunately, is not sufficiently appreciated at home and abroad, however, is that Hamburg is one of the most beautiful cities in the world, not only symbolically, as a stead of work and as a community which has flourished on a lofty ideal, but also in the true sense of the word, with its Alster and its parks, its avenues, offices and warehouses, its ocean giants on the river, its picture as a whole. This is a fact which awakens the admiration and delight of all those whose travels take them to the old Hanse City. May this magazine serve to bring beautiful Hamburg to the knowledge of a wider circle of friends. May it be the means of inducing many a reader to pay a visit to Hamburg – a visit, I am convinced, that will remain in his memory, as one of his most delightful experiences.[5]

For some visitors, Hamburg's bohemian vibe and thriving cultural scene needed no alteration. One of them, thirty-year-old Irish writer Samuel Beckett, curious and raw before his fame, stepped ashore at Hamburg's Landungsbrücken pier on the morning of 2 October 1936 with the intention of improving his German and getting to know the city's art and artists. Over the coming months, his 'artistic pilgrimage' would lead him to Munich, Berlin and Dresden. 'What moved Beckett to this journey was to escape from his domineering mother, to see paintings and to buy and to read books – intensively,' says Roswitha Quadfliegm, a Swiss writer who studied Beckett's adventures in Germany.[6] 'In each town he visited public art museums, private galleries and bookstores.' In the soaking autumn of 1936, Beckett never saw the Nazis but Quadfliegm says he couldn't help hearing their over-orchestrated voices. 'For example, loudspeakers blared out

Adolf Hitler and Goebbels opening Winterhilfswerk. He wasn't a visionary, but he felt the spirit of the language the Nazis were using.'[7]

The young writer initially lodged near Hamburg's main train station, but soon switched to a barebones guesthouse in the Grindelviertel where he jotted his daily impressions in two grubby notebooks. Most days he could be found plodding along the grimy strip of taverns, where a room cost RM5 a night and getting a prostitute to share a bed was just as cheap. Everywhere he went, Beckett copied poems, idioms and even vulgarities word for word, leaving a diary littered with a peculiar mix of German and English constructs. 'Aside from Beckett's encounter with the visual arts, I believe his foremost interest in German was to experience the language from a completely different aspect than that which he had gleaned from Goethe and Klopstock,' says Quadfliegm. Beckett was fascinated by slang and the language of the man on the street. 'In fact,' adds Quadfliegm, he started interspersing his diary with more and more German expressions and that is exactly what makes the diary extremely amusing. 'Phrases heard during dinners at his boarding house and profanities scrawled on the walls of public urinals were as important to him as texts in art catalogues.'

Running to several hundred pages, Beckett's notes provide a fascinating glimpse of Hamburg in 1936. The only sand in the oil were his constant toothache, abscesses and flu, conditions compounded by grey, wet and miserable weather. There are frequent entries like 'Hundewetter again', 'another filthy day' and 'out early, despite the weather'. The pursuit of art took him to the gallery eleven times and the Museum of Art and Industry, with its domed tower, on seven separate occasions. He mentions almost 200 artists in his diary whose works he gazed at for hours on end. He met the painters Gretchen Wohlwill and Friedrich Ahlers-Hestermann, among others, and was ushered into private galleries to admire the exquisite collections of Rose Schapire and the Sauerlandt and Hudtwalcker families. However, he developed an aversion to the much-vaunted paintings by Philipp Otto Runge in the Kunsthalle, which were regularly recommended to him.

'A whole room of nonsense. They make me feel ill,' he recorded with merciless candour.

In his free time, Beckett drank and ate just about everywhere, but his favourite perch could be found at restaurant on the corner of Dammtorstrasse and Valentinskamp where the food was cheap and the service fast. He tired of stews and 'eternal cakes' but was keen to taste specialties such as eel soup. In the city park he knocked back 'a large Löwenbräu in one gulp' and felt 'most happily melancholy'. From the tower of the Süllberg restaurant, he admired the river over a dinner of watery crab soup, fried plaice and a stodgy dessert.

Beckett had left Germany by the time the Duke of Windsor and Wallis, his duchess, arrived in early October 1937. Having abdicated the British throne, the duke planned to tour factories and research working-class social and economic conditions. While the trip was embarrassing to Edward's brother King George VI, it was a propaganda coup for the Nazis and especially Robert Ley, who took charge of arrangements. During their twelve-day stay, the Windsor's kicked back in Hitler's personal train and were greeted by enthusiastic crowds; the duchess was even accorded her royal title, much to her delight.

Accompanied by his new blonde wife Inga, a young soprano picked up at the Friedrichstadt-Palast theatre, Ley put on a magnificent banquet for the Windsors with Goebbels, Hess, Himmler and Ribbentrop in attendance. British Ambassador Sir Eric Phipps remarked that Ribbentrop declared that 'HRH will someday have a great influence over the British working man'. Indeed, British intelligence documents released by the Public Record Office later revealed the Nazis expected assistance from the duke and duchess, 'the latter desiring at any price to become queen'.

In the short term, though, given the huge international press interest, it was hoped the 'royal tour' would provide a shot in the arm for foreign tourism. American magazines were particularly attracted to photos of the duke hopscotching around the country and enjoying ale at a Munich beer hall. Between long-winded speeches, Ley whisked the couple to factories, hospitals and youth camps in Dresden, Stuttgart and Munich. They inspected a coalmine deep in the Ruhr and toured a welfare centre, a factory and the Reichsbahn sports ground as well as examining model workmen's dwellings.

For one of the engagements, the duke travelled along the autobahns on a luxury coach specially equipped with a kitchenette, where the Hotel Kaiserhof's head waiter prepared the meals. In Nuremberg, the duke inspected assembly grounds used for Nazi Party rallies. They proceeded to an elaborate pavilion built for the KdF movement before driving through the picturesque old part of the town up to the ancient citadel. There was also time to make a lightning visit by bus and plane to the construction site at Prora to inspect Ley's KdF holiday camp. According to *Time* magazine, Ley proved himself a buttonhole orator, talking loud enough to be heard by correspondents above the whirr of machines. On one occasion, dressed in a tatty raincoat, Ley stubbed out a cigarette before lamenting:

> This was a great rubbish heap – this factory! It was worse than a rubbish heap because it was fouled by communists. And then the Leader Adolf Hitler came along and all that was changed! Look at the happy workingmen! LOOK AT THEM!!

Like the thousands of KdF visitors before them, the Windsors' trip climaxed with a visit to Hitler's Berghof at Berchtesgaden. Dressed in a beige tunic, his eyes shining with pleasure, Hitler personally pointed out the views along the valley to Salzburg before leading the duke off for a private discussion in the presence of translator Paul Schmidt, who later quietly recounted there was nothing to indicate whether or not the duke sympathised with the ideology and practices of the Third Reich. 'Apart from some appreciative words for the measures taken in Germany in the field of social welfare the former king did not discuss political questions. He was frank and friendly with Hitler, and displayed the social charm for which he is known throughout the world.'

After two hours, Hitler bade farewell to his guests. One of the reporters observed that Hitler took the hand of the duchess between both of his and shook it cordially. 'Then he turned to the duke, shook hands with him, and gave the Nazi salute, which the Duke returned.' With a farewell wave, Hitler turned to his interpreter and chuckled smugly that the duchess would have made a good queen. A *New York Times* journalist wryly remarked that 'the duke demonstrated adequately that the Abdication did rob Germany of a firm friend, if not indeed a devoted admirer, on the British throne'.

15

NUREMBURG'S JOLLY GATHERING

Certain locations in Germany acquired an almost mythical quality during the years of National Socialism. For nearly a week, Mrs Jackson – the lady who had kept her eyes peeled for Jews in Cologne – meandered through the cobbled streets of Munich soaking up its magical combination of art, history, music and – as a fairy tale would have it – Nazism.

Under summer sun and clear blue skies, she stuck her head through the doorway the Hofbräuhaus, the grubby, windowless beer hall with peeling plaster where Hitler announced the first Nazi manifesto in 1920. Then, by foot, she set out to see all the gimmickry at the Feldherrnhalle, a vast shrine to the martyrs of Hitler's putsch on Königsplatz. 'A soldier stands to attention on either side of the plaque and as one passes, one raises the right arm in salute. Even cyclists and car drivers do so too,' Jackson observed.[1] (Non-Nazis avoided the structure by using a little bypass behind the hall, nicknamed Drückebergergasse, meaning 'shirker's lane'.) Venues connected with Hitler were proudly included in a lavish booklet published by the Verkehrsverein (Tourist Association) highlighting 'must visit' locations on a big, colourful map. It included apartments on Schleißheimer and Thiersstrasse where a young Hitler lived, the Nazi Party offices at Sterneckerbräu, Corneliusstrasse and Schellingstrasse, the famous

Braunes Haus, Ehrentempel, Führerbau, Burgerbräukeller and the Adolf Hitler Kaserne. Instead of a foreword, the guide opened with a quotation from *Mein Kampf* in which Hitler mentioned how impressed he was on his first visit to 'this remarkable German city'.

The American Socialist W. E. B. Du Bois was also impressed with Munich. During his visit, he settled into a modest pension in the somewhat gritty Altstadt. 'It is a city of the theatre, of music, of marvellous old buildings, and of beer,' he noted approvingly.

> Americans who have tasted strong beer made for long keeping, wide distribution, and exportation have no idea of the delicacy and satisfying quality of the best German beer astonishing, especially in South Germany, to see how much time is spent in the beer hall; and yet one is still tempted now, as in other day, to say that it is hard to see how ordinary, educated human beings could spend their time better. Certainly, in America the movie, the cabarets, and the card parties would not provide an enticing substitute. The beer halls are large and well aired. The proportion of alcohol in the best beer is very small, and the social intercourse of friends with friends and of strangers with each other gives a public courtesy which one cannot find in the American attempt to be at once exclusive and public.

Budget travellers soon discovered the cheapest dark beer, noted for its strength and flavour, could be found at a small bar at the main railway station, the starting point for pilgrims steaming to Nuremberg for the annual rally, where Hitler proclaimed important ideology.[2]

Officially known as the National Socialist Party Congress, the annual Nazi jamboree in Nuremburg was organised by Robert Ley and the sort of jackboot event that could only happen in Germany. However, by the 1930s, as faith in Nazism grew stronger, meetings had grown to unprecedented proportions, trebling Nuremburg's normal population of 450,000 and causing hotels, pensions and campsites to overflow. 'The hardest job of work I have tackled for long time has been trying to get a bedroom in Nuremberg for a friend who is anxious to see the Nazis in Congress next week,' the author of the *London Letter*, a syndicated column, noted tetchily. 'Every hotel in the town is crowded, and none of the tourist agencies can find an empty bedroom in a private house. One British general, who was to have been a guest of the German War Ministry, has had to be told that he accepted too late.'[3]

It became the norm for the foreign diplomatic corps – which included seven ambassadors and thirty-five ministers – to bed down in a Pullman train near the station, while KdF tourists were rewarded with a bunk in the collapsible 'Strength Through Joy' village, the same wooden structure used at the Olympic Games. Other billets were provided in school buildings and public halls, where 180,000 metal beds were erected. Many teenagers slept under canvas in 2,750 huge tents – a system which became problematic when 900 BDM girls were found to be pregnant after returning from the 1936 rally. One of the expectant mothers named thirteen Hitler Youths as possible fathers.[4]

Every year, Hitler and his cohorts installed themselves in the small but ornate Hotel Deutscher Hof, scene of the most lavish receptions and parties. Just as Hitler loved the 'Hof' in Nuremburg and the Kaiserhof in Berlin, other Nazi leaders had their own hotel preferences. For example, SS chief Heinrich Himmler ordered his officers to stay in the hotel Vier Jahreszeiten during any official or events in Munich but expressly forbade his men visit or eat in Berlin's Hotel Excelsior. 'This prohibition also applies to the Hotel Auf der Wartburg near Eisenach, which has the same owner,' the order explained. It transpired that in addition to being a 'high-grade Freemason', the owner had once ushered Hitler from his room before check-out time in order to accommodate new arrivals – a slight which was evidently never forgotten.

Hitler faced no such embarrassing episodes in Nuremburg, where every detail was meticulously planned. 'His standard was run up on the roof,' a journalist observed, 'while in the street below assembled the black uniformed guards whose business from now until the end of the rally is to prevent all pedestrians and vehicular traffic from approaching the hotel.' Diplomats, security officers and well-heeled party donors also filled the hotel, eager to rub shoulders with the Führer's inner circle. 'It is so full of celebrities,' a reporter radiantly declared, 'that Herr Hitler might walk into the bar at any moment and find that his whole Cabinet was there.'[5] At the annual Göring party, champagne corks popped as VIPs – many spruced up with garish uniforms – arrived from various fronts throughout the evening. Standing wide-legged in a sky-blue tunic, Göring regaled his guests with tales of his patched-together flying career, his hunting conquests and details of his ever-expanding art collection.

In many ways the rallies could be described as a kind of national love parade for the public too. Most days, the Wehrmacht, SA, SS, Hitler Youth, Reich Labour Service and Bund Deutscher Mädel marched in arenas, public spaces and the main market – all connected by over 200 miles of wire attached to loud-speakers.[6] Finnish writer Olavi Paavolainen was among a handful of writers from the Nordic countries invited to participate in a retreat of German writers supported by the Nazi government. 'It is an old truth, that fanaticism does not tolerate bantering,' Paavolainen observed. 'The young Nazis, who, under normal circumstances are joyful, sociable and great humorists, turned grave like Repenter monks when the conversation turned to the dogmas of national socialism.' During his trip, Paavolainen was shown northern Germany, but the highlight was a prized seat at the Nuremberg Rally, an event etched on his mind ever after. 'The march past of 45,000 men in dark brown trousers begins,' he commented admiringly. 'It takes two hours ... Young men from all walks of life ... brandishing spades gleaming like mirrors on their shoulders instead of a rifle and singing like only the Germans can! There is no end to the cheering and enthusiasm of the audience ...'[7]

The rallies always opened to a crush of international reviews. 'For the past three days scores of special trains have been bringing thousands of Germans and foreign visitors from all parts of the country,' a newswire writer explained, describing a town enshrouded in banners bearing Nazi slogans. 'Throughout last night the streets and cafes were scenes of the wildest revelry with Nazis singing and dancing to the strains of their national songs.'[8] Indeed, if residents couldn't see the commotion, they certainly heard it. From belfries over which fluttered the swastika flag, the church bells of Nuremberg rang for an hour to proclaim with religious note the beginning of the rally.

Albert Speer created an almost 'mythical' place which, he hoped, would attract visitors and tourists for generations to come:

> The Party Rally terrain was also intended, in the course of generations, to grow into a district given over to spiritual ceremony. The rally area itself was only to be the first stage and the nucleus of the whole. Oak groves had already been planted and staked out. All sorts of buildings of a religious nature were to be erected within them: monuments to celebrate the concept of the Movement and its victories; memorials to outstanding individuals ... I secretly decided to place my own tomb by the grand processional avenue, just where the avenue crossed the lake.

As well as the usual demonstrations of German nationality – flag waving, roll calls and commemorations – the event offered a sporting and cultural programme that transformed the whole city into a huge festival area. However, the most important aspect was the almost religious orientation towards Hitler, as a British correspondent learned when he watched 70,000 spectators gather to witness the Führer speak on a sun-splashed meadow.

> The rally will be marked by one of the greatest electric lighting displays ever achieved. All around this huge space have been erected 150 giant searchlights. Simultaneously they will send their rays into the sky. Fifty more searchlights will cast a brilliant glow on to the stand on which Herr Hitler himself is taking the salute. All Nuremburg was awake at 8am for the very good reason that 400 of General Göring's Air Force planes had arrived overhead. They are to take part in Monday's great air display. Hearing the thunderous roar, aliens ran into the streets and gazed wonderingly at the fighters and bombers gleaming in the sun.[9]

A works outing. During the 1920s, as more employers realized the benefits of a contented workforce, leisure organisations emerged to cater for the workers. 'The Friends of Nature' promoted 'a feeling for the outdoors' through regular hikes and rambles, while a plethora of small independent agencies sprang up offering day trips and multi-day excursions.

The travel scene expanded before the war when the major steamship companies hit financial troubles and launched luxury trips, giving birth to the lucrative pleasure cruise.

Workers enjoy a drink at the local Bier Stube. KdF rolled out education programmes, excursions, sports activities and social evenings held either in the factory canteen or at a local pub.

Robert Ley's office complex on Fehrbelliner Platz, from where he oversaw the DAF and KdF. (Photo: Nathan Morley)

Above left: Factory workers take a bike ride into the country. Members opined that to belong to a KdF sports club was a grand thing, as good as any private society.

Above right: Learning to ski at work. Special KdF skis, roller skates and tennis rackets were provided by the movement. Skiing lessons were held in factory dining halls and on artificial snow, and those taking the courses usually signed up for holidays in the mountains during the winter.

A KdF group enjoys a ski trip in the Alps. Everything from boots to goggles were supplied by the KdF.

Above left: A female worker gets stuck into a sports session after work. As an incentive, many workers aimed at obtaining a Reich sport badge, an idea initiated at the turn of the century and revived by the Nazis. By 1934, over 300,000 badges were won each year.

Above right: Workers check the latest KdF activity programme. Over time, factories appointed a *KdF-Wart* (representative) to promote outings and cultural programmes as well, generating enthusiasm about forthcoming trips.

In 1934, 1,000 factory and office workers arrived at this station Berchtesgaden, a village nestled high in the Alps, for the first KdF Bavaria holiday. (Photo: Nathan Morley)

Visitors to Berlin Zoological Gardens – Germany's oldest and most illustrious zoo – were able to admire 433 species of mammals including hippos, a well-stocked antelope house, a yawning Asiatic lioness and giant Indian elephants.

Having worked up an appetite for Hitler, Berlin Zoo's director, Lutz Heck, was quick to bring the zoo into line with the goals of national socialism.

Hitler declared that the two great roads being constructed through Berlin, known as the North–South and the East–West Axes, 'were planned to carry the traffic of the year 2000 or 2500 and not of 1940'.

Tourists inspect the Brandenburg Gate in central Berlin. A brochure titled *Beautiful Berlin*, published in German, English and French, described Berlin as a city 'set in emeralds'.

An evening class for young workers. DAF also assumed influence in the field of vocational and professional development and introduced correspondence study programmes to attract night-workers and those in the countryside.

Above right: The impressive new autobahns received international acclaim. By the mid-1930s, over 120,000 workers were directly employed in their construction, as well as an additional 270,000 in the supply chain for construction equipment, steel, concrete and maintenance equipment.

Below right: A worker heads south for a much needed vacation in Bavaria. The *Völkischer Beobachter* reported in September 1934 that the KdF had ferried 44,771 tourists to Upper Bavaria during the previous eight months.

Below: A group of friends enjoy the Baltic sunshine. Schoolboy Willy Schuman remembered that 'every year more summer visitors came to enjoy the magnificent snow-white sandy beaches' of Prerow, an up-and-coming Baltic spa resort four hours from Berlin by train.

Construction work at the world's largest resort set amid the sand dunes at Prora on the Baltic island of Rügen.

Tempelhof Airport became an architectural advertisement for the thrill of air travel: a glorious entryway into the new Germania in the heart of Berlin. (Photo: Nathan Morley)

The check-in desk at Tempelhof. Lufthansa, Imperial Airlines and KLM were busily developing new tourist routes crisscrossing the continent from Helsinki in the north to Lisbon near the tip of Africa.

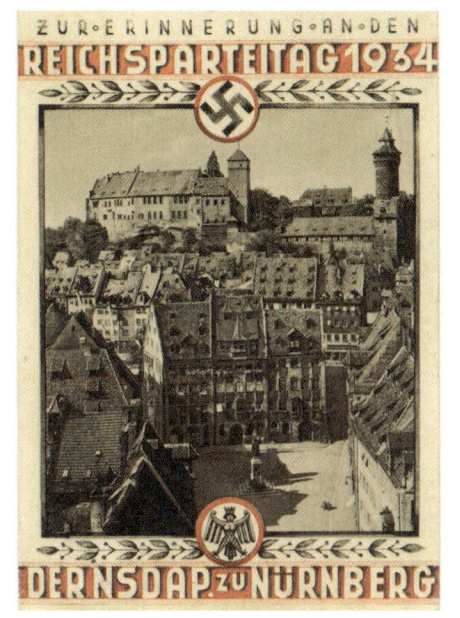

Above left: Officially known as the 'National Socialist Party Congress', the annual Nazi jamboree in Nuremburg was organised by Robert Ley and the sort of jackboot event that could only happen in Germany.

Above right: A KdF tour group inspects the Nazi rally grounds at Nuremburg. In many ways the rallies could be described as a kind of national love parade for the public too. Most days, the Wehrmacht, SA, SS, Hitler Youth, Reich Labour Service and Bund Deutscher Mädel marched in arenas, public spaces and the main market – all connected by over 200 miles of wire attached to loudspeakers.

Tourists flock to Hitler's Berghof. Baedeker described it as a 'stately mountain retreat in one of the most picturesque spots in Europe 60 miles along the motorway from Munich, near the Austrian border'.

Left: During the long dry summers, most visitors found time for a splash at Wannsee beach in the forests west of the capital. Offering fresh air and nature – it served a release valve for all of Berlin.

Below: Factory workers enjoy a weekend in the Baltic. Such excursions were popular and affordable from 1934.

The Nazis quickly dominated proceedings at the annual Munich beer festival as this postcard from 1935 shows.

KdF's first purpose-built liners, the *Wilhelm Gustloff* and *Robert Ley*. The limits of KdF's popular appeal were never more apparent than when ocean liners set out on trips to Portugal, Spain, Greece, Yugoslavia and Libya representing a vast expansion in the holiday programme.

KdF vacationers drove through a merciless ocean of sand dunes to inspect the excavations of Sabratha, 80 kilometres from Tripoli. 'The city, originally founded by Phoenicians, later ruled by Carthage and finally by Rome showed the magnificent Roman culture which united this country,' *Arbeitertum* noted.

KdF tourists inspect the ruins of Pompeii.

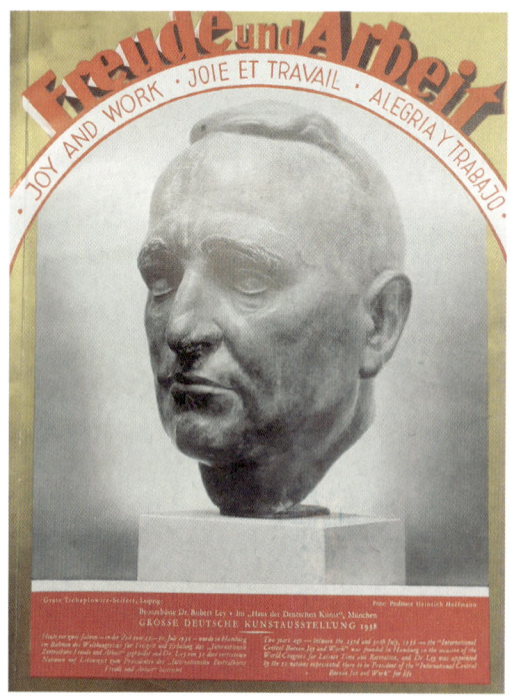

Above left: Robert Ley immortalised. Ley was appointed the head of the 'Action Committee for the Protection of German Labour' in 1933 and forcibly dissolved unions and absorbed their assets into a new Deutsche Arbeitsfront, known as DAF, a National Socialist undertaking.

Above right: Although a thoroughbred Nazi, Herman Esser was not widely beloved among his colleagues; even his boss Joseph Goebbels developed a powerful dislike of this 'thoroughly rotten character'.

As a point of pride and propaganda for the regime, the *Hindenburg* was described as Germany's 'Grand Hotel' of the air with accommodation for fifty passengers and two promenade decks.

Above left: Soldiers enjoy a break in the Alps. In the first years of the war, German policymakers, motivated in large part by a fear of tired and demoralised troops, promoted 'purposeful travel' such as short excursions and vacations.

Above right: Hitler was determined to pull the country from the Old World by making 4 million Germans car owners by developing a new Volkswagen, or people's car, designed to his personal specifications.

Top left: German soldiers take a break during a journey to France on a Reichsbahn train. From 1939, the priority of the railways was shifted from civilian to military movements, which, under the strain, struggled to maintain an adequate timetable.

Below left: German troops in Paris. Over time, either in the line of duty or on leave, German troops saw Prague, Paris, Rome, Athens, Crete and Tobruk during their military service.

Below: A popular postcard showing a soldier dashing for the 'leave train', taking him home or to a recreation centre or resort.

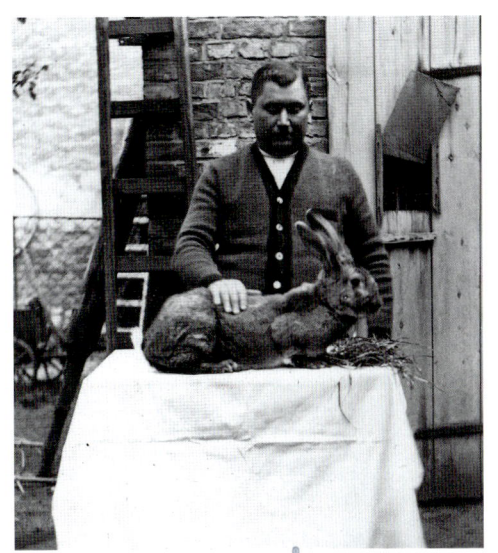

Above left: For the creative, there were many inventive ways to supplement meagre food supplies. Rabbits – which became known as 'balcony pigs' – often made up the main course on family occasions, while it was also rumoured – but never really proved – that cats were nicknamed 'rooftop rabbits' for obvious reasons.

Above right: From 1942, life on the home front became increasing difficult. Many women were mobilised for either factory of farm work.

Football remained a popular pastime with both workers and the military during the war. Although a welcome distraction, Joseph Goebbels thought football useless for propaganda purposes as he noted in his diary when Sweden beat Germany 3-2 at the Olympic Stadium. In his usual acidic way, he scowled that the 100,000 spectators 'cared more about the game' than the capture of any city in the East.

The only domestic travel pamphlet published in 1944 was commissioned by the SS and dropped by plane over the advancing US armies. Designed to lower morale (and encourage defections), the mockingly titled *Go South to Sunny Germany* leaflet – based on the design of pre-war tourism material – featured a smiling, bikini-clad beauty plugging the seductive line, 'A land of sun and smiles awaits you.'

On 25 April 1945, Hitler's beloved Berghof, the site of so much holiday fun and happiness, was blown to smithereens by RAF bombs.

Nuremburg's Jolly Gathering

Watching from below, future British Prime Minister Edward Heath 'saw it all, every day for three days' during his student travels. 'This was when I realised what they (the Nazis) were really like,' he recounted. In contrast, John Baker White, an ardent anti-communist and latterly MP for Canterbury, fell all over himself praising the rally, noting 'not one single attempt was made to pump us full of Nazi creeds and philosophies':

> We were left absolutely free and unfettered to form our own opinions, to go where we pleased without hindrance and were given no propaganda material of any kind. Our efficient, always charming, always patient guides, with one exception all officers in the SS guards, took every care to see that we reached the Congress and demonstrations in comfort and in proper time, that we were fed as comfortably as Nuremberg could manage and that we were returned to our hotel as soon as arrangements allowed. Nobody could have carried out a difficult task with greater efficiency.[10]

At its peak, the military and oratorical display at Nuremberg, which initially lasted four days, then seven and finally eight, brought a million visitors to the city. Foldout maps and detailed guides to the arena, Luitpold congress hall, the stadium and other attractions were printed in English, Italian, French and German.

An unexpected sidelight for locals was the frequent appearance of foreign tourists and dignitaries. For example, in 1938, 100 Arabs sailed from Palestine to attend the rally – paid for by Germany. 'These are surely queer guests for the great Nazi festival,' the British press mused. 'There is something more than suspicion that Italy and Germany have had a hand in encouraging the Arabs of Palestine in their revolt against the Jews and against British authority.'

Albert Speer's work at Nuremburg secured his meteoric rise to the top of the National Socialist hierarchy. All the more surprising was that Speer was hardly a stereotypical Nazi either – being handsome, multilingual, well-educated and dignified. As a young architect, Speer had been responsible for the planning of all major mass rallies since 1933, and designed Hitler's New Chancellery at the horrendous price tag of RM 90 million – corresponding to almost a billion euros today. The showpiece of the structure was a 146-metre-long marble gallery leading to Hitler's majestic 'office', which, at 390 square metres, was the size of a small supermarket. Hitler, who helped design some of the building himself, also took the precaution of installing an underground bunker, which, as will become clear, turned out to be a valuable asset.

Speer was also busy with another job, having been handed the task of refashioning Berlin into the future 'Germanic capital' of the world. In 1938, his grandiose plans were carried a stage further as work began at sixteen different points in the capital and its suburbs, with Hitler personally trampling through a muddy construction site to lay the foundation stone of the House of German Tourist Traffic on the Potsdammerstrasse. Göring boasted to British Ambassador Eric Phipps of plans for a magnificent avenue from the Spree to a greatly enlarged Tempelhof Airport along which a number of ministries would be erected.

> A 'colossal' luxury hotel will be placed there, with another one less luxurious though equal in size for the 'Strength through Joy' organisation, so as to show the German workman that he also counts in the new Reich. The course of the Spree is to be deflected, and a huge embankment built so that the Spree will be 'wider than the Seine'. A triumphal arch will span the new avenue (the largest arch in the world). 'That street in Paris,' said General Göring, (presumably referring to the Champs Elysées), 'is only 78 metres wide, this avenue will be 148 metres wide.'

The whole of the famous Avenue of Victory, with its thirty-two statues of the rulers of Brandenburg and Prussia, one of the best-known sights of Berlin, was shifted to another part of the Tiergarten in the course of the reconstruction. While some were dazzled by this vision of Germania, others quietly denounced the project as a *folie de grandeur*. In his speech, Hitler declared that the two great roads being constructed through Berlin, known as the North–South and the East–West Axes, 'were planned to carry the traffic of the year 2000 or 2500 and not of 1940'. At the same time, work was started on two new railway stations – one for the west-bound traffic and the other for east-bound traffic. As huge swathes of the city centre were earmarked for destruction to make way for the project, Speer noted Hitler's enthusiasm about the future touristic possibilities.

> The Finance Minister could realize what a source of income to the state my buildings will be in fifty years. Remember what happened with Ludwig II. Everyone said he was mad because of the cost of his palaces. But today? Most tourists go to Upper Bavaria solely to see them. The entrance fees alone have long since paid for the building costs. Don't you agree? The whole world will come to Berlin to see our buildings. All we need do is tell the Americans how much the Great Hall cost. Maybe we'll exaggerate a bit and say a billion and a half instead of a billion. Then they'll be wild to see the most expensive building in the world.[11]

16

THE TIDE TURNS

Throughout the late 1930s, tourism remained remarkably robust, despite international crises in Abyssinia, the Rhineland, Spain and Czechoslovakia. 'If there's one thing I'm certain of,' rhapsodised Eric Taverner in his book *These Germans*, published just prior to the German absorption of Austria, 'is that the last thing Hitler wants is war.'

Taverner based his work on pedestrian encounters gained during a driving holiday through Germany, but above all he was interested on British opinions of Hitler. He sniffily surmised a popular view:

> Some people object to him because they consider him just a nobody. What the devil can he know about governing? 'He was only a house-painter,' they say. Was there not once a common carpenter who has had quite a large influence upon the history of the world? Ex-painter and ex-corporal he may be, but the present dictator, far more correctly described as the leader of Germany, is today essential to the life of the State.

Taverner, therefore, must have been genuinely shaken when Hitler's troops marched into Vienna on 13 March 1938, occupying police stations, transport hubs and government offices. National Socialists, fellow travellers and opportunists threw flowers at Wehrmacht troops on the streets, evoking images of liberation. Barely twenty-four hours later, Robert Best, the British United Press special correspondent, watched the sun blaze down on Hitler as he drove into Vienna to the thunderous screams of '*Ein Volk, ein Reich, ein Führer!*' At various times, Best was deafened by the commotion. 'His car moved along the Ringstrasse while Vienna echoed to the thunder of cheering. He was standing in his car, returning the Nazi salute of the crowds, who were packed to suffocation along the route.'[1] Shivering with excitement, Hitler phoned Göring a few hours later. 'You just cannot imagine. I had completely forgotten how beautiful my country is,' he gushed tearfully.

The highlight of the day, for propagandists, at least, was a wet-eyed Hitler standing beside his parents' grave near Linz, where he gave a performance designed to underline the emotionality of bringing his homeland into the Reich. After the triumphant reception from locals, Hitler personally took over the 'sponsorship' of Linz, which henceforth became known as 'Hitler's Patenstadt' and received special designation, placed before other municipalities in matters of budget, culture and development.[2]

As exciting as all this was, for the average tourist stuck in the middle of the commotion the exhilaration was short lived. 'Women who were there say it was a nerve-racking experience,' the *Belfast News* reported. 'In any case, the old charm of Austria must to a great extent have vanished, and the delightful hospitality the people will have been overshadowed in some degree by their own national problems.' In fact, many British tourists massing around the embassy complained of receiving heavy-handed treatment from Nazi officials. Already jittery, some telegrammed experiences to Fleet Street reporters. 'Travellers arriving in Switzerland from the Tyrol and other holiday resorts in Austria report that every corner of the land is full of German police and German troops,' a newswire informed. 'Dour, overbearing Prussians have taken over the posts of smiling, helpful Austrian policemen. Troops have taken the best accommodation, even in the holiday resorts, and it is said the charm of Austria as a holiday resort has already been ruined.'[3] As early as 14 March, the *Völkischer Beobachter* reported Austrian police had become 'a reliable National Socialist popular instrument of power in the hands of the Führer'.[4]

Before Germans had a chance to catch their breath, Hitler's lust for territory continued when a fortnight later he laid claim to the Sudetenland, sparking an emergency meeting of Hitler, Italian leader Benito Mussolini, British Prime Minister Neville Chamberlain and the French leader Édouard Daladier. Their talks, held at Berchtesgaden, resulted in the so-called 'Munich agreement' requiring Czechoslovakia to vacate its Sudeten regions. While Chamberlain – brandishing the agreement and 'predicting peace in our time' – believed he had saved the day, Hitler inched a step further in the war he was planning to secure *Lebensraum* in the east.

Meanwhile, as echoes of the old Austria were being wiped away, Hitler's political opponents were packed off to Dachau and measures were adopted against the Jewish population as the so-called Nuremberg Laws excluded Jews from business and social life.[5]

American author and adventurer Negley Farson, famed for penning the classic *Going Fishing*, witnessed Jewish intellectuals and prominent philosophers forced to scrub sidewalks. 'When a Nazi band from Vienna stampeded into my friendly old hotel,' Farson recounted, 'I told the proprietor whom I had come to know so well that, in saying goodbye, I was probably seeing him for the last time.'[6] Farson's initial reaction to this apparent madness was to question how Austrians, blessed with a 'fascinating mountain life, so exhilarating with its deep pine forests and perpetual snow on the mountain peaks', could fall for the cruelty embodied in Hitler's Nazism. 'Yet they fell.'

In protest, a group of influential celebrities – including Fred Astaire, Bette Davis and Edward G. Robinson – were especially critical of the situation in Austria and called upon President Roosevelt to sever economic relations with Berlin and boycott

The Tide Turns

German goods. As the Nazis committed outrage after outrage in Austria, the protests from Washington and London remained protests and nothing more. However, as it turned out, public anger saw many foreigners shunning holidays in Austria and instead opting for Switzerland, Scandinavia or even Romania, which was actively seeking tourists. The growing distaste for the Hitler regime had already seen the British Transport and General Workers' Union address the issue and recommend a boycott on holidays in Germany: 'My advice to this Congress is to tell affiliated members to keep out of Germany until a decent moral standard of government is in force there,' Mr J. Porter from Distributive Workers in Manchester told delegates.[7]

As a countenance, although rather weak, the 'Link', a British–German friendship group with thousands of members, many with fascist leanings (it styled itself as a non-political group designed to promote Anglo-German friendship), encouraged its members to take holidays in Germany and Austria. Such trips were heavily promoted by the *Anglo-German Review* (AGR), a magazine not only sympathetic to Hitler but also possibly bankrolled by the Nazis. Many AGR contributors were also expert in using some of the old writing ploys to make points, slipping in arguments about how ostracizing Germany would not improve the situation of the Jewish population.[8]

Knowing first hand how devastating a boycott could be, commercial travel agencies, including MER, began diverting German tourists to Austria to plug the shortfall in foreign tourists.[9] At the same time, the Nazi press played its part in rousing public enthusiasm. The world-famous Capuchin mountain in Salzburg was renamed Strength through Joy Mountain, and before long the medley of foreign languages once heard in Vienna was replaced by assorted German accents. KdF budget trips provided a short-term increase in overnight stays – for instance, on Mother's Day weekend, Salzburg welcomed 1,456 KdF overnight guests from Munich, Augsburg, Ludwigsburg and Nuremberg. By the end of 1938, every tenth KdF trip was to Austria; one year later it was every second trip. Austria quickly became the most popular travel destination in the Reich.[10]

Austrians were swiftly ushered into most KdF programmes, including sea cruises to Norway and Helgoland.[11] Another source of revenue came from German soldiers frittering away their pay at beer halls in the Prater, an eclectic jumble of fairground attractions between the Danube and the canal in Vienna, where they helped to increase national beer consumption by 5 per cent in the first four months of annexation.[12] When Hermann Esser's organisation assembled the 1938 edition of the Reichs-Handbuch Der Deutschen Fremdenvekehrs-Orte – a guide for travel agents – the authors imbued Hitler's boyhood home town of Linz in Austria with distinction. A wistful accolade paid tribute to the years Adolf Hitler spent in Linz up to the death of his mother at Christmas 1907: 'These were decisive for the formation of his character and worldview.' Furthermore, tourists were strongly advised to visit the town hall, 'from where Hitler merged Austria to the German Reich from the balcony, liberating the people of Ostmark on March 13 1938'.[13]

In an attempt to attract wealthy customers from friendly countries, Indian nationalist Habib ur Rahman was commissioned by the Nazis to write an article on the ancient Austrian spa of Bad Gastein, which had been in the resort business for 500 years. However, the whole feature is so nickel-and-dime that one suspects it was a reminiscence of a hack from the Ministry of Propaganda. 'Because of beautiful surroundings and incomparable healing properties Bad Gastein has the reputation of an international spa,' 'Rahman' began. The visitor's book, he observed, showed guests from every climate and shore came seeking new strength and healing for their ills.[14]

> The foreign writings make up a truly mosaic pattern, the European writing, the Oriental, starting from left to right, such as Hindustani, Arabic and Persian. The local authorities take great care that internationally famous guests enter their names in the visitor's book and there are many delightful inscriptions and many words of praise dedicated to Bad Gastein in it. In between the American and Arabic names there are also Chinese and Japanese characters which denote Chinese and Japanese guests who also visit Bad Gastein in considerable numbers.

The Tide Turns

In the Gastein thermal water and flowing gasses there is an unusually large amount of radioactive emanation. The amount of this emanation in the thermal water varies from spring to spring. According to investigation it is assumed that within the depths from whence spring the Gastein thermal waters there are great quantities of stone with radioactive emanation and because of the extraordinary similarity of action there can be no doubt that here the radioactive body is radium itself. The thermal water itself is pure and clear.

Bad Gastein can boast that every hotel and pension is in itself a Kurhaus, that is, in every house the thermal baths necessary for the cure have been built in, and in the form of Roman bath cabins. The guests have every different kind of hotel at their disposal. There are very elegant hotels, complete with every modern appliance and the last word in comfort, as for instance the Grand Hotel de l'Europe, where there was a reception recently to give an enthusiastic welcome to Dr. Goebbels, who arrived suddenly on a visit. Dr. Goebbels showed particular interest in the baths and everything connected with the character of the town as a health resort. Bad Gastein has a great future before it and expects that it will occupy the place to which it is entitled through the National Socialist regime.[15]

The flipside of the sudden surge of traffic to Austria was that, predictably, German domestic tourism suffered. After losing their share of vacation spending to their neighbour, the good folk of Berchtesgaden were left with a new dilemma. While tourists still crowded the mountain tracks, cafes and hotel lobbies, there were fewer of them. 'This decline was to be expected,' the Berchtesgaden Travel Council bravely noted. Careful to avoid any mention of Austria, it surmised that 'Berchtesgaden must make every effort to keep its winter traffic and not to fall too far behind in other areas due to the lack of mountain railways'. The fact remained that Berchtesgaden had assets that would be the envy of many mountain resorts, including a modern rail station, highway connection and raft of accommodation at all prices.

Meanwhile, the government was searching for ideas to bolster hotel occupancy rates after a drop in British tourists was blamed on the seizure of Sudetenland. Adding fuel to the fire, German exile organisations, church congregations and Jewish groups in Britain actively called for boycotts of Germany. 'We have examined the reasons for these cancellations,' Franconia's governor Julius Streicher haughtily noted in his *Fränkische Tageszeitung*. 'We have learned that those Englishmen who almost became our guests declined because they believed that they would thus put themselves within the range of Czech guns. This information consoles us for we know that the Czech cannon are not long enough to disturb us. It may be assumed that the knowledge will also eventually spread to England.' Furthermore, Streicher chided that English absentees must be satisfied with less beautiful and eventful vacations. 'Indeed, it serves them right for letting themselves get excited by scare talk.'

In stark contrast, at the same time the island of Sylt was attracting tourists, but the wrong type. As Jews were pushed out of resorts in Bavaria and the Rhineland, the Gestapo expressed alarm that many Jewish guests continued arriving on Sylt, a ruggedly beautiful island off Germany's north-west coast. In particular, a police report noted they were comfortably ensconced in the pretty towns of Westerland, Wenningstedt and Kampen. 'Inexplicably, in these seaside resorts the Jews are still more or less welcomed with open arms, since the mentality of the islanders considers profit over the National Socialist worldview.'[16] The report fumed that no special hours of use were set for Jews in the recreation centres and cafes, nor were special cubicles made available to Jews in the lido at Westerland. 'The entire beach is still available to Jews to use freely. A special beach for the Jews has not yet been created.' The police chief ended on a stern note:

> I intend to prohibit Jews from staying in the seaside resorts of Kampen, Wenningstedt and List. I see myself compelled to take this measure, as several Reich Ministers intend to spend their vacation in Kampen, including Field Marshal General Göring and his wife as well as Reich Minister Darre.

The Tide Turns

The reference to Göring was indeed no exaggeration. Flush with financial success – including her RM22,000 salary from the State Theater – Emmy Sonnemann had built a beach cottage on the Rote Kliff sand dunes between Wenningstedt and Kampen. She'd often drive to Hamburg and then fly to Sylt, which she described as her very own 'paradise of peace and quiet. I used to spend a month there every summer. It was the best relaxation of all for me.'[17] By time the Görings became honorary citizens of Kampen the Jews had long gone. The mayor of Wenningstedt also had signs nailed to beach railings forbidding 'taking pictures of Colonel General Göring and his wife while bathing'.

Meanwhile, the spirit propelling the anti-Jewish action was in full swing in Garmisch-Partenkirchen. During March 1938, the local council was 'taking strident and vigorous measures to tackle the "problems" caused by Jews and Free Masons,' as the Monthly Work Report reveals:

> The high point of activity was a rally in the ballroom in Garmisch on the topic 'Tourist Season without Jews'. This manifestation was extremely well attended, and expressed the general consensus that in the district Garmisch-Partenkirchen, Jews are likewise seen as undesirable. There was a very extensive positive response to the call to affix anti-Jewish signs to hotels, restaurants, boarding houses, stores, etc. Some business persons, hotels, and the like have still not responded by action to the call. It is reported from Grainau that the Jews consider these defensive signs to be ridiculous, and that they will not let themselves be deterred by them from entering the shops. Some business persons are of the opinion that if Jews are already banned from entering German shops, they should likewise not be allowed to travel by means of the German Reichsbahn Railway. In Ettal, previously a popular destination for Jews, they have stayed away this winter.[18]

Ruffled by the boycott of Austria, Goebbels quickly learned that life could hurl thunderbolts and assured the international community that Germany did not want to shut itself off from the world. The frontiers, he said, were open wide to all those who wished to visit.[19] Pushing the point further, Hermann Esser, in his capacity as Secretary of State for Tourist Traffic, insisted that 'understanding between nations would be unconceivable without tourist traffic'.[20] He also asserted that political leaders could use tourism 'for the furthering and realisation of their aims since it meets an important means of reinvigorating, strengthening and unifying the citizens of a nation and in addition thereto, it is a significant instrument for the attainment of goals in foreign policy'. He continued:

> To define the issue in an unequivocal manner: The intensive furthering of tourist traffic is valuable internally from a political point of view in that it increases the capacity for achievement and secures the wellbeing of the nation, thus seeking to bring about his recreation in contentment and peace. It is valuable from the point of view of foreign policy that it furthers understanding in the world and thus prepares the path leading to the attainment of the success of which National Socialism, due to its political outlook, has attained in the field of tourist traffic. The recognition of an important fact has become general, namely that national policy and tourist traffic policy are inseparably connected. The expression 'Tourist Traffic Policy' can therefore have but one meaning. It signifies that the fundamental principles of political state leadership must apply to all endeavours for the promotion of tourist traffic.

Strangely enough, and in contrast to Esser and Goebbels's assertions, Berlin – more by stupidity than judgement – provoked puzzlement in the summer of 1938 by demanding British passport holders obtain a visa before holidaying in the Reich. 'The recent events in Germany and Austria had already caused many British tourists to change their minds about having a holiday in those countries,' a talkative London travel agent remarked. 'This latest regulation about visas will undoubtedly cause a further decrease in the number of British visitors this year.'[21] As it happened, 578,880 British tourists took holidays that year, a figure only eclipsed by the 1.3 million guests from Czechoslovakia, mostly Sudeten Germans. Official figures show the Belgians sent 120,060

The Tide Turns

guests, Bulgaria 36,754, Denmark 342,327, France 210,819, Italy 466,008, Japan 19,339, Yugoslavia 154,778, the Netherlands 607,433, Norway 89,659, Poland 164,727, Sweden 43,191, Spain 38,925, Turkey 47,040 and the USA 447,640.[22]

Every visitor returned home with a story, impression or emotion. Some told of their experiences seeing cruelty to Jews, while others lamented the massive rearmament and militarisation of the country. Even foreign correspondents in the Reich became increasingly alarmed at the hostility towards Germany in the international press. One of them, an idealistic Berlin-based journalist named Philip Gibbs, cautioned his readers on the subject, claiming that most Germans had no interest in politics. In a kind of glancing commentary, he complained that newspapers – and many individuals – fell into a habit of speech which was disastrous to a proper understanding of life:

> I have to plead guilty to that myself. It is the custom of speaking about Germany or France or Italy or any other country, as though it were a psychological unit – a hydra-headed monster with all its heads thinking the same thoughts, reacting in the same way to any event – delivering judgment as one mind and body upon all questions of national importance. That is profoundly and grotesquely untrue, as all of us know by a moment's thought but constantly forget say that Germany is intolerant, Germany is militarist, Germany is oppressed, but when one goes to Germany one finds crowds of careless youth singing old songs in the Rhineland, if the sun is shining, and anxious men and women hurrying on their business in Berlin, and lovers holding hands in the Tiergarten, and young students with their noses in their books on the university steps, and millions of individual dreams, and difficulties of daily life, World Politics, or what the special correspondent of the London Times wrote the day before yesterday, does not assume such importance in German minds as the question of where they will spend the summer holidays or whether eggs are more plentiful in the markets.

17

FOLLOW THE SUN

The limits of KdF's popular appeal were never more apparent than when ocean liners set out on trips to Portugal, Spain, Greece, Yugoslavia and Libya, representing a vast expansion in the holiday programme. Stealing the show was KdF's first purpose-built liner, the *Wilhelm Gustloff*, a sleek, modern vessel topped with a white smokestack. Sprawled over ten decks, it offered passengers seven bars, a cinema, smoking room, winter garden, library, swimming pool and a fully equipped gymnasium.

Almost immediately, the sheer size of the *Gustloff* aroused considerable speculation in the foreign media about its 'true purpose'. With its long upper deck obstructed only by the funnel, some reporters mulled that it could easily be converted into an aircraft carrier. *Reynolds Sunday News*, a British tabloid popular with the working classes, quoted a shipping expert as saying that the deck could be lengthened to form a landing strip and the vessel's speed could be readily increased. Thus modified, it could accommodate thirty-five aircraft – half the number accommodated by Britain's supercarrier *Ark Royal*.

The Nazi press brushed off such speculation as 'nonsensical', as did its first passengers. 'The *Wilhelm Gustloff* is a ship to celebrate and be happy,' declared Gertrud Meyer, a fashion designer and enthusiastic KdF beneficiary. Exploring the *Gustloff*, she marvelled at the 'five dance floors, a concert hall and cinema … It has everything.' Likewise, propaganda described the ship as the most 'visible proof' that there was no class distinction in National Socialist Germany. 'It is a ship without class,' *Arbeitertum* asserted in a four-page profile.

> The 1,460 passengers and the crew are billeted in identical accommodation. Every single cabin has an outward view. According to this principle, the ship has been built to avoid constructing inner cabins without natural light.
>
> Each cabin contains either two or four beds. There is a wardrobe and a chair for each passenger, as well as a sink with cold and warm water. At the window there is a sofa in each cabin with a table. All the cabins are heated by means of steam heating and have ventilation systems and are spaced over five decks.

Additional publicity could be heard loud and clear. DAF produced a short film, *Schiff ohne Klassen*, showing the pennant-festooned vessel steaming to Madeira as holidaymakers relaxed on sun loungers, played table tennis and flailed about in the swimming pool. 'All German districts have sent workmates to enjoy this first great KdF voyage,' *Arbeitertum* gleefully reported. However, the main gossip that first day was the untimely death of fifty-five-year-old Captain Lübbe from a heart attack. 'At the funeral service onboard, the vacationers clustered on the deck said goodbye to the departed to the sound of the German hymns,' *Arbeitertum* noted solemnly. In her day-by-day chronicle, passenger Elisabeth Dietrich described how they dropped anchor off Dover and unloaded Lübbe's coffin onto another ship. Once the tide of emotion had faded, the *Reiseleiter* (cruise leader), assisted by the ship's first officer, handed out entertainment itineraries, which were hungrily inspected and debated. On the regular trips, the daily routine began with a trumpet 'wake-up call' at 6.20 a.m. followed by breakfast, exercises on the sports deck, morning music over the public address system, a lecture about attractions, a performance from the band, evening dancing, and so on. With strict adherence to the law, the barman shut the grill across his bar at 23.30 and 'quiet hours' were enforced from midnight.[1] For passengers not used to barrack-like life, the noise and tumult onboard could be suffocating. The aforementioned Gertrud Meyer complained of a total lack of privacy, with 'no corners to isolate'.[2]

Luckily, unlike the cruises to Scandinavia, those seeking an escape from the claustrophobia enjoyed trips to Lisbon and the surrounding area or to Sintra on the Atlantic coast as well as daytrips to Madeira by bus or car.[3] On-board parties organised in cooperation with the Portuguese leisure organisation Alegria no Trabalho were always a highlight. As one writer put it, 'the world was open to the working man like an enchanted garden; the sun of Africa greets him'.[4] Archibald Crawford KC, organising director of the British Economic League and a sympathetic supporter of the Nazi regime, was invited to join a two-week KdF cruise on the *Gustloff* to Lisbon and Madeira. During his trip, entertainment included the 'best marionette troupe in the world, leading opera singers, several orchestras and pocket money in Portuguese currency when on shore'.[5]

Life on board soon fell into a regular pattern. At sundown, the first stalwart punters began to drift to the public bars as waiters and porters scurried through alley entrances to the centers of the ship's night life. 'It is strange how quickly every mistrust fell,' recalled Maria Förster during a cruise around the Italian coast. 'It lasted only a few hours, and then what emerged was a great and trusting comradeship. Here sits the factory worker next to the young office employee, the country woman next to the city woman. There are no differences.'

During the voyage, there wasn't an inch of the ship that passenger Elisabeth Dietrich failed to carefully inspect. 'I visited the kitchen located on the A-Deck behind the front dining room where a young chef from Garmisch explained everything,' she commented admiringly. 'There are seven large kitchens, four large electric ovens and various other machines for everything. The meat is taken in frozen.'[6] She jotted down details of a lifeboat drill, visited the radio station, viewed the laundry and drying room and attended an on-board lecture entitled 'The Machinery of the *Wilhelm Gustloff*, which she transcribed in its entirety. 'The entire German industry was involved in building the *Wilhelm Gustloff*,' she began. 'Unfortunately, I couldn't hear this interesting presentation up to its end as the horn was blown for the 1st group to eat.'[7]

Dietrich would have no doubt been impressed with the subtly lit dining room adorned with mahogany furniture, red sprigged carpet and tables set with silver cutlery. It was a sight that dazzled holidaymaker Max Ehlert: 'In the huge, wonderful dining rooms, meals are served at tables laid with white cloths – most passengers are amazed. Nobody expected such catering.'[8]

The fare was copious, from the hors d'oeuvres to the fruit and cheese. Breakfast consisted of oatmeal with milk, scrambled eggs with chives, cold cuts, jam, honey and bread as well as tea, coffee, hot chocolate and milk. Lunch featured a saucer of semolina soup, roast veal, spinach with butter, potatoes and, for dessert, chopped cherry with whipped cream. A rich three-course dinner at 7 p.m. was the most important meal. Passengers feasted on cauliflower soup as a starter and fillet steak with potatoes, a side dish of peas and carrots, and ice cream and waffles for dessert. Snacks and sandwiches were offered from 10 p.m.[9]

Given the plush surroundings, it was hoped passengers would display discipline and – despite regional and class boundaries – exemplary camaraderie. Travellers on these first cruises were made aware of the need to convey a positive impression of the 'national community' abroad. A detailed example of general measures can be found in the travel booklet *With KdF on Southern Seas* from 1936:

> When you are abroad, note the following: Follow the laws of your host country and do not interfere in its politics, not even in conversations. Behave politely and correctly during your excursions and walks, respect the manners and customs of other peoples. Always remember that you are a representative of your nation. The way you are judged, your fatherland is judged. Be proud to be a German, be especially proud to be a German National Socialist.

More importantly, they should also give the outward appearance that the social situation of Germans had improved since Hitler's ascent to power. To accomplish this, the KdF often loaned box brownies to make the less affluent passengers appear wealthier during shore trips (they were handed back on return to the ship). Creating the 'right impression' became an obsession with KdF managers – and paid dividends:

> The Portuguese with whom a German traveller and his comrades came into contact could not believe that the Germans were workers because they appeared to be so well dressed. Only when the tourists showed their hands to their hosts did the latter become convinced![10]

In less than five years, KdF holidaymakers were traveling in strange lands without knowing a word of the language and certain that they would never be lost, hungry or uncomfortable. They could also experience a selection of unusual locations. In Libya, a guide leading an excursion to the Italian colony extolled the vibrancy and industry of the 'Italian settlers' carving out a future of modernity in North Africa. Vacationers drove through a merciless ocean of sand dunes to inspect the excavations of Sabratha, 80 kilometres from Tripoli. 'The city, originally founded by Phoenicians, later ruled by Carthage and finally by Rome showed the magnificent Roman culture which united this country,' *Arbeitertum* noted. 'The excavations are ongoing and with carried out with infinite love and care.' Sandblasted and sunburnt tourists were served eggplant broth, mixed with onions and raisins over a communal mountain of brown couscous. In addition to wandering among the famous ruins at Leptis Magna in Tripoli and browsing dirty stalls selling cold fried fish, peanuts and fruits, passengers were invited to see first hand the 'lousy filth' of a Jewish neighbourhood,[11] while in Venice and Genoa, visits to the poor periphery and squalid dwellings became fixtures.[12] Although not to everyone's taste, Alfred Rosenberg believed in retrospect that such outings strengthened Germans' love for their homeland and impressed them with the fact that 'more was done for them at home than for workers elsewhere'.

However, for most travellers, it was the sweeping views of Africa's coast and contact with locals which made memorable vacations. 'Eating with other peoples is always one of the most revealing impressions,' noted a *Völkischer Beobachter* reporter who embraced the 'charm of the unknown' by sampling foreign foods. 'We will never forget the lunch that we had in Santa Lucia. Two tenors competed to sing us the most beautiful Neapolitan songs, and the band even played a Rhine song in our honour.'[13]

Under 'balmy skies', *Arbeitertum* journalist Kurt Schaaf reported from the 'threshold of the Orient' when he joined a KdF group onboard the *Oceana*, which docked at Piraeus near Athens. The young journalist was soon immersed in 'an unusually lively scene where street traders touted for business and shopkeepers spread wares out in front of their doors unbothered by dust and flies'. The group visited cafes and the Parthenon, and took a city tour by coach.[14]

Although DAF and KdF periodical features painted an idyllic picture of tourists roaming freely, an SS officer working as an agent during an Italian cruise was shocked at how everything was regulated down to the precise minute.

> The KdF vacationer had nothing to do but to let himself be led around. There is no period during the entire time that an escape can be had from this. Even the enthusiasm of the vacationers is regulated so that greetings and jubilation can be produced 'on command' so-to-speak. Nothing is left to chance or to the Italians. If the traveller is anxious for new experiences in a foreign country but can do nothing on his own; when all his steps are carefully regulated and commanded, he often ends up doing things against his will.[15]

Journalist Ferdinand Tuohy set his sights on a party of Germans in Venice, where three KdF ships docked for shore excursions. In a biting critique, he lamented that Venetians got little joy as 'each German was doled out ten lire a day for shore spending and they brought their own rations along. It was seeing Venice for nothing, in the locals' view. And the Venetians always were sharply critical.'[16]

Like Tuohy, Mr. S. S. Wilson keenly observed the comings and goings of KdF tourists during a visit to Italy. 'They are busy making friends with their new allies,' he joked in a letter to the *Chelmsford Chronicle* in which he detailed the military build-up in Italy. 'We were not allowed to go near Genoa as it is now a large war base from which aeroplanes bomb Spain. Large notices in four languages are posted in all the hotels warning foreigners to keep away from all military areas.'[17]

When the first KdF tourists berthed in Naples, along with Robert Ley, they were treated to a carefully scripted welcome from a simple metalworker:

> This is actually the first time that thousands of workers travel from one country to another to meet their comrades in work there, to get to know and understand fellow workers who speak another language and have another blood in their veins and to establish brotherly relations with them.
> This fact, that will not remain hidden even from our greatest enemies, we owe to the genius of our two great leaders, Hitler and Mussolini. National Socialism and Fascism bring new culture to the word.
> I am proud of the honour of being able to receive you today. You are workers like ourselves, workers of an industrious, strong and united country. And therefore, this day, a day on which we once more celebrate work, is a day of joy, a festival, a symbol of common friendship and common ideals. Your visit marks the beginning of an entirely new kind of relation between our two nations.[18]

Although some factory workers did get to enjoy such trips, especially in the first few months of their operation, many cruises were too expensive for blue-collar workers, a fact noted in an underground SPD report from a mechanic in the Rhineland. 'Often it is the better-off citizens and the Nazi bigwigs, of course, who take advantage of the KdF,' he stated. 'In our company of around 20,000 employees, only two men have been allowed to travel to the Azores for free.'[19] American chargé d'affaires in Berlin Hugh R. Wilson drew similar conclusions:

> The long excursions are apparently still beyond the means of ordinary workers, which would seem to show that low as the prices are, and although adapted to the situation of the lower middle classes, Strength through Joy has not yet succeeded in extending its maximum travel benefits to the ordinary worker. Various devices, such as raffles of free trips paid for by the employer, do not solve the difficulty.[20]

Before long, a second KDF liner, the *Robert Ley*, began plying the same routes. However, dissenters complained about its sanitary facilities. Although the décor was plush, there were only forty bathrooms serving 1,600 passengers (and just one hundred showers). As if this wasn't bad enough, during winter trips a lack of stabilisers left 'traces of seasickness visible everywhere ... gradually everyone disappears below deck, many muttering "never again!"'[21]

Despite the criticism, Robert Ley loved the ships and occasionally took advantage of a complimentary suite onboard the *Gustloff*. In his book *Caesar's in Goosestep*, author Norman Bayles told how he met a sorry-looking Ley in his cabin one evening 'still drunk from the night before and one of his assistants had to be carried out as he was so plastered. The cabin stank of old blood sausage, stale booze, and cigarettes.'

Quite apart from all this, events onshore frequently conspired to steal the thunder of KdF adventures in the Mediterranean. German tourists were often baffled by the hostile reaction from the locals. For example, in Split, Croatia, an excursion party were left open-mouthed when teenagers sarcastically shouted, 'Germany, Germany under everything' – a derogatory twist on their national anthem.[22] In Istanbul, a KdF tour party made sly digs at the local guides, accusing the Turkish government of having 'sold their country to Great Britain'. 'The guides thereupon refused to conduct the tourists any farther,' news media reported. An uglier incident occurred when a group of German tourists ordered two Jews to leave a coffee shop, causing a raucous outcry. 'Turkish customers rose and declared that Turkey was not Germany. The two factions came to blows and afterwards the partisans of Strength through Joy picked themselves up from the pavement and retreated in disorder.'[23] From the German point of view, this story – which appeared in many European newspapers – was an utter catastrophe.

On another occasion, a visit by 3,500 KdFers to Naples led to trouble for the management of the Opera House. The Germans were the guests of the civic authorities, and it was decided to give three performances of Puccini's opera *La Boheme* exclusively to the KdF. All tickets sold to the general public (including other foreign tour groups) had to be returned, as the theatre could only hold the KdF groups. After the concluding performance, the theatre management sent a bill to the government, but this appears to have offended the authorities, who immediately issued an order that the theatre be closed until further notice on the grounds of the unpatriotic and un-fascist manner in which they treated German Nazi visitors.[24]

As if the shenanigans and embarrassments in southern Europe weren't bad enough, a similar picture emerged from Sweden where KdF patrons left an equally poor impression. However, what was really striking, as a young journalist recognised, was the total lack of shame:

> Once upon a time there were individual restaurants that were world-famous for their smörgasbord. You enjoyed all the delicacies and nibbled here and nibbled there – you took one or the other twice – but it tasted too good – but everything was within the limits of decency – until a KdF party made Sweden insecure when uncultivated hordes stormed restaurants like swarms of locusts eating the tables bare. After months of such abuse, the most expensive delicacies were replaced with liver sausage. The lobster disappeared to make way for larger herrings with jacket potatoes, and the roast chicken was replaced by pork knuckle.[25]

18

1939

On 27 January 1939, Hermann Esser arrived on Wilhelmstrasse to take up his post as State Secretary for Tourism in the Reich Propaganda Ministry. Having served as chairman of the Reich Committee for Tourism (RAFV), he never tired of emphasising that tourism had to be a useful tool for the leadership to strengthen public health.

Although a thoroughbred Nazi, Esser was not widely beloved among his colleagues; even his boss, Joseph Goebbels, had developed a powerful dislike of this 'thoroughly rotten character'. Having earned his stripes brawling during the Munich beer hall days, Esser even brought a sneer to the lip of Gregor Strasser, a prominent Nazi in the early days, who considered him a vulgar scoundrel. As one writer put it, however, 'Hitler found him useful. And that clinched it.' A loyal scoundrel, it seemed, was better than a man with a mind of his own. Indeed, Esser was a swaggering hothead who loudly boasted of being 'kept in comfort' by lovers throughout the Reich, leading to cynical observers remarking it was never established how many children he fathered. He craved glory and publicity by penning his anti-Semitic magnum opus *Die Weltpest* (*The World Plague*), which was said to be a personal favourite of Hitler's.

During his first weeks in the job, Esser began sermonizing about an article in the SS newspaper *Das Schwarze Korps* which huffily demanded railway sleeping cars be reserved for Aryans as 'Nazis could not be expected to share compartments with Jews'. The diatribe – along with Esser's harrying – pushed operator Mitropa to ban both German and non-German Jews.[1] Increasingly nervous and frightened, Jews were still permitted to rent rooms at railway station hotels but were instructed to 'take their meals in their bedroom'.[2] For example, at the Reichshof in Hamburg, small stickers plastered on bathroom mirrors requested 'guests of the Jewish race' also eat in their rooms, and stay clear of the restaurant and bar.[3]

Even as this dastardly persecution persisted – and worsened – some foreign celebrities made appearances at German venues. Henry Hall, for one, was eager to snatch a hefty pay packet and took his formidable band to the Berlin Scala with the promise not to play a single tune by a Jewish composer. Arriving on the day that Jewish dentists and vets were barred from practising, Hall objected to being singled out 'to meet the accusation that I am acting in an unworthy manner when at least one other well-known band and numerous variety artistes have accepted similar contracts'. Furthermore, he scoffed, 'We and everybody else know that tunes composed Jews are barred in Germany, and so the only reasonable thing to do was not to include them our programmes.'[4] Instead, Hall promised old favourites like 'The Lambeth Walk', 'The Donkey's Serenade' and other tunes written by non-Jews. 'I do not want anybody to think that I'm concerned with German politics. We have to approach the matter in a reasonable common-sense way.' To add insult to injury, Hall clarified that no Jews were included in his twenty-two-man band (he did have Jewish musicians on his roster; they had been left in London for the duration of the four-week contract). Funnily enough, by the end of the engagement, Hall became fed up with wrangling and endless interference from the Ministry of Propaganda, which led to a BBC broadcast from the Scala being censored and his opening monologue cut. Hall had prepared a script about his impressions of Germany, sent it to London for approval, and it was returned to Berlin; however, just before transmission, the BBC received a telegram from Hall simply saying: 'Sorry, cannot talk tonight.'

Jews, of course, were nowhere in sight at the 1939 Berlin Motor Show, where every one of the party's prominent figures gathered at the Messe to stage a giant pep rally for Robert Ley's gleaming new Volkswagen. The event, obsessively covered by the media, gave Hitler the chance to launch a monologue about the dangers of speeding and road safety, two of his pet subjects. 'He who rides in a car is responsible not only for his own life but also for the lives of other people,' he roared into the microphone as he promised to make Germany the busiest from the point of view of traffic but also the safest.

> Every six years the German people suffer just as many dead in traffic accidents as the Franco-Prussian war of 1870-71 claimed altogether. This is an intolerable situation. Those who involve the nation in about 7,000 dead and from 30,000 to 40,000 injured annually are enemies of the people. It is necessary to exterminate dangerous drivers just mercilessly as road bandits.

The Motor Show was good copy right from the start. Hitler posed for the cover of several magazines inspecting engines, tyres and diagrams, while other snaps showed him beaming behind the wheel of a Volkswagen polished to a gleam. One magazine ran a six-page feature accompanied by no fewer than twenty-five photos. On the airwaves, the listening public were transfixed by descriptions of the new Austin, Sunbeam, Talbot and Humber. However, even the spanking new Hillman model – complete with powerful engine and blood-red paintwork – was outshone by the hoopla caused by the KdF-Wagen, which *Arbeitertum* predictably hailed as a 'socialist and technical miracle'.

In way of compliment, a British motoring expert said it was 'not at all freakish-looking … it has extremely modern lines, closely resembling a commercial make sold at over three times its price'. Dubbed the 'little wonder', it could seat four to five people and was equipped with a rear air-cooled engine which gave a speed of 62 mph. Its petrol consumption was 40 miles to the gallon and its tires were made of Buna, an artificial rubber, while the interiors used artificial silk and textiles instead of cotton, cutting down the need for imported materials.

The Motor Show was a roaring success, clocking over 825,000 visitors through the turnstiles. More to the point, many visitors arrived under the dubious assumption that their own KdF-Wagen subscriptions would soon bear fruit. However, some of the 250,000 buyers were already expressing genuine anxieties about the issue. While it is known 150,000 people were paying weekly instalments and expected to wait five years for delivery, the remaining 100,000 subscribers – made up of DAF officials and party members – cautiously hoped to receive their ignition keys by Christmas 1939.

Reflecting on the development of the KdF-Wagen, party ideologist Alfred Rosenberg thought it had turned out to be fast, solid and convenient but, in typical fashion, singled out the car for disapproval, saying that each one sold meant one child less to each family: 'The Volkswagen definitely did stand in the way of attempts to assure a large and healthy new generation.'

At the end of Motor Show, Goebbels sent a dozen trucks to the Messe to haul away the decorations to be recycled for celebrations to mark the Führer's fiftieth birthday. Hitler had officially become part of the calendar, and to create an event 'worthy of an emperor', council workers erected grand stands and filled the streets with decorations, along with twenty huge pylons topped with flat bowls in which fires were lit after dusk, harking back to familiar Roman themes. Gilt-edged flags fluttered from lampposts, roofs, steeples, balconies and hotel entrances. In typical grandiose style, Robert Ley decorated the exterior of the KdF offices as if it were a civic building, not just with bunting and giant swastikas but with a huge gold-framed portrait of Adolf Hitler. It was an astonishing sight.

As with the Olympics, private travel agencies and KdF worked on parallel tracks, each striving to get as many visitors to Berlin for the big occasion. Excitement mounted as the capital prepared for 'a day history would remember'. When it happened, a carefully choreographed parade lasted five hours and involved more than 40,000 soldiers and 1,500 officers, as well as 600 tanks. For more than four hours Hitler stood, almost continuously saluting, while soldiers goose-stepped and armoured vehicles roared and rumbled past. It turned out to be a very odd sort of parade in the eyes of CBS's William Shirer. He sat open-mouthed when heavy artillery roared passed the crowd, prompting spectators to clap enthusiastically. 'How could you applaud inanimate things like cannons and tanks?'

However, the local press were certainly impressed, as were foreign visitors like British motoring correspondent W. A. Gibson Martin, who happened to be visiting the city:

> ...it provided an interesting experience in evolving a traffic-free route, enabling me to bypass the military procession and go about my legitimate business. I had no difficulty in passing in front of, or behind, the procession which extended for some miles and took five hours to pass the saluting base. The main street – Unter den Linden – and its approaches were all closed to traffic of every kind for more than six hours, yet I was able to make several visits to places north and south of the procession route – which ran east to west – and still was able to return to the Adlon Hotel and see Herr Hitler pass along the Piccadilly of Berlin!

Predictably, Goebbels was jubilant. 'A brilliant picture of German power and strength,' he gushed. 'The Führer is celebrated by the people like no other mortal person has ever been celebrated. So that's how we stand. The goddess of victory shines in the glaring sunlight, a wonderful omen.' For the occasion, Goebbels had commissioned opulent leather-bound book of poetry dedicated to Adolf Hitler. 'That God gave you to us is our greatest happiness,' began the first contribution. Another, filled with religious fervour, declared him a 'burning soul' endowed with 'faith, through solitary grace'. Further in the volume, another scribe asserted that 'blessed are the people who received him'. The fact that Goebbels allowed such a publication testifies to the atmosphere surrounding Hitler at the tail end of the 1930s. The regime, however, did draw a line: Hitler was allowed to be called 'Redeemer' and 'Saviour', but there was to be no direct connection between him and Christ.

The 'Redeemer' was especially jubilant given that a month earlier he had seized the rump of Czechoslovakia, enslaving a non-German people. Still on the warpath, he demanded the cession of Danzig from Poland, leading Warsaw to secure French and British guarantees against German aggression. Unimpressed, a visibly angry Hitler renounced an Anglo-German Naval Agreement and the German–Polish Non-Aggression Pact. Taking their cue, the Nazi press launched an assault of unrestrained anti-British rhetoric, alarming the tourism industry. Everton and Stoke City football clubs cancelled German tours 'in the best interests of everybody', while Arsenal abandoned a match in Hamburg.[5] There followed a raft of other cancellations from sporting, educational and scouting groups. More than 100 British schoolchildren packing for a 'friendship holiday' to Cologne and the Rhineland planned by World Friendship Tours were told to unpack due to political circumstances.[6] In this volatile climate, some Britons considered it morally wrong to visit Germany and provide Hitler with 'good English currency',[7] while Americans, afraid of getting caught in an outbreak of war and finding themselves interned, began eyeing other travel options.[8] Needless to say, visitor numbers in the Reich plummeted, with some areas recording an 80 per cent drop in foreign holidaymakers.[9]

Reeling from the losses, German travel agents hastened to assure the British that holiday traffic remained safe and unaffected. In a last-gasp effort to revive the season, a pamphlet titled *Tourism and Hospitality in the New Germany*, rallied against the negative headlines by condemning the 'nonsense written about our Germany everywhere in the world':

> ... and how much of this nonsense is still believed. How much nonsense is still written about our Germany everywhere in the world, and how much of this nonsense is still believed. But all the efforts of the tendentious instigators would be futile had it been possible for every member of other nations to form an independent opinion about the German people and the German land.[10]

Meanwhile, British travellers' experiences in Germany were eagerly pawed over by the public. Letters to the local press show a mixture of joy and irritation among the testimonials. Some observed more petty officialdom, and tighter passport controls, while others adopted a softer tone. 'I cannot say that any of the nonsense talked about their making things uncomfortable for British visitors this year has any truthful basis,' surmised Hugh Gillies, a Scottish holidaymaker writing from Bavaria. Gillies did, however, note the paucity of food and goods on offer, 'particularly that the delicatessen shops had very meagre displays in their windows, mostly dummy cartons, and the former abundance of gigantic Wienerwurst and other German delicacies are no more. The working people seem to be half starved. It will be a great pity if war should come because there are no kindlier people under the sun than the Southern Germans.'[11]

'P. R. E.', a correspondent to the *Leeds Mercury*, wrote a flattering sketch of hospitable and humorous Germans. 'Hamburg gave us the best welcome we could wish for by letting us through the Customs in five minutes and leaving our baggage unopened,' he wrote, noting his group –which tramped around the Rhineland – were often mistaken for Americans, Swedes, Danes, Spaniards and Italians.[12]

> The oft repeated *'wir sind Englisch'* brought surprise to most faces (the English tourist traffic has declined heavily of late), but in no case any diminution of friendliness. In German eyes the English are set apart from the rest of Europe, and undoubtedly are the objects of very special interest at the present time. The speedy return of Danzig to the Reich was taken for granted and any suggestion that Great Britain might fight to prevent it was received with incredulity. References to the Italian nation seemed to provoke mirth. The young Axis partner is the butt of many an unsubtle joke in Germany, especially in cafes when beer is flowing freely.[13]

Other such sentiments continued to be sliced and diced in the press, some clearly concocted at Germany's behest. Rattled by the impending disintegration of British traffic, MER[14] took large spaces in the British press urging people to spend their August holidays in Germany. 'Land of hospitality' – a phrase that was constantly evoked – became the go-to slogan in 1939. As a sweetener, 60 per cent discounts were dangled along with other perks. In tandem, the German Railways Information Bureau bombarded the London press with full-page adverts filled with poetic text and landscapes.

> No country is more easily seen. From Schleswig to Carinthia, Silesia to the Rhine, great arterial roads supplement the railways. Above all, a German holiday is good, simple fun. It is jolly to sit at a lakeside restaurant, listen to the band and watch tow-headed babies splashing in the blue water. It is amusing to sample Rhine wine in the vineyard where it grew. It is fun to paddle down the Isar in the deepening twilight and hear the Wandervogel singing. To learn the Tyrolean part songs for yourself perhaps a step or two of the folk dances to wear lederhosen or a Dirndl dress and discuss life with mine host of the Hirsch over a stein of Schwartzbrau, to enjoy the good humour of the throng which crowds Salzburg, Bayreuth, Munich and many other cities during the festival season. There are the little things that linger in the mind the goodness of the Kuchen, the girl you danced with in the Platz, the fragrance of a moonlit night in the Black Forest, the stillness of a Tyrolean lake, black glass, mirroring the stars. Of such is a German holiday.[15]

With fewer French and English accents heard in German resorts, the burden to drum up domestic tourism was great. That summer, a flurry of brochures hit the home market advertising breaks in Carinthia, Styria, Lower Danube, Upper Bavaria, Tyrol, Black Forest, Franconia, Lake Constance, Palatinate, Moselle, Thuringia, Harz, Silesia, East Prussia and the Baltic, a favourite haunt for the family of schoolboy Willy Schuman. 'Every year more summer visitors came to enjoy the magnificent snow-white sandy beaches, the spectacular dunes, and the large Darss forest,' he radiantly declared of Prerow on the Baltic, an up-and-coming spa resort four hours from Berlin by train. 'The forest was so dense and relatively wild that Herman Göring had a herd of bison imported and released into the wilderness. The water of the Baltic was unpolluted. After breakfast, we would spend three or four hours swimming, playing ball in and out of the water and building sandcastles.'[16]

The choice of destinations on offer was seemingly endless. ILF, a subsidiary of MER in Leipzig, published colour photographs in their 1939 *Spring and Summer* brochure promising an overwhelming landscape and enchanting wildlife: 'Your heart and soul will be filled with joyful happiness, all at an affordable price.' Car owners were encouraged to try the ILF road trip across the Alps to Lake Garda and to Venice, which included reserved hotels and pensions along the route. The return leg took in Austria and the Grossglockner, the highest mountain in Germany.[17] A 'classic trip to Rome' promised a 'detour' to the Pontine Marshes, a swathe of reclaimed land championed by Mussolini, a feature added in keeping with the political zeitgeist. Italian publishers Bestetti & Tummanelli flooded the German market with guidebooks promising 'fair weather' even in the middle of winter, when 'Italy can enjoy numerous beautiful sunny days and starry nights'.

> The huge Alpine chain protects Italy from cold north winds. The winter climate is particularly mild on the Ligurian Riviera, in Naples, Merano, Arco, on Lake Garda, in Abbazia and on Sicily.

Bestetti & Tummanelli boasted that those seeking culture would hear fine music not only in theatres and convention halls but also in public places where there was 'often an opportunity to hear the best classical music performed by excellent orchestras':

> The same goes for the theatres. Even though in Italy one generally prefers the more melodious operas, those in which the symphonic element predominates also have a large audience. There are no permanent theatrical and operatic stages in Italy. There is an annual season in the opera houses, during which the artists are recruited on a case-by-case basis, while the drama companies move from

town to town, in some only giving guest performances and in others staying for longer seasons.

Many tourists took advantage of the KdF's new holiday programme, which included the Sudetenland. Hermann Esser also fixed reciprocal arrangements whereby Czechs could be induced to spend their holidays in Germany in return for German visitors in Prague.[18] At the Czechoslovak Travel Agency in Lower Regent Street, which flanked the German Railways Information Bureau, posters advertised the country as 'The Hunter's Paradise in Central Europe'.[19] Another campaign touted 'Sudeten German Mineral Springs' such as Franzensbad, where guests could benefit from twenty-seven curative springs, mud and carbonic baths 'long proven for women's diseases, childlessness, heart and vascular disorders'.[20] Čedok, the leading Czech tour operator, which had been forcibly incorporated into the MER, led the advertising campaign.[21] One of the pamphlets, advertising Sudetenland holidays for spring 1939, fell through the letterbox of a journalist in London:

> With it was another leaflet setting out the attractions of the rest of Czechoslovakia. This is actually a publication of the Czech Railways; but a slip has been pasted over the front to explain that the country is now German, and a rubber stamp has put a Printed in Germany in the place of the Printed in Czechoslovakia which it bore.[22]

However hard the Germans tried, the British media remained hostile. The syndicated *London Diary*, published in the regional press, declared summer tourist traffic to Germany would hit a record low given the winter had been a disappointment with foreigners boycotting the Austrian winter sports resorts. 'At the height of the season a friend of mine stayed in a German hotel near Garmisch,' the London diarist recounted. 'It had 300 bedrooms and only four guests. Austrians there have coined a new slogan for the hotel industry – "One people, one nation, one ruler – one visitor."'[23]

Such bleak assessments were supplemented by accounts from tourists like student Frank Lee, who was left flabbergasted after checking into a Bavarian hotel. 'It was ceremoniously desolate, a far cry from a year earlier,' he complained. 'The orchestra played but the waiters looked a very sad race, with nobody to serve and no tips.' Aiming to give a positive assessment, Gwen D. Hoult joined natives in savouring the crisp air but couldn't resist mentioning the prevalence of synthetic food during his sojourn through the south of Germany:

> You ask for coffee and are informed by a friendly neighbour that you're drinking acorn and maize – that his suit is wood, not wool as Germany is too poor to buy the real thing. True cocoa and tea is expensive, so wine is substituted whenever possible. There is no waste. We were requested to leave no butter or jam on our plates or a bad impression would be created. The flavour of their grapes and peaches, the taste of coffee and black bread, passes into oblivion.[24]

Another traveller, David Wynn, was left equally unimpressed. A quiet and cultivated American reporter, Wynn recalled how every family, without exception, with whom he lodged suffered from a scarcity of food and complained about prices. 'These conditions were typical not only of the peasant farmers but also of shop people, factory workers, intellectuals, and even the wealthy retired who were perhaps the loudest complainants.'[25]

One of the plethora of jokes about price rises described how an old man stopped before a shop window in Berlin and said to his wife, 'The prices aren't so bad. Look at that tag on that blazer – that's only RM5.'

'Yes,' his wife replied with an exhausted sigh, 'but that's a drycleaner's shop.'

19

THE END OF AN ERA

British tourism to Germany all but ended with the signing of the Molotov–Ribbentrop Pact, which secured the neutrality of the Soviet Union and cleared the way for Hitler to march towards war. This non-aggression deal, signed on 23 August, saw Berlin and Moscow agree not to go to war and carve up the conquered east between them. It also ensured Soviet non-intervention for any German invasion of Poland.

Almost immediately, newspapers whipped up emotions, fuelling a panic across the continent. A journalist from the *West Middlesex Gazette* heard the news during dinner at a brasserie in Belgium. While starters were served, his Romanian friend chortled as he described the Molotov–Ribbentrop Pact as 'the greatest comedy he had seen'.[1] However, there was no laughing in London. Prime Minister Neville Chamberlain recalled Parliament, put the Royal Navy on a war footing, cancelled all military leave, called up military reserve forces and placed Civil Defence workers on alert.

At the same time, Nazi authorities called all their steamships home, disrupting transatlantic services and shocking anxious travellers. 'American embassies have been besieged by jittery Americans anxious to get home,' Felix Cotton from the *Washington Post* reported. 'Travel between the two continents has been predominantly a home-coming with only the crews in some cases going back.' Sniffing around the piers of New York, Cotton noticed American authorities taking 'great interest' in the German Lloyd liner the SS *Bremen*. 'The ship sailed out of New York harbour, without passengers, late Wednesday, after being detained for a day and a half while Federal agents searched her for guns.' As it slipped away from the 55th Street terminal on New York's West Side, Cotton caught the echoes of military music from the ship's band and shouts of 'Heil Hitler' across the water.

Not since 1918 had Europe witnessed a drama comparable to that taking place during the summer.[2] With demand for passage exceeding capacity, the *Queen Mary*, en route to New York, managed to squeeze a record 2,385 people on board. Banker J. P. Morgan gave up part of his luxurious suite when he heard of the crush of passengers, keeping only a bedroom to himself.

Meanwhile, the young reporter from the *West Middlesex Gazette* had moved to Liege, 30 miles west of the German border, where the air was thick with apprehension. 'Soldiers, loaded with their cow-hide rucksacks, were reporting for duty or being drafted to their posts,' he recorded on 26 August as Belgium called up its reservists. 'Sobbing women, some on the point of collapse, were saying goodbye to their sons, husbands, lovers.' After taking stock of the situation, a precipitous rout followed as the reporter, like most other tourists, headed for Ostend and passage home. 'The boat returning travelled under orders with no deck lights showing, and ironically was largely occupied by a party of British ex-servicemen who had been visiting in Flanders an area of former battle.'

Meanwhile, time weighed heavily for foreigners over in Vienna. One British tourist never forgot the pandemonium of 28 August when the railway station was crowded with 'panic-stricken people – Italians, Jews, Carinthians – all trying to leave Vienna'. After securing a seat, his adventures were by no means over as the train was held up eleven times to give way to troop trains. At Villach, 140 miles from Vienna, there was a tragedy: 'The many Jews on the train were bound for Italy, where they hoped to embark at Italian ports. News came that all Italian sailings had been suspended. The Jews were ordered to leave the train. It was heartbreaking to see them and the little children with them.'³

In Berlin, holidaymakers converged on the British Embassy, joining the small colony of expatriates – depleted by a mass exodus in the previous months – waiting calmly for advice. Employees from Shell Oil, British-American Tobacco, Dunlop, Cunard White Star, Kodak, British Metal Corporation, Anglo-Persian Oil and Anglo-Argentine Cold Storage were long gone. At the same time, French residents were taking to their heels and bewildered Poles fumed that their government had given no inkling of what might happen, nor had they provided instructions.⁴

Returning holidaymakers used the press as a useful font of grievance. A group tour returning from a motorcycling holiday had some sharp words about the police investigating photographs they had taken on their travels. One of the group, Norman Balinforth, told *The Yorkshire Observer* that they were stopped on the Darmstadt–Heidelberg autobahn and taken to the police station at Mannheim where they were held for seven hours while their possessions were examined and were told that a cine-camera film would be developed. 'We were asked to account for our movements but it appeared the local police were well informed of our movements,' Balinforth bitterly noted.

A bare week later, the world changed forever when German troops marched into Poland. An urgent telegram from the Foreign Office in London to the British Ambassador at Berlin was shot off at 5.00 a.m. on 3 September 1939. In what was effectively an ultimatum, it stated that unless Germany ceased its military action against Poland by 11.00 a.m. that day, Great Britain would consider itself at war with Germany.

> Please seek interview with [German] Minister for Foreign Affairs at 9 A.M. today, Sunday, or, if he cannot see you then, arrange to convey at that time to representative of German Government the following communication: 'In the communication which I had the honour to make to you on 1st September I informed you, on the instructions of His Majesty's Principal Secretary of

State for Foreign Affairs, that, unless the German Government were prepared to give His Majesty's Government in the United Kingdom satisfactory assurances that the German Government had suspended all aggressive action against Poland and were prepared promptly to withdraw their forces from Polish Territory, His Majesty's Government in the United Kingdom would, without hesitation, fulfil their obligations to Poland.' Although this communication was made more than twenty-four hours ago, no reply has been received but German attacks upon Poland have been continued and intensified. I have accordingly the honour to inform you that, unless not later than 11 A.M., British Summer Time, today 3rd September, satisfactory assurances to the above effect have been given by the German Government and have reached His Majesty's Government in London, a state of war will exist between the two countries as from that hour.[5]

The German reply came at 11.20 a.m., twenty minutes after the deadline of the British ultimatum expired. As expected, Berlin refused to pull out of Poland. The two countries were at war.

20

WAR

The Second World War had an astounding effect on Germany. As if a switch had been thrown, every aspect of life changed. Unprecedented cuts were imposed on social and cultural projects, while car use was virtually prohibited, with special permits needed to buy gasoline. All privately owned rubber tires were declared property of the state, while in restaurants Mondays and Fridays were proclaimed 'meatless days', prompting one customer at a large Berlin hotel to grumble that the menu offered soup, rice and cauliflower, with cake for dessert, 'but the prices remained the same'. Almost immediately, cities and towns were blacked out and would remain so until May 1945. At the same time, the priority of the Deutsche Reichsbahn was shifted from civilian to military movements, and it struggled to maintain an adequate timetable under the strain.

For many people, the blackout – or *Verdunkelung* – was a menace instead of a protection. Across Germany, courts handed down harsh punishments for crimes committed under the veil of darkness. In one case, the death sentence was passed for bag-snatching and a special court in Halle condemned a young man to death after he was caught robbing a house. Such crimes prompted those of a nervous disposition to install extra latches and deadbolts. In the home, people learned to prevent slits of light escaping the edges of curtains and doors. Street lights showed only tiny green flames on amber mantels. Buses ran with a single ghoulish blue light, while tram cars had faint illumination on their route numbers but inside the lamps were shrouded in black cloth hoods.

The death toll on the streets and on the railways seldom appeared in the press, but some papers did publish advice for greater safety at darkened train stations where many passengers had mishaps on stairs, platforms or on the trains. Motor car headlights were blackened, except for narrow slits, making it almost impossible to see, even on clear evenings. Such conditions led to an alarming spike in traffic accidents, with 70–100 per cent of mishaps in North Rhine Westphalia occurring in darkness during December 1939. (An SPD report attributed 80 per cent of the crashes to pedestrians.) In an effort to provide some visibility, curbs, road crossings and railway platforms were coated with luminous paint while small glowing phosphorous buttons were attached to overcoats – kids had them stitched into hats and satchels. The extra vigilant wore white gloves, or attached little bells to their buttons; some used their voices for signalling by impersonating the hoot of an owl. Rubber-soled shoes could not be heard in the dark, unlike soldiers clumping along noisily in heavy boots.

It's hardly surprising that under such conditions prostitution thrived, as sex workers haunted the freezing streets in search of work. The corner near Bulowstrasse in Berlin, not far from the Sportspalast, was a popular pickup spot where women past their prime sought new opportunities. An American journalist remembered being propositioned by a pensioner with spindly hands and deep-set eyes. 'Even the old girls, the wrinkled ones, stood on corners with their ugly features safely hidden in the darkness and shone their flashlights on their legs in invitation.'

Despite draconian sentences, police recorded a spike in rapes during the first eighteen months of the war. Prostitutes were not safe, especially from soldiers on leave. The cover of darkness also gave opportunist sex pests ample protection to stalk, molest or make inappropriate advances on women. Police reports noted molestation and the groping of women's breasts had become common. Berliners, usually willing to think the best of their police force, were dismayed by the lack of action and demanded a better response.[1]

The war meant the promised advent of the revolutionary Volkswagen was gradually pushed into the background as the showpiece Fallersleben factory was given over to military production, protected by a 2-square-mile security zone ringed with barbed wire, searchlights and gun emplacements. Inside, aero engines were churned out under American licence using parts originally intended for the Volkswagen engine. It didn't take long for the public to get wind of the news. An old joke, according to Richard Grunberger's *Social History of the Third Reich* went:

> Optimists and cynics alike chuckled at the story of the Volkswagen employee, who, having sedulously filched all the cars components from the factory, assembled them at home and wound up with a Bren gun carrier.

There was another joke along the same lines:

> Hans: Why don't you take a piece of the car home each night and then assemble it yourself?
> Peter: No, that won't work.
> Hans: Why not?
> Peter: I've done that already and put it together three times, but every time it comes out a cannon.

Despite great disappointment, there was no national controversy about the KdF-Wagen delays. Subscribers received a receipt instead of a car and were promised their car when peace returned. 'All savers should be certain, your KdF-Wagen will be manufactured immediately after the war,' *Arbeitertum* assured in March 1940. 'Even during the war, the work at the Volkswagen works will continue to make progress. Immediately after the end of the war, the factory will fulfil its task and realize the motorization of the whole German people.' 'It was the biggest pre-payment swindle of all time,' was the hushed verdict of one angry subscriber. As it happened, not a single Volkswagen was ever delivered, nor refunds offered.

At the same time, construction at Prora came to a screeching halt when builders were reassigned to defence duties or to the V-Weapons plant at Peenemünde, leaving a vast concrete shell in a sea of mud.[2] Surviving brochures show seven of the eight accommodation blocks were topped out, while the theatre and cinema remained empty shells and the swimming baths, festival hall and docks never materialised. However, the rail connection was built. If the complex had been completed, it would have been the biggest holiday resort in the world. Instead, it would be used as a refugee camp, a hospital and a training school for the armed forces.

Few magazines in Germany embraced the coming of war with as much bluster as DAF periodicals, which had hitherto dwelled upon vacation trips and cruises. Before a month of war had passed, the KdF monthly was given over entirely to features on a bewildering variety of home management tips – along with a hint that more women would be needed in factories and agriculture.[3] There were articles dedicated to needlecraft, home upholstery, leatherwork, physiology, infant and child welfare, first aid and home nursing. Furthermore, articles about new food regulations were common; meat, butter, milk, cheese, sugar, jam, bread and eggs had been put on ration.

Hoteliers complained that from the outset the bulk of the best imported meat was directed to the Army, and home-killed joints – mostly bone and gristle – were placed on the domestic market. The public endured the austerity measures with astonishingly good grace, despite a few notable incidents such as when the price of butter rose and the cost of margarine fell in late 1939 – a move seen as a 'gift to the well-off'. Poorer folks also complained that horse meat – a staple of the working classes – was being snapped up by everyone because it was available ration-free, leading to depleted stocks. But, all told, the pre-war diet – which seemed to be adequate, although not comfortable – had prepared the nation for leaner times.

Meanwhile, as the phoney war dragged on, troops from the British Expeditionary Force landed in France to shore up the French defences. At the same time, a British naval blockade targeted Nazi shipping in reprisal for the sinking of the *Athenia* and the *Simon Bolivar*.[4] However, Berlin's greatest worry was the safe return of passenger liners running the gauntlet to reach home ports or sanctuary in neutral harbours – those that failed to make it home were confiscated by the Allies. Significantly, there was also another reason for the dash home: the cost of laying up ships in foreign ports coupled with the difficulty in obtaining foreign exchange. By December, there were still 400 German ships in foreign ports, with harbour dues amounting to at least £4 million per year. Some of the harbour charges were already overdue. If the Germans were unable to pay, the various harbour authorities were legally entitled to auction the German ships to recover their money. 'In this way the Allies might be able to obtain valuable additions to their merchant shipping reserve,' the British press observed. 'Some ships will attempt to get through the blockade; others will be scuttled. Our sailors will attempt to bring in as many prizes as possible.'

Needless to say, at the outbreak of war, German liner positions were sent to the Admiralty and, as seen below, many valuable vessels were in dangerous positions (marked in bold type).

BERLIN, Norddeutscher Lloyd steamer, built 1925, 15,286 tons. Under repair in Germany after casualty.
BREMEN, Norddeutscher Lloyd steamer, built 1929, 51,731 tons. Left New York, August 30.
CAP ARCONA, Hamburg South American steamer, built 1927, 27,561 tons. Arrived Hamburg, August 25.
COLUMBUS, Norddeutscher Lloyd steamer, built 1922, 32,565 tons. Left Havana, September 1, after landing cruise passengers.
DEUTSCHLAND, Hamburg American steamer, built 1923, 21,046 tons. Left Southampton, August 24, for Hamburg.
EUROPA, Norddeutscher Lloyd steamer, built 1928, 49,746 tons. At Bremen.
GNEISENAU, Norddeutscher Lloyd steamer, built 1935, 18,160 tons. At Bremerhaven.

HAMBURG, Hamburg American steamer, built 1926, 22,117 tons. Due New York, September 1, from Hamburg.

HANSA, Hamburg American steamer, built 1923, 21,131 tons. At Hamburg.

MILWAUKEE, Hamburg American steamer, built 1929, 16,624 tons. In German waters.

NEW YORK, Hamburg American steamer, built 1927, 22,337 tons. Left New York, August 28, for Hamburg.

POTSDAM, Norddeutscher Lloyd steamer, built 1935, 17,528 tons. Left Hamburg, August 19, for Far East.

PRETORIA, German East Africa Line's steamer, built 1936, 16,662 tons. At Lourenco Marques.

RELIANCE, Hamburg American steamer, built 1920, 19,580 tons. At Hamburg, with fire damage.

ST-LOUIS, Hamburg American motors hip. built 1929, 16,732 tons. Left New York, August 28, for Hamburg.

SCHARNHORST, Norddeutscher Lloyd steamer, built 1935, 18,184 tons. In Japanese waters.

WINDHUK, Woermann steamer, built 1936, 16,662 tons. At Lourenco Marques.

A cruel twist – for the Nazis at least – came when 500 French paintings and drawings were seized by British authorities at Bermuda after being discovered on the *Excalibur* en route to the United States. The cargo, which came under the Nazi classification of degenerate art, was being sent for sale. There were works by Renoir, Cezanne, Monet, Manet and Picasso. For the British public, it was amusing to read about the virtuoso performances of German ship captains across the seven seas. The German liner *Cap Norte*, which slipped out of the Brazilian port of Pernambuco on 17 September, was captured in the South Atlantic. Similar examples of bad luck saw Hamburg America and Norddeutscher Lloyd liners *Nordmark, Vogtland, Rendsburg, Cute, Naumburg, Essen, Stassfurt, Franken, Bitterfeld, Wuppertal* and *Rheinland* and the Hansa steamer *Soneck* impounded, while the SS *Bremen* found refuge in the Soviet Arctic harbour of Murmansk and then dashed to Bremerhaven, where it was used as a barracks ship. German liner *Watussi* was also lucky; its crew had taken refuge in Mozambique harbour in Portuguese East Africa on the outbreak of hostilities but managed to lift anchor and slip quietly away to home waters.

Luckily for the German military, the KdF ships SS *Berlin*, *Wilhelm Gustloff*, *Robert Ley* and *Stuttgart* were in home ports and converted to hospital ships and transporters for the wounded, their funnels painted with a large red cross. On the SS *Berlin*, the KdF entertainments crew was replaced by twenty-two doctors, and former cabins and dayrooms were equipped with operating theatres and X-ray apparatus. Five specialist departments – internal, surgery, eyes, mouth and jaw – were established in the lower decks, while its staterooms became wards with 400 beds.

21

1940

Hidden behind frosted glass, Robert Ley spent much of 1940 holed up at his new white granite office complex on Fehrbelliner Platz. Although the brakes had been slammed on the Prora and KdF-Wagen projects, his life remained busy. When Axis powers sought to expand tourism connections, Ley welcomed Japanese travel officials brandishing plans for a Berlin office, marking a new tourism policy. Given the positive military facts of the moment, Russia's Intourist agency began distributing Soviet travel brochures at exhibitions in Leipzig and Berlin, where their office expanded to employ five Germans and three Russians in full-time positions.[1]

In stark contrast, authorities in Great Britain were busily expunging the Nazis from the local landscape. In Glasgow, the local council auctioned the furnishings of the German Railways Information Bureau – a sale which saw one bidder walk off with three photographs of Hitler in different poses and a large Swastika flag.[2]

There is little doubt that Robert Ley had reached the zenith of his Nazi career as he faced the balancing act of adapting KdF to military-focused tasks while pushing industrial workers to increase arms production, a job complicated by manpower resources being stretched to the limit and a freeze on overtime pay, salary bonuses and statutory holidays.[3]

Poor weather in early 1940 was particularly persistent and especially bad, disrupting tourism and slowing production. During January, hoteliers in the mountains fretted over the desolation of the season as the harshest of conditions in 115 years paralyzed Europe. Along the Alps, from ski resorts to clifftop restaurants, people whose livelihoods depended on tourists prepared for a lost season. The view wasn't much better in Berlin. Gazing out at the snowscape from his office opposite the Kaiserhof Hotel, Goebbels scowled that the cold 'makes one sick', a sentiment shared by CBS's William Shirer, who was forced to type his despatches from under a blanket at the Adlon: 'There is nothing like continual cold to lower your morale,' he sighed.

As conditions worsened, exacerbated by fuel famine, Lufthansa grounded its fleet and navigation was suspended as many rivers, including the Danube, froze. To the north, a vast ice sheet covered the Baltic disrupting traffic between Berlin and Copenhagen, halting the supply of eggs, butter, bacon and other provisions. Strikingly, however, Berlin continued to buzz during the cold with a cacophony of nightlife. The Frasquita Club and the swanky Femina, with its rising dancefloor and chorus girls in four-inch heels, drew widespread attention. (Goebbels would soon prove eager to put an end to such decadent endeavours.)

'Such establishments,' American journalist Otto David Tolischus observed, 'were packed mostly with young people facing conscription for war duty who wanted a last fling.' Everywhere among the revellers were uniforms – soldiers in field grey, airmen in light blue, Nazis with a Swastika band on their arms and SS men in black. The Delphi, an almost mythical club behind the velvet ropes, remained the place for cooing and flirting while the Golden Horse Shoe fused a restaurant, lounge and dancefloor into a single two-level space. For those loath to go to bed, smooth romantic melodies filled the air at the Eden Hotel roof club until the early hours.

In an effort to gauge how Germans were coping with the war, former SPD Party members jotted down mood reports for the Party's leadership in exile. Normally, these ideologically motivated memos were gingered up to fit their own narrative; however, the example below acknowledges that Berliners were displaying a lust for life that winter.

> It is still almost impossible to gain a uniform impression of the mood of the Berlin populace. It is interesting to note that despite the rising prices of food and drink, the declining quality of beer and the use of ersatz foods, restaurants and cafes are doing a booming business. At certain times of the day it is nearly impossible to find an empty seat. The cinemas are also extraordinarily full. This phenomenon is an expression of the fatalism that has become widespread. People want to spend their money because it makes no sense to save anymore, and they don't want to sit at home because they need diversion. Should Germany win, they say, it won't do us any good, we won't be any better off than now. Should Germany lose, we may be much worse off. Basically, whatever happens it doesn't really matter.[4]

This description tallies with an account from Heinrich Hauser, a German exile who returned to Berlin as a tourist in late 1939. In his book *Battle against Time: A Survey of the Germany of 1939 from the Inside*, he described a city morphing into a Mecca for pleasure-loving Germans:

> Nightlife is just as international as before except there are far fewer Englishmen and Americans to be seen,' he observed. 'Instead there are many more Rumanians, Hungarians, Greeks.
> The Hitler revolution at first swept away all this somewhat spectral internationalism of Berlin's nightlife, and for the next several years the amusements were decidedly dull. But now a new dance on the volcano has begun a craving for pleasure and nightlife no less febrile than the past.[5]

As people consciously tried to drown themselves in indulgence, Hauser described nudity as a narcotic – the Berlin shows were more daring than 'those almost anywhere in the world'. He lamented the fact that drunkards, once a rare sight, could be seen everywhere. 'Alcoholism is spreading to such an extent that the government not long ago started a campaign against it by imposing severe penalties.'[6]

Hauser couldn't fail to notice the decrepitude of the railways on which more than 500 people had lost their lives in accidents since the war began. With the conflict thinning the ranks of the Reichsbahn workforce, passenger numbers rocketed, tracks creaked and the freight business – the lifeblood of the Reichsbahn – was given over to military movements. Problems were exacerbated by the Anschluss, which saw the incorporation of the Austrian railways into the Reichsbahn. Then, in May 1938, work on fortifications in the west came to require about 8,000 rail wagons daily. Three months later, the burden of mobilisation and the partial occupation of Czechoslovakia heaped more strain on the network. Rolling stock continued to decline throughout this time, with essential repairs impossible due to a lack of raw materials, and when war broke out the Reichsbahn was utterly unprepared for the additional strain of the Polish campaign. Even in the months preceding the war, accidents had risen to astonishing levels. Tens of thousands of Germans who had arranged travel during the 1939 Christmas holidays were left disappointed, sometimes waiting for hours on icy railway platforms only to be told that no more trains would run.

Harry Flannery observed that the 8 a.m. train from Cologne to Berlin arrived at half-past five in the afternoon: 'Nine and a half hours for a trip that took five hours before the war.' Flannery was all too keenly aware that the Reichsbahn had become a byword for overcrowding, delays and understaffing. 'One German told me he had bought a first-class ticket and stood for eleven hours between Munich and Salzburg'. Another story told how a female musician – tormented by the constant jarring and rattling – sat hunched on the floor of shabby carriage with two broken windows in a temperature of -12°C. A *Handelsblad* correspondent saw passengers elbow and jostle into packed compartments descend into hysterical rages, 'people must be prepared to stand ten hours in an unheated corridor':

The dislocation of traffic has gradually assumed a catastrophic character. The rush hour in Berlin is torture. Buses, trams, and tubes are regularly so overfilled that it is astounding that the number of accidents is not much greater.

The sufferings of passengers on public transport paled in comparison to the immeasurable cruelty visited on the Jewish population that winter. Reich Minister of Economics Walther Funk forbade them from buying clothes, and only millboard – a weak cardboard substitute – was allowed for resoling shoes, further compounding an already diabolical existence. Other acts of persecution included telephones being forcibly removed from their homes and shops displaying posters stating that 'purchases may be made by and for Jews only between 4 p.m. and 5 p.m.' (by which time most of the stock had been sold). On top of that, Jews received only half the normal coal allocation. These directives were only the beginning of the nightmare that would unfold over the coming year.

Germany had endured fifty-six days of snow when the bitter cold finally made its exit, allowing farmers to belatedly begin spring sowings. With the onset of warmer weather, there was a return to tourism as locals and visitors from friendly countries enjoyed holidays and excursions. At first there was no urgency in passing legislation limiting tourism given the understanding that an annual holiday was essential to the well-being of the industrial worker and his family. Travel agents were given wide latitude for the most part, but the Kdf's era of crusading vacations was at an end.

In many districts, hotels and guesthouses were converted into military sanatoriums or requisitioned to serve sick troops or those on leave. Even plush resorts like Tutting am Starnberger See, hitherto a magnet for the rich, was forced to adapt to the new military 'clientele' (many hoteliers harboured modest hopes the conflict would end sometime in 1940). As always, trips to Berchtesgaden, Baltic beach retreats and jaunts on Rhine river steamers lived up to expectations. Keen to keep morale high, the government did little to interfere with the smooth running of tourism, fearing a repeat of 1918 when nerves were shot and morale slumped. Maintaining the façade of normality was seen as crucial to the functioning of ordinary life. This position was confirmed by Hermann Esser in early 1940 when he told travel industry representatives it was the 'will of the Führer that the work of tourism continues'.[7]

For the most part, private travel operators committed themselves to a strategy based on weekly excursions which would persist, in substantial measure, until late 1943. Tramondo Reisen offered package tours from Berlin to the Harz Mountains, Tirol, Thüringer Wald and Vorarlberg, a mountainous district in western Austria. Their *Pauschalriesen im Sommer 1940* leaflet shows trips starting at RM57.60 (for Harz) up to RM120 (for Tirol). Surprisingly, given the war, terms and conditions had a remarkably 'peacetime feel' about them. Single-room surcharge for all trips was RM5 per week; if a pre-paid single room was not available, the surcharge was refunded or a double room was given instead for an additional surcharge of RM2 per week. Furthermore, the leaflet stated:

> The travel prices include: return train journeys (as far as possible with express trains) and connecting journeys with coaches (except for St. Andreasberg in the Harz), accommodation and food (breakfast, lunch and dinner – excluding drinks) electricity, shoeshine (1 pair daily) and service, visitor's tax, and other sundry charges, care of holidaymakers by the spa administrations or local tour guides. Catering begins with dinner on the day of arrival and ends with lunch on the day of departure. For full-day excursions, a packed lunch is provided and warm meals are served in the evening. Each participant asked to take care of their luggage on the outward and return journey and also at the destination.[8]

During the glorious summer of 1940, as the sun shone over Germany, newspapers were larded with stories of peaceful vacations. Members of the Westphalia pharmacists' association enjoyed a trip to Bad Meinberg where they spent, as the editor of the *Münstersche Zeitung* reported, 'three wonderful days that had absolutely nothing to do with the war ... it was total paradise. One just could not grasp that somewhere in the world there was a war going on.'

In the period that followed, the KdF – which had provided holidays for 10 million people since 1933 – was reshaped to serve the armed forces. By agreement with the High Command, it took over the cultural care of the army, with the exception of motion pictures. Scrambling to get organised, the KdF engaged the services of 1,000 artists to entertain more than a million soldiers at 2,423 welfare events at hospitals, naval ports and flak positions during 1940.[9] The same motley troupe of professionals which had previously entertained autobahn workers, signed up for the new Zelt theatre – an outfit similar to Britain's ENSA – following in the wake the Wehrmacht, lugging a portable stage (sometimes erected in the corner of a field). The crude scenic arrangement – a collapsible stage and painted cloth backdrop – was outshone by the enthusiasm of the audiences.

Launched in the presence of Ley and Goebbels, the Zelt theatre was born with a performance of *Lothar*, a patriotic drama from 1912 by Dichters Walter Flex.[10] Over time, the troupe delivered both serious and light material, encompassing everything from Shakespeare to knockabout comedies. As the workload grew, so did pressure on the artistic community to join in this vast patriotic effort. However, the romantic idea of entertaining the armed forces irked many artists, including the ravishing Ilse Werner, who had no emotional attachment to the nation's soldiers and despised being forced to play in front of troops when 'ordered'. Her colleague Anton Dermota was equally scathing, complaining of appointments 'from which one could not escape'.[11] Likewise, the sweet-faced Evelyn Künneke fumed at being 'posted like soldiers. Appearances here ... appearances there.'[12]

22

DRUNK ON VICTORY

On the second weekend of April 1940, Berliners streamed out to the suburbs to enjoy the fine weather. As some headed to the zoo to see the new acquisitions stolen from Warsaw Zoo, others flocked to watch local bands and Italian opera singers that were screeching their way around the country. *Palla de Mozzi* by Italian composers Giovaccino Forzano and Gino Marinuzzi attracted crowds to the Deutsches Opernhaus, while in Cologne, *Alexander in Olympia* by Marc-André Souchay opened at the Opera House. Ticket returns show the most popular composer was Wagner, followed by Verdi, Puccini, Mozart and Rossini.

At the cinema there was the premiere of the spy flick *Der Fuchs von Glenarvon* (The Fox of Glenarvon), about Irish freedom fighters, and at the same time, *The Postmaster*, based on the novella by Alexander S. Pushkin and starring Heinrich George, opened in Vienna. American films remained extremely popular, but the stark difference between lavish Hollywood productions and the rather austere efforts of local studios irritated Goebbels. He promptly slapped a ban on American colour films, which he felt highlighted the superiority of US cinema.

Paper shortages hadn't yet impacted the publishing industry, which continued to churn out guidebooks for destinations across Europe. Bookworms devoured the children's tale *Häschenschule*

(Bunny School) by Fritz Koch-Gotha, which sold more than 250,000 copies that year.

Sports fans delighted as cyclists Gustav Kilian and Heinz Vopel from Dortmund won a 145-hour race in Cleveland, but there was disappointment at an international football match when Yugoslavia thrashed the German team in front of 50,000 spectators in Vienna.

The unquenchable spirit of the Berliners sustained the Haus Vaterland on Potsdamer Platz with its Wild West Bar adorned with pictures of Lincoln and Jefferson. Harry Flannery, not a night bird by nature, occasionally popped in and found the staff obliging and cheerful. He was often served by blond waiters in bright cowboy shirts and cowboy hats:

> Outside the door of the Wild West Bar, I stopped beside a light-gun machine, by which the operator could aim and shoot at pictures of passing planes. Two young anti-aircraft soldiers were busy there. I watched them. One fired away intently and then stepped back, patted himself on the chest, and boasted of his perfect score.

As Berlin became a favoured spot for troops on leave, Richard Fleischer, director of the Haus Vaterland, was quick to cash in on the huge influx. In the spring of 1940, for the first time, 400 soldiers were 'invited' for coffee, cake and entertainment, with the idea being to get them spending at the bar. Buoyed by this new revenue stream, Fleischer opened the so-called Wehrmachtkabarett, with live shows every evening from 23.30 until 02.00. *Weisse*, a light beer with a shot of blackcurrant syrup, became a firm favourite with the Wehrmacht.

As the days grew longer, German housewives who already had long training in queuing began to notice shortages of staple foods. Journalist Oswald Villard moaned that 'there is food enough to keep going on, but there is not much variety. The menus are very much cut down.' Marie Vassiltchikov, a Russian émigré living and working in Berlin, was appalled during a luncheon visit to the Adlon. 'We had hoped to have a good meal there, but it turned out to be *Eintopftag*, "one-dish day" – a tasteless stew that all restaurants are obliged to serve once a week.'

As a rule, waiters dished out fish (usually pike) on the two meatless days a week, but 'potatoes were served with every meal in the restaurants, always boiled. The Germans did not fry potatoes because of a lack of fat, but they did not bake them either,' Villard grumped. Sparse menus were not the only change diners experienced, as the oily Hermann Esser insisted that restaurants and hotels tune into radio news broadcasts for the mandatory benefit of workers and customers. This absurd directive was dreamed up after he witnessed 'uncouth guests talking loudly and unconcernedly during a news broadcast'.

The peaceful atmosphere of spring was disturbed on 9 April when German troops invaded Denmark and Norway,[1] causing outrage in neutral countries and particularly in the United States. *The New York Times* ran off a special edition which snarled, 'Without any more warning than a gangster gives his victims, and without the shadow of justification except that of brute force, Denmark, another free nation, was murdered in cold blood this morning.'

On the home front, Germans were alarmed to hear Karl Lange, a member of the Reichsbank directorate, forecast increased taxes and austerity. His utterance added to longstanding nervousness about the economy which had already led shrewder members of the population to seek long-term financial security by purchasing furniture, plots of land, pianos and works of art. An article in the SS-mouthpiece *Das Schwarze Korps* foolishly revealed plans to partially pay some staff wages by means of a voucher, further stoking fears about the fragility of the national currency.

As the war progressed, Ley quietly but openly visited occupied and friendly countries, ostensibly for discussions on tourism cooperation. Perspiring profusely in the sunshine of Sofia, he beamed after obtaining permission from the Bulgarian government to send large numbers of tourists (including thousands of wounded soldiers) to the Black Sea resort of Varna that summer.[2] At the same time, Hermann Esser was knocking at the door of the Yugoslavian government with a request to let 10,000 German tourists spend the summer there – his wish was granted on condition the tourists were only women and children under fifteen,[3] as German tourists were suspected of being part of a Fifth Column working obediently to the instructions of Berlin.

Remarkably, given the fragile situation on the continent, American tourists were still flocking to the Channel coast, the French Riviera and Paris, buoyed by the presence of the British Army along the Maginot Line. 'All along the Rue de Rivoli around the Opera and the Madeleine one sees them in light gowns and lounge suits anticipating summer,' a journalist wryly noted. 'These early birds arrived by clipper and others are coming, according to the newspapers, by liners as well as plane. Paris accepts the compliment of their confidence in Allied protection on sea and land.'[4]

However, that confidence was shattered just a month after the invasion of Norway, when German troops launched a lightning strike through the Ardennes that ended with the occupation of Belgium, Luxembourg, the Netherlands and France. As the British forces and tourists scampered for safety, Winston Churchill was installed as Prime Minister in London, replacing the beleaguered Neville Chamberlain, who, as well as suffering a political blow, was already weakened by bowel cancer, to which he succumbed seven months later.

Across Germany, as people stormed newsstands and fought for papers, stationers reported a run on maps as everybody wanted to pinpoint the location of new acquisitions. Gloating returned to the front page of the *Völkischer Beobachter*, which surmised that even though Germany's wine stocks were considerable – despite fears of a bad harvest and growing consumption – imports of French wines would keep the drinks flowing, 'with the bonus of being cheaper as well'. With Champagne, Burgundy and Bordeaux under occupation, soldiers were paying 40 pfennig for a bottle of good champagne, while a litre of red or white cost around 20 pfennig. The article disdainfully remarked, 'No real German can suffer the Frenchman – but he likes to drink their wines.' The military victories helped the perennial summer rush, especially in Berlin and resorts in Bavaria and Franconia, which saw a 35 per cent jump in overnight stays compared with 1939.

23

HITLER'S TOURISTS

In the first years of the war, German policymakers, motivated in large part by a fear of tired and demolished troops, promoted 'purposeful travel', such as home leave, short excursions and vacations to other occupied territories. Over time, either in the line of duty or on leave, German troops saw Prague, Oslo, Copenhagen, Paris, Rome, Athens, Crete and Tobruk during their military service.

With the fall of France, the immediate benefit for the home front came in the form of the systematic pillage of food and natural resources as the occupiers exacted a huge toll in their new conquest. Thousands of tons of oats, leather, aluminium, manganese, oil, grease, coffee, coal, grain, scrap iron, whale oil, cattle and pigs for slaughter and wines were shunted off to the Reich. To add insult to injury, the French were forced to feed their new masters, who continued to spill over the frontier in increasing numbers.

By now, Hitler had reached the height of his power. On 6 July 1940, his special train rolled into the Reich capital for a hurriedly organised party to celebrate the conquest. Crowds stretched from the city cathedral to the Adlon Hotel. Party officials led community singing from a balcony at Café Kranzler as huge crowds joined in on the boulevards. Dorothea Günther, a twenty-two-year-old resident, never forgot the delirious joy of the public: 'Hitler was glorified more than ever as the "final victory" seemed within reach':

How could there ever be doubters? The German army moved into Paris. There French perfumes, lingerie and other Parisian chick sold-out. The victory parade that swept through the Brandenburg Gate in Berlin was simply bombastic. Dunkirk was hailed by the Nazi press as the victorious end of the greatest battle ever.

Monitoring the jubilation, police reported the 'steadfast enthusiasm of the last few weeks has turned into a festive mood marked with silent, proud joy and gratitude for the leaders and the Wehrmacht'.[1]

For the wider public, newsreel announcer Harry Giese provided the picture: 'Berlin hailed its first returning division with resounding jubilation – the German nation and its soldiers, an inseparable community-in-arms.' The clipped tones of Giese – a thirty-seven-year-old actor from Magdeburg – had become the dominant fixture of cinema newsreels, as his machine-gun commentaries provided the soundtrack of Germany at war.

There was even more to celebrate on 14 June, when German tanks rumbled into Paris past the Arc de Triomphe down the famous Champs-Élysées to the Place de la Concorde. Over in Berlin, journalist Ruth Andreas-Friedrich – who had secretly been helping Jews threatened with deportation – was startled by the excitement caused by the fall of Paris:

> As the report came over the radio … we were just having lunch in the canteen. Hurrah was suddenly heard from a corner of the room. One of the cleaning women jumped up, grabbed her glass, and cheered: 'Long live the Führer!'[2]

German soldier Felix Elger had little idea of the whirlwind that was about to engulf him when his company entered Paris a few days later, as he wrote to his wife:

> In the early hours of the morning your husband marched as a German soldier through the capital of France, through Paris. I have drawn our route for you on the enclosed map. My personal impression of Paris was a very positive one. I have to admit frankly

that I have never seen a more beautiful and elegant city. The residents are extremely amiable, as is every French, by the way. I would like to visit this beautiful city with you, beloved woman. The suburbs, the industrial districts with the slums stand in stark contrast to the splendid inner city.[3]

That same week, Adolf Hitler touched down in the French capital for a fleeting visit. Speaking of their visit to the great Opera House, his valet, Heinz Linge, remembered that 'Hitler knew it so well from his book studies that he could act as the tourist guide and astonished everybody, including the Paris experts Speer, Arno Breker and Hermann Giesler, with his detailed and comprehensive knowledge'.

On Hitler's heels, another army of sorts followed with trowels, pickaxes and spades. Organisation Todt, named after its leader Fritz Todt, the man responsible for the autobahn network, adopted a *blitzkrieg* approach to repairing roads, laying out aerodromes and other facilities for German forces in occupied countries. They refurbished restaurants, theatres and clubs for soldiers as well as renovating hotels and guesthouses. An early conversion project was a venue for the KdF in Paris at the Theatre de l'Empire, Avenue de Wagram, as *Arbeitertum* reported:

> When the guns are silent, the muses have the floor. As soon as a ceasefire has occurred on any section of the front, the High Command of the Wehrmacht, in cooperation with the Nazi community Kraft durch Freude, draws on artistic forces which, through their performances, are to bring our soldiers the spiritual relaxation so necessary after hard battles.

Singer Erna Berger was thrilled with her Paris experience, which culminated at the opera. 'It was just a pleasure for me. We were able to sing in the Grand Opera, which is otherwise reserved for French artists, which was a special joy for every singer because of the unique acoustics. I did not realize then that it also meant a hostile demonstration of power in front of the defeated opponent.'[4] Of course, there were other benefits for the touring troupes. Singer Lale Andersen, known for her hit 'Lili Marlene', remembered how 'everyone marvelled at us like mythical creatures that had opened the door to paradise'. Everything was obtainable. Actors and soldiers became dedicated hoarders. 'A bar of Danish chocolate, knitting wool, Chanel five, a packet of Houten cocoa, a cake of French bath soap...' the list was endless, Anderson recalled.

The hoarding was relentless. Actor Hans Söhnker even bought tinned vegetables in Paris, hoping for peas or mushrooms; he was eventually disappointed to find that he had bought diced turnips. It was hardly surprising that with this so-called 'Hamster mentality' KdF engagements in occupied Western Europe became sought-after postings within the artistic community, while assignments in Poland and the Balkans were less popular (Russia would later be considered a waste of time). In response to the massive stockpiling of goods, from 1942, Hitler ordered that food and luxury items taken into the Reich from occupied territories by soldiers, businessmen or entertainers were exempt from control and confiscation (as long as they could be carried by the owner).

Day after day, German troops filled shops buying up all the chocolate they could find, encouraged by an exchange rate of 20 francs to the Reichsmark (compared to a pre-war exchange rate of 12 to 1). From then on, traders and occupiers entered a mutually beneficial dance of co-dependency. American reporter Harry Flannery observed that 'butter was such an unusual thing that the men bought it everywhere and ate it as they walked along the streets without bread, like ice-cream cones'. But there was more: 'The successful purchaser of a cake of soap is liable to see a German walk out from the same shop with a whole box full', and 'silk stockings, one of the special purchases of the Nazi soldiers, were almost all gone. Those that remained and had cost 25 to 30 francs a pair had risen to 70 and 100 francs a pair.'

Else Wendel remembered the joke at the time being that 'the really clever girls were those who changed their escorts as we conquered each country. A smart girl could have all the luxuries she needed from Norway, Holland, Belgium, France and now onto Greece and Italy.' Wives whispered to their soldier husbands not to forget to buy sweets and French perfume, or delicious sausages from Poland – and, if things turned out well, a tweed suit from England. It came as no surprise when a sudden glut of French champagne, cognac and perfumes started weighing down shelves in German shops. Newlywed Ilse Schier was the grateful recipient of presents from her husband Reinhardt, who was serving on the Atlantic coast in France: 'He sent Chanel No. 5 perfume and Breton handicrafts,' she recalled. His daily letters home apparently showed his posting was no hardship:

> He had participated in the blitzkrieg and fortunately survived everything unscathed. It was an unforgettable tourist experience (for him). They got the opportunity to participate in sailing trips and otherwise get to know life in France, which they really enjoyed.

It only took a few months for Paris to resume most of its daily occupations and nightlife. By August, the German Railroads Information Office reopened on the Avenue de l'Opéra in Paris to 'advise and assist French travellers and those from other countries visiting France who wanted to extend their trips into the tourist paradises of the Reich'. The company expected a rapid revival of foreign tourist travel in Germany as plans for an extensive programme of art, sports, music and other festivals got underway.[5] The cobbled streets of Paris could be lively after midnight, especially as young troops hit the town fortified by Calvados, a very potent apple brandy.

In virtually all activities Paris again became the 'City of Light'. Air-raid precautions were still in force but the curfew was relaxed, and restaurants, nightclubs and bars recorded brisk business, swelled by German soldiers who replaced the tourists. Hitler's weary men had taken some hard knocks, particularly in Belgium and Holland, but in Paris they considered themselves veteran troops. 'Until now this war has been one big KdF trip,' one soldier joked to his parents after the fall of France.[6] Almost immediately Paris cemented its place as a city of rest and relaxation, a haven for sex and gastronomy. The sheer volume of German troops swarming France was alarming, as one disgruntled local writer complained: 'Biarritz, La Baule Deauville, Le Touquet. Nazis, Nazis everywhere trying in vain to pal up to the locals.' In fact, many resistance pamphlets urged citizens not to be hoodwinked by friendly manner of German troops. 'Don't be under any illusion: these people aren't tourists. Take your time, ignore what they say, shun their concerts and their parades.'[7]

By late summer, German military authorities had established a special unit of the Wehrmacht organising tours in Paris.[8] A 'special correspondent' writing in *The Scotsman* saw buses shuttling troops to Montmartre, Montparnasse, Notre Dame, Bois de Boulogne, Napoleon's Tomb and other sights of the city and suburbs. 'Tours for German officers have been arranged to the countryside and the seaside in Normandy and Brittany, while troops are resting in preparation for whatever next move may be contemplated.'[9] A separate organisation, Jeder Einmal in Paris (meaning Everybody in Paris Once) ferried in soldiers from as far as North Cape, Greece and the Ukraine to the French capital for excursions.

War news never dominated the front page of the *Deutsche Wegleiter*, a weekly guide published by the Wehrmacht offering restaurant recommendations, theatre programmes, profiles of art galleries like the Louvre and Musée d'Orsay and a sporting guide complemented by pages of small advertisements for local businesses. Contemporary history came to life for many visitors to the Maginot Line, the supposedly impenetrable French defence against German invasion. Visitors were able to inspect bunkers, minefields, supply lines and anti-tank installations. The locations where the German army punched through in 1940 became especially popular attractions. In some areas, vast troves of captured armaments were available for inspection. There was also the possibility of taking a break in Alsace, which one guidebook noted was 'once again a living member of the German Reich and belongs among the most beautiful and valuable travel destinations available to Germans'. The KdF later took the opportunity to mount a barbed attack on the French, describing the cultural situation in Alsace as bleak: 'Under French rule the government had never taken any initiative to satisfy the cultural needs of the rural population,' noted the pamphlet *KdF-Arbeit im Elsass*. 'Nor had anyone else taken care of this.'[10]

From dawn to dusk, soldiers flocked to Parisian bars and cafes along the Seine sweating in grey woollen uniforms. The Métro subway provided a new experience for many, while others were vastly exhilarated by the Eiffel Tower and scratched their names on the beams with pen-knives. Wehrmacht officer Ernst Jünger spent a tour of duty in Paris. In his journal, he noted dining at the Tour d'Argent on supreme of sole and the famous duck. 'Sitting in the dining room is like being in a large airplane looking out over the Seine and its islands,' he observed. 'In times like this, eating well and much brings a feeling of power.'[11]

What struck many French citizens was the obvious youth of the German occupiers. In a feature, 'Tourists in Uniform', published in *L'Illustration*, the writer observed that under their grey uniforms 'we couldn't distinguish social class, or profession':

> But we could sense that there were many intellectuals among these young people, university students, who would take up their interrupted studies and who would profit from their visit to learn about French culture and to increase their learning and experience. They probably had only a bookish knowledge of our culture. This occasion would help them, to their benefit, to see the real face of France, to be able to get to know its citizens, and to familiarize themselves with our customs and our spirit.

Indeed, many German soldiers buzzed around Pablo Picasso who could usually be found at the restaurant Le Catalan, near the Saint-Germain-des-Prés intersection.

At the same time, female companionship was affordable and available at bordellos throughout the city. Eighteen-year-old gunner August von Kageneck recalled that even though most of his platoon were the sons of farmers and had never left their home village it didn't take long for them to find a knocking shop: 'Ah, soldiers,' he laughed. 'You always sniff out a brothel easier than a church.'[12] (Many troops circulated a list of Paris brothels and their addresses, while Wehrmacht medics warned of venereal disease, which was common in the city.) French author Jean Guéhenno was appalled at the influx of troops and their open relationships with prostitutes. 'They are everywhere,' he complained on a visit to Versailles.

> There were three of them in the restaurant, big, pot-bellied, unbuttoned, slumped in their chairs, nostalgic, in the hands of three horrible whores billing and cooing, caressing them, pampering them. All of them were stretching and grunting together with pleasure. O German virtue! O Siegfried! It's true that the whore and the soldier are international types. But ordinarily they hide their amorous frolics. A conquering soldier openly flaunts all his rights.[13]

Bathed in the glorious French sunshine, Corporal Werner Monk, a radio operator, quickly morphed from a soldier to a sightseer during his deployment in France. Based in Saint-Omer, near Calais, Monk threw himself wholeheartedly into the experience, living freely and unbound. 'Our wages, which at that time were still paid in francs, were very generous for us,' he recounted,[14] noting a 'front-line allowance' meant soldiers received the equivalent to double wages so that it was possible to 'live like a God in France'. He recalled that alcohol was always plentiful, be it from the sutler's store or at local shops. 'There was no shortage and the wines, cognac and every kind of alcohol was inexpensive. I, too, was always well supplied with spirits.'

For most German soldiers, alcohol was a constant companion in the evenings, especially on payday. Monk's local pub, run by French women, became a favourite spot for recreation.

> The guests in this pub were German and French, they all drank either their aperitif, or their beer, or their wine and that without any problems. Without any anger or hostility, not in words and not in gestures.
>
> Whenever possible, I went to the pub, and not just because of the alcohol. After the anisette liqueur, I also got to know and

appreciate the Pernod. A lot of bad news was said about the Pernod because of alleged health problems, but we thought it was a rumor and enjoyed this typically French drink with enthusiasm. We were particularly impressed by the national drink of the French, the anisette, which was said to make you stupid, some said, and others said it gave more strength to men. Apart from the Pernod, I had found my very special drink in the pub, or had copied it from the French. That was 'Vin blanc avec citrone'. Not only did it taste great, it was also much easier to digest. Above all, you didn't get as 'drunk' from it as from the liquor from the bottles, the many types of schnapps and liqueurs.

A special preference was the French cheese, the real Camembert from Normandy. It was a real treat for us, we bought this cheese in a shop in Trouville, where we were soon known as good customers and were served as such. That was a great additional meal that was enjoyed with a bottle of red wine. But the French cigarettes just tasted better, but mainly because they were so unfamiliar. And it was easy to buy, there was no restrictions as there were no smoking rations in France.

During the first year of the war, Wehrmacht troops were pampered endlessly. Adolf Hitler thought there was no greater sadness than orphan soldiers forced to spend a holiday alone. In an effort to spread cheer, those without families or vacation companions could benefit from Adolf-Hitler-Freiplatzspende ('Hitler Vacations') and recuperate in private households or, in special cases, at spas and recreation homes. As *Arbeitertum* explained, the scheme was a fertile breeding ground for kindness. 'In most cases, a cordial friendship is established between guest and host that will survive the war.' Special requests were met whenever possible. For example, some men wanted to visit Berlin, Munich or Vienna while others preferred a seaside trip or a break in the Warthegau. Such requests were collected at the Office for People's Welfare and sent to field post offices.

In any case, the donor can be convinced that through his sacrifice he is helping one of our heroic front-line soldiers to recover and that he is grateful to the men who defend the front with constant commitment to the homeland and help create the new Europe.

'This time I really had a vacation,' wrote a rifleman on his return to the front lines. 'It was an unforgettable experience for me, and it is impossible to describe what beautiful and good things I have experienced!' The respite in somebody else's home clearly did him good. He told *Arbeitertum* how he was fussed over and pampered endlessly, before giving readers a potted summery of his unfortunate life. His father died in France in 1918 and his mother passed away soon after. He and his two brothers grew up without loving care and it was only during his labour service in RAD and during his military service that he got to know the 'concept of mutual care and solidarity through the deep experience of comradeship'. The war came, and he and one of his brothers were drafted. His brother 'fell' in Poland, while he himself took part in the Maginot Line breakthrough, and in the late summer of 1940 he was invited to spend his vacation with a host family through Adolf-Hitler-Freiplatzspende.

> Every day I had the feeling of the great German national community that our Führer had created – filled with a new social spirit. Strengthened in body, mind and soul, I happily returned to my company, to my dear comrades. Again, and again, I had to tell them about my wonderful vacation. Now we go back to the service in order to give my contribution to the glorious victory of Greater Germany, to which the Führer will lead us, through the final fulfilment of our duties.

The year 1940 ended on an optimistic note for the Nazis. Robert Ley, writing in the *Völkischer Beobachter*, forecast the imminent collapse and defeat of Britain. 'It is now only a question of time,' Ley promised, 'that all workers will share in the treasures of this world after the defeat of Britain. You German workers will participate in the spoils. The one thing National Socialists promise you after victory is that you will be able to realise all your Socialistic ambitions. You will have much better time after this war.'

24

A NEW EUROPE

Although British travel writer Ferdinand Tuohy had his share of worries about the direction of the war in 1941, he found time to ponder the plight of Europe's famed resorts. From his desk in London, he considered the emptiness and sadness of the stilled and ghostly holiday spots. 'Imagine all the garaged-up motor coaches, the boarded-up tourist offices, the vanished army of guides, the closed casinos, the hotels running to seed, the tied-up river and lake steamers, the skeleton staffs, the shuttered shops, bars and cafes, the silent rail terminals.' He lamented the plight of waiters and wine stewards forced to cater for Nazi appetites.

> Tourism used to be the fourth industry of France. At its highest pitch, 700,000 were employed. Pretty well the only tourists today are Nazis and their relatives settled like locusts on the French scene at twenty (forced) francs to the mark. It is hard to picture all the lovely places Brittany, Touraine, Savoy, Normandy, the Pyrenees, and the Alps given over wholly or partly to the Nazi jackboot. The Germans always were bad visitors. They went at things too determinedly, glued to their guide books.

For the German public, the delights of France remained off-limits during 1941. Instead, that summer the public jockeyed for the best holiday deals to the farthest-flung regions of the Reich. Bavaria continued to welcome trainloads of guests, many on the hunt for a hearty and satisfying meal. According to the SS mouthpiece *Das Schwarze Korps* – a publication mistrustful by nature – culinary geography dictated holiday choices:

> The tourists go to where the food is good and eat them bare. Hardly had it been possible to forge a united German nation in which the Bavarian no longer looked upon the Prussian as coming straight from hell, than these tourists arrived and threatened to break up this unity once more by their greed.[1]

Over in Munich, Lord Mayor Karl Fierler was eager to secure his slice of tourist traffic and convened a meeting of the Party, Reichsbahn, hotel owners and restaurateurs to come up with ideas. The previous year had seen Munich enjoy record visitor numbers, boosted by 'military vacationers' alongside many Italians. Two attractions were heavily promoted by Munich council in 1941. The first was a special exhibition called Art of the Front, using artwork created by soldiers posted across the occupied areas. The second was a small folk festival designed to replace the annual beer festival, and this proved to be a great success.

On the national scene, Hapag set the presses rolling to produce an eight-page *Summer 1941* brochure featuring Bavaria, Austria, Sudetenland and the Baltic resorts, while Carl Degener revived 'dreamlike' breaks near Salzburg and Tyrol, Mayrhofen, St Gilgen and Golling priced from RM153. The price included a room, return rail tickets and food (breakfast, lunch and dinner – excluding drinks), electricity charge (for lights), shoeshine (one pair daily), visitor's tax and local tour guides. For those wishing to venture further, ENIT Tourismus Reisen (Berlin and Vienna) offered a range of Italian breaks, including two-week stays at private beaches on the Adriatic.

Tourism in the north began to suffer, however. That summer there was a shortage of adequate lodging for tourists along the Baltic and North Sea coast as guesthouses and sanatoriums were requisitioned and filled with injured soldiers or evacuated mothers with their children. All evacuees told the same story about life in the west: sporadic bombings interspersed with periods of calm followed by growing tension. As the pattern of RAF bombing became more established, the onslaught created several islands of calm in Germany. In the lowlands, for example, or in many rural small towns, daily life went on as usual, whereas in industrial regions and big cities – though seldom in the suburbs – the bombing upended everyday existence.

As the summer pushed on, authorities privately derided the hordes of holiday traffic clogging up the transport networks. With the situation worsening, press articles appealed to the public to choose less popular resorts and spread vacations throughout the year so that the countless convalescing soldiers could enjoy vacations.[2] In an editorial, the *Völkischer Beobachter* advised vacationers to go to the Black Forest, Sudetenland or Silesia for their holidays. Furthermore, it opined, holidays should only exceed three weeks in special cases, such as for health reasons: 'A four-week holiday should be the absolute maximum.'[3]

As the year progressed, there was plenty of excitement on the war front. German troops entered Athens, followed by an airborne invasion of Crete. On the high seas, the battleship *Bismarck* sank HMS *Hood*, killing all but three crewmen from a total of 1,418 aboard the pride of the British Royal Navy. Soon after, the *Bismarck* was blown out of the water in the North Atlantic, killing 2,300.

On the German home front, the signs of economic malaise were unavoidable, even in resorts where many hotels and restaurants were accused of exploitation. In one racket, diners were obliged to hand over twice the number of fat coupons for a meat dish. It was just one of many scams *Das Reich* described as fleecing: 'It has also become the custom to demand fat coupons for dishes not cooked in fat. This is unbearable, and it has now become necessary for the Government to intervene and ration fat coupons for every dish.' The absence of 'quality control' in tourist establishments and restaurants meant that adulteration was commonplace.

A New Europe

The squeeze was even felt in the major hotels of Berlin, where American journalist Harry Flannery sought good-quality booze. When he first arrived in Germany in 1939 all hotels served Canadian Club, but by 1941 the only whisky available was a watered-down, 'un-drinkably bad' local concoction. 'Most of the Germans drank a white fluid that looked like gin and that I thought tasted like gasoline.' Likewise, American journalist Howard K. Smith discovered that even the bar at the Adlon – still the best hotel in Berlin – was squeezed for refreshment: 'It caused visible pain to the old bartender to answer an order for a cocktail saying he was dreadfully sorry, but today, precisely today, he had run out of ingredients.' Smith thought it 'almost pathetic' watching fine old hotels with glorious pasts struggling to keep up appearances. At the Kaiserhof, the barman set up a display of bottles of coloured water against the mirrored background of the counter.

> Actually, all he had was some raw liquor the management had managed to squeeze out of a farm house outside Berlin, 'Himbeergeist,' or fake vodka that took the roof off your mouth, or wood alcohol with perfume in it which was served under the name 'Sclibovitz,' two fingers to a customer and no more, but tomorrow, meine Herren, maybe. The coloured water trick was applied widely after that, but it became embarrassing when thirsty citizens began plaguing the places which displayed flagons of it to sell a bottle or two. One fancy delicatessen on the Kurfürstendamm eventually placed a frank sign in its window, 'These bottles are filled with coloured water and nothing else. They are purely for the purpose of decoration. We have no liquor, so please do not bother our sales staff, which is short due to the war.'[4]

There were few smiling faces at pubs either. On arriving in Berlin, a Swedish correspondent spat out a mouthful of ale he had been served, which he described as 'gassy coloured water'. As he discovered, a decree forbidding deliveries of hops, ersatz hops and malt to breweries had devastated quality as the last genuine ingredient was removed. Before long, beer contained virtually no protein, no fats, and not a single vitamin – even the calorific content was vastly reduced.

Another correspondent, William Bayles, remembered being served a pint which 'would have made any Bavarian *braumeister* blush with shame':

> It was announced some time ago that the amount of grain allowed for beer had been restricted, and with the demand increasing, there is no solution but the water-tap. Certain famous breweries are to receive permission to keep their quality at par and to increase the price as the supply of grain is reduced.

Another gripe with the hospitality trade was rude service, combined with long faces and grumbling. The issue became so serious that Goebbels launched a campaign for politeness, as public concern over abrasiveness and the infrequency of such words as 'please' and 'thank you' became more widespread. Swedish journalist Gunnar Pihl explained to his readers how the scheme worked:

> The public wrote in and suggested people who were especially polite; the Minister of Propaganda distributed prizes, a thousand marks, a radio, and twenty theatre tickets to the four politest ones. Politeness was filmed and shown in the movies. Polite people received a pin as a sign of their civility, a pin with the Berlin bear on it. When distributing the pins, Goebbels declared that the people of Berlin were fundamentally tremendously polite.

Journalist Harry Flannery was sick and tired of the apathy and rudeness in restaurants, especially when waiters ignored the calls of customers:

> They knew they could not be dismissed, and service generally depended on the character of the individual. The waiters in Berlin were typical of other workers. As a result, a life that brought one in contact with workers was continually marked by unpleasantness. I have seen a German woman crying after being roared at by a

post-office clerk merely because she had neglected to bring one of her many identification papers, and a German housewife in tears at a grocery store where she was registered and which she had to patronize. She had delayed a few minutes to look over the stock. A clerk came up. 'Well,' he said, 'make up your mind. We have other people to take care of.'

Although the alcohol shortage caused distress, of all the suffering privations in daily life it was the lack of soap, perfumes and toilet preparations that was most unpleasant – and this in an age before spray and roll-on deodorant.

Rationing meant the public received a single three-ounce soap tablet per month. This scentless grey 'war soap' replaced brands like Palmolive and Kaloderma, which vanished from sale. War soap was blamed for causing skin irritation, particularly among babies and toddlers – hardly surprising given it contained a mixture of soda, sand and argillaceous earth. The smell of unclean clothes, body odour and tobacco was enough to drive some commuters off public transport, added as it was to the misery of increased flatulence thanks to a widespread diet of foods rich in starch. Again, Howard K. Smith suffered when confronted with strong stenches:

> To see the people, you take the subway. You also smell them. There is not enough time, nor enough coaches for coaches to be cleaned and properly ventilated every day, so the odour of stale sweat from the bodies that work hard and only have a cube of soap as big as a penny box of matches to wash with for a month lingers in their interiors and is reinforced qualitatively until it changes for the worse, qualitatively as time and war proceed. In summer it is asphyxiating ... dozens of people, whose bodies and stomachs are not strong anyhow, faint in them every day. Sometimes you just have to get out at some station halfway to your destination to take a breath of fresh air between trains.[5]

During May, the month in which Rudolf Hess parachuted into Scotland claiming to be on a peace mission, the RAF unloaded more than 1,000 tons of bombs on Brest, Hamburg, Kiel, Bremen, Cologne, Hanover and Mannheim as British military planners set about destroying the morale of the civilian population. Terrified by the onslaught, many wealthy Germans wended their way to the Alps, Black Forest, Thuringia, Silesia and Sudetenland to seek shelter. The massive influx saw the Bavarian resort record 51,000 'holidaymakers' in contrast to 22,000 a year earlier. Such stories infuriated NBC's Berlin correspondent Charles Lanius, who shamed wealthy families for keeping safe while the wives and children of the poorer classes had to stay and suffer the air raids. 'These are the people,' Lanius tersely noted, 'who would normally be wintering at Biarritz or Monte Carlo.'[6] On the same theme, American reporter Edward F. Balloch claimed Garmisch had been adopted as the 'funkhole' for a select band of Nazi leaders and their families who did not stint themselves when it came to enjoying life. His comments were almost certainly prompted by a report that Milan's La Scala orchestra performed in Garmisch at a lavish banquet for a little circle of men in peaked caps with their spouses.

One Nazi never accused of avoiding the RAF onslaught was Robert Ley. As he stomped around the country addressing factory workers, news arrived that Inga – five months pregnant – was injured in a riding accident after a whistle from an approaching train startled her horse, throwing her to the ground: The baby survived unscathed and was born prematurely three months later.

While comforting Inga, Ley oversaw the creation of excursion trips designed to help the public identify food sources in the countryside or in woodland, indicating that authorities were getting jittery about future food supplies. DAF's Dr Werner Bockhacker took factory workers on daytrips to familiarise them with shrubs, roots, berries and other species. By this point, coffee was already being made from flower bulbs using tulips and crocuses. To ensure supplies, other chemically prepared substitutes included artificial chicken, eggs and yeast products made from wood, which was surprisingly rich in proteins. The Wehrmacht at this time was nourished with powdered apples, cheese, jams, vegetables, tomatoes and spinach.

Robert Ley was exceptionally proud to report that, by late 1941, 163 troupes were performing KdF shows in the Netherlands Italy, Norway, Denmark, North Africa and on the Eastern Front. In addition to entertaining active-duty military troops, shows were also provided for Todt workers building the vast Atlantic Wall stretching from France to Norway.

Although Holland was theoretically out of bounds, German vacationers with military connections occasionally snagged a room at Amsterdam's Krasnapolsky, one of Europe's great hotels. (Baedeker described it as the foremost meeting place in Amsterdam, with one of the largest cafes in Europe complete with garden and billiard table.) A year after the occupation, the Netherlands Labour Front (NAF) – a Dutch copy of the DAF – was founded after existing trade unions were dissolved. The so-called Congress for Joy and Work, a KdF spin-off, operated in Holland arranging symphony concerts, variety and cabaret under the baton of Joop Termeulen, the Dutch leader of the KdF-Orchestra. In The Hague, in association with Deutschen Theatre in den Nederlanden, the KdF staged an impressive production of *Madama Butterfly*, while the NS-Symphonie-Orchester – billed as the 'Orchestra of the Führer'– played a series of concerts across the Netherlands from Eindhoven to Groningen. Similar events were held in Belgian factories for workers in addition to vaudeville evenings in Brussels and the provinces.

Despite travel being discouraged among the Dutch population, local authorities sometimes pushed the public to take excursions. For example, when the historic home of Peter the Great was touted for demolition because visitors were scarce, the Germans acted. Hand built by Peter in 1632 and preserved as an architectural monument, the dwelling served as his personal abode and had been a great pre-war attraction. In an effort to save the property, the Nazi-run Society for Tourist Traffic in the Zaan district initiated a drive to make people visit the house in order to affect its continued existence.[7]

Over in Poland, lights still shone bright from the larger hotels reserved for the exclusive use of Germans. Although stripped of character, dismembered, looted and bereft of food, Poland proved a remarkably attractive prospect for many German travellers. As the territory welcomed both military and civilian tourists, the iconic Baedeker company set about producing a special travel guide, which, when published a few years later, came complete with a foreword by Governor Hans Frank. Baedeker's *Das Generalgouvernement* promised readers a journey of excitement and wonder: 'The land by the Vistula, together with its towns, has gained a completely new face since the German Reich took over its administration.' Visitors were guaranteed all the charms of home, including a newly named Adolf-Hitler-Platz. (A short entry for Auschwitz casually lists it as a railway station, while the guide also noted that Lublin was *judenfrei*). There was practical advice to the German traveller: 'For longer distances and during night-time driving it is recommended that you bring a gun with you.'

Since 1939, establishments catering for German troops and visitors continued to spring up. In Breslau, the 'thoroughly deloused' Hotel Monopol offered rooms for RM4, with tea at 5 p.m., a grillroom, evening concert and 'American Bar'. In Krakow, the Hotel Royal was rebranded into House Tyrol, offering full board, 'good beer' and 'good music' in the evenings. In the south-east, the Hotel Deutscher Hof in Przemyśl was the 'best and cheapest place to stay' for the *Reichsdeutschen*.[8] For entertainment, in addition to the ubiquitous KdF, travelling circuses were popular with troops, as were the newly established German cinemas, such as the Scala in Krakow.[9] In Lodz, the Diocesan Museum – a valuable repository of ecclesiastical art, archives and texts – was commandeered by the Germans and turned into the KdF office. 'The library was destroyed and the collection devastated.'[10] Posen – a former German territory lost after the First World War – became so jam-packed with excursionists that military personnel, many with bolt-action rifles slung over their shoulders, struggled to find places on trains.[11] The crowds were constant. According to scathing SS reports, holiday traffic was rough and unceremonious as many passengers (including serving soldiers) were squeezed into lavatories, while some even disembarked through carriage windows.[12]

In Warsaw, locals responded with stunned incomprehension as soldiers cheerfully snapped pictures of the ghetto and the Jewish cemetery near Okopowa Street, which became a principal attraction. Resident M. Zylberberg described graphic examples of this new phenomena. 'It was not only the funeral processions that made the cemetery so strangely lively,' he observed, 'but the constant presence of hundreds of German soldiers. They gleefully photographed the dead and the accompanying relatives, and even went as far as taking snapshots of the corpses as they were laid out in the mortuary.' The Nazis were particularly active in this respect on Sundays, 'when they would visit the cemeteries with their girlfriends. This, rather than the cinema, was a place of amusement for them.'[13]

25

BARBAROSSA

Berlin's 'unbreakable ties' of friendship with Moscow, lauded in the German press since the signing of the Molotov–Ribbentrop Pact in 1939, ended with Hitler's surprise invasion of Russia on 22 June 1941. The invaders kicked off hostilities from points along a front which extended from northern Finland to the Black Sea – a distance of roughly 1,500 miles. Over 3 million men, 600,000 trucks, 650,000 horses and 2,700 Luftwaffe aircraft were mobilised with the help of Finland, Romania and Italy.

For many Germans, a two-front war was a nightmare come true, bringing with it more uncertainty. However, early fears were soon soothed by the ruthless efficiency of the Wehrmacht, which punctured a hole 80 miles wide in Russian defences. Within a week, Minsk, the capital of Belarus, had been captured; by 10 July, the Soviets had lost thousands of tanks, aircraft and men.

Hitler treated military commanders to long monologues about his future plans to populate the immense spaces of the Soviet Union – a vast and varied land of forests, rivers, rolling steppes, sub-tropical gardens, lakes, golden deserts and rugged sea coasts. He fantasised about developing Sochi, a Russian resort on the east shore of the Black Sea, into an exclusive holiday retreat along with Kemmern, a spa 30 miles from Riga.

> We'll give this country a past. We'll take away its character of an Asiatic steppe, we'll Européanise it. With this object, we have undertaken the construction of roads that will lead to the southernmost point of the Crimea and to the Caucasus. These roads will be studded along their whole length with German towns, and around these towns our colonists will settle ... For Ley, it will be the job of his life to drag that country out of its lethargy.

In the future, Hitler promised, every worker would have his holidays and could indulge in a few days in each year 'which he can arrange as he likes'. Together with Ley, he indulged in plans about the endless possibilities for tourism: 'The beauties of the Crimea, which we shall make accessible by means of an autobahn – for us Germans, that will be our Riviera,' Hitler boasted in July. 'Crete is scorching and dry. Cyprus would be lovely, but we can reach the Crimea by road. Along that road lies Kiev! And Croatia, too, a tourists' paradise for us. I expect that after the war there will be a great upsurge of rejoicing.'[1]

For many soldiers, the adventures across Europe and eastwards into Russia became one gigantic adventure. A young corporal with a platoon heading for action in the Soviet Union wrote to his parents:

> I can tell you, in order to requite your understandable curiosity, that I have behind me a very big trip until the Russian border. We drove through half of Europe, no exaggeration. Again, many new impressions pour in and again one gets to know many new and interesting things. My military service so far has been almost entirely an educational trip![2]

During these early days of Barbarossa, Ley was in euphoric mood. On 27 June, Inga gave birth to a baby girl, named Gloria in tribute to the early successes in Russia.[3] Howard K. Smith thought the best evidence that the German High Command believed in a swift victory came on 13 July, before the invasion was a month old, when a communiqué declared 'the Soviets were showing signs of dissolution and collapse'. At the same time, the *Völkischer Beobachter* added to the excitement by announcing that Stalin's army was down to its 'last reserves'.

As in the French campaign, the KdF followed on the heels of the advancing troops and requisitioned theatres and concert halls in the Soviet Union. In Vilnius, the Lithuanian capital, KdF marched into the cultural centre known as the House of the Red Army and set up a theatre for occupying troops. As always, *Arbeitertum* followed events. 'When you want to pursue the area of activity of the KdF today,' it reported, 'you can no longer get by with a map of Germany!'

> Wherever the German soldier stands, be it under the midnight sun in northernmost Norway or under the piercing rays of the Libyan sun, KdF is with him. Every day our artists are on the move and have covered 77,000 km within a year, a distance that is twice the circumference of the earth!

Describing itself as the 'medicine man for Europe', the organisation boasted an extremely versatile face. Theatrical performances such as opera and operetta predominated, but cabaret also came into its own. But the KdF wasn't just on the front lines, *Arbeitertum* reminded readers: '40 million national comrades on the home front experienced the counterbalance to their hard work by enjoying theatre events, concerts, art exhibitions, folk evenings, amateur art performances, film screenings and colourful social evenings.'

Although the press continued to whip up triumphant emotions, the reality was that throughout July, August and into September, the Russian adventure was falling short of expectations. The first snowfalls on the Russian front in September came as German troops looked with trepidation at the winter before them. In the unfriendly vastness of the Russian landscape, nature can be brutal as cold winds scream across the plains; temperatures plunge to -20°C and vegetation struggles for life. Back home, it didn't take long for the population to become disillusioned, as the Nazi Women's Organization (NSF) noted in a report from the largely Catholic village of Steinwiesen, in the district of Kronach in Bavaria:

> Every day there are losses on the Eastern Front and the population is beginning to complain. Wherever one goes there are little huddles complaining, crying or grumbling. The black blood really comes out here. They run off to church like mad to seek comfort.[4]

Month by month, in spite of substantial victories, the path to victory looked ever more distant, leading to growing doubt in the minds of the German people. 'By this time victory was overdue,' Howard K. Smith remarked after observing a scratching of heads and wonderment in Berlin. 'But the matter was far more serious than simply a psychological impatience for the end.'

> This campaign, unlike all the others, was making itself materially felt. Little items, little amenities were disappearing from the shops and big items were growing scarcer. The number of letters returned to their senders every day marked 'fallen' in red ink, increased portentously.[5]

As General Halder recorded in his diary, Hitler's short, sharp blitzkrieg, which had impressed everyone back in June, was turning into a prolonged offensive.

> We have underestimated the Russian colossus ... [Soviet divisions] are not armed and equipped according to our standards, and their tactical leadership is often poor. But there they are, and if we smash a dozen of them the Russians simply put up another dozen. The time factor favours them, as they are near their own resources, while we are moving farther and farther away from ours. And so, our troops sprawled over an immense front line, without any depth, are subjected to the incessant attacks of the enemy.[6]

The feeling wasn't lost on the Berlin correspondent for the *Neue Zurcher Zeitung* who saw a tetchy public 'waiting with great interest and even anxiety to hear details of the great successes promised by the Nazi High Command'.[7] By November, according to German calculation, Russia should have been out of the war – but the fighting continued. As the Battle of Moscow began, temperatures around the Russian capital dropped to -12°C and the Soviet Union launched ski troops for the first time against the freezing German forces. The most trustworthy barometer of morale on the home front was the volume of anti-Jewish rhetoric, which fell when things were going smoothly but rose sharply when the population sensed danger or failure. Newspapers continued to scream that the war was started by Jews in the Kremlin, Wall Street and the City of London. Such nonsense was repeated more often as the military situation deteriorated.

As if things weren't bad enough, on 7 December 1941 a Japanese attack on the American naval base of Pearl Harbour brought the USA into the conflict. Soon after, inexplicable as it still seems, Hitler declared war on the United States. That same morning, in a short meeting with American chargé d'affaires Leland B. Morris, Ribbentrop read the declaration, which concluded with the line:

> ... Germany too, as from today, considers herself as being in a state of war with the United States of America.[8]

Decline set in rapidly after that. The year ended with the German people having seen their supposedly invincible armies driven back as they faced another winter under the shadow of terrible casualty lists.

26

1942

The year 1942 had a gloomy start both for the country, which was succumbing to another round of Allied bombing, and for the Russian campaign, with continuous setbacks hampering the Wehrmacht.

On the home front, the clarion call of belt-tightening was heard everywhere. Wines and spirits were scarce, pharmacists sold goods in tiny quantities, and fruit and potatoes remained hard to obtain. Meat, butter and bread rations were reduced and shopkeepers selling bottled goods, wines, vinegar, or anything requiring a cork were ordered to demand one used cork per bottle sold. With a heavy increase in smoking due to the strain of the situation, it also became a struggle to source well-known cigarette brands like Lord Chesterfield, Kemal, North State and Juno – a name ubiquitous with its slogans '*Berlin Raucht Juno*' (Berlin smokes Juno) and 'our cigarettes are fat and round'.[1] When available, 4 pfennig would buy a six-pack but supplies became erratic, as journalist John McCutcheon Raleigh discovered during a shop-to-shop crawl for Virginia Blend. On a visit to the AWAG department store, he saw four or five pillars of display boxes stood on the counter, all containing paper replicas of popular brands. Customers also complained that cigarettes shrank – losing a quarter of their length – and there emerged unknown brands such as Cocktail American Bridge Club, which, despite its artisan packaging, tasted disgusting.[2]

As companies were asked to collect waste paper for recycling, calls were made for 'voluntary donations' of copper, bronze, brass, tin and other metals. Across Germany, council workers sawed off decorative iron railings surrounding civic spaces, gravestones and gardens to be melted down for war use. The strains imposed on manpower and civilian life by the fortunes of war saw DAF programmes sharply reduced, but the KdF survived although the variety and scope of its activities – especially on the home front – were severely curtailed. The chronic shortage of materials ended its 'beauty of labour' campaign, adult education classes were scaled back and musical concerts declined. Although sports activities managed to survive, they were gradually reduced as the year progressed.

One of the most astonishing – and, for the army, undignified – happenings of the war occurred when the government appealed for the public to send clothing to the troops freezing in Russia. In some cases, cardigans and jumpers were handed out at train stations to soldiers destined for the front lines – giving the impression of an Army in mufti, as they donned pompom hats, bright scarves and fox furs. By mid-January, German troops suffering from frostbite in Russia totalled 50,000; among those, 1,856 amputations were conducted. The myth of the invincible German military machine was finally being shattered.

For the German workforce, life on the shop floor became increasingly oppressive. Employers were given the green light to punish absenteeism, late arrival and offences endangering order and security. Even though such punishment was not provided for either by law or labour control regulations, the docking of wages became the weapon of choice.

Given this atmosphere, it's hardly surprising most Germans hankered for a holiday or, at least, a short break. Scarcely a day passed without schmaltzy pop hits such as 'Wenn ich Urlaub hab' – which included the line 'When I'm on vacation, dear darling, you're mine!' – blasting from radio sets. During spring and summer, holiday traffic roared on at almost full pace. Up until the Easter, the Reichsbahn continued to add extra passenger trains to the schedules around holidays, prompting accountant Harald Endemann to take advantage of a special offer. He chuntered off for a few days away in the Hanseatic city of Stade in Lower Saxony, where he watched a performance by the Spanish prima ballerina and soloist Manuela del Rio. In a letter to his wife, Charlotte, Endemann described a lovely, 'pretty old and yet lively' typical North German town...

> ... with wonderful brickwork, gabled houses, old defiant churches, a small colourful harbour, beautiful old secular buildings. Yesterday KdF were here – I almost fainted! – I saw Manuela del Rio, the ticket cost RM1.80 (which I paid despite being tight on funds). She was very good, as if made of porcelain; her partner and the guitarist were also good. The castanets technique was amazing. I enclose the programme.[3]

In Berlin, almost 850,000 day trippers enjoyed the Wannsee beaches while plans for the genocide of the Jews was being decided on the other side of the lake. At the great Anhalter station, staff adapted to dealing with troop transports, holidaymakers end excursionists and, by June 1942, the deportation of Jews.

Porters helped guide elderly Jews onto trains bound for Theresienstadt concentration camp, a task undertaken amid the normal hustle and bustle of station traffic. As the public set off to enjoy excursions, two third-class coaches loaded with Jews were coupled to the regular passenger trains destined for Dresden and Prague departing from platform one at 6.07 a.m. From the point of view of the Nazi government, the MER tourist agency had acquired enough expertise to help facilitate the deportation of Jews to concentration camps; from 1942, many 'Jewish special trains' were organised by MER.

As war increased the public's appetite for escapism, every week hundreds of thousands of people plodded off to football matches in search of entertainment, even if games were often postponed or scheduled at short notice. Although a welcome distraction, Joseph Goebbels thought football useless for propaganda purposes, as he noted in his diary when Sweden beat Germany 3-2 at the Olympic Stadium. In his usual acidic way, he spat that the 100,000 spectators 'cared more about the game' than the capture of any city in the east.[4]

A more productive source of propaganda saw Goebbels throw himself behind a special exhibition entitled 'Soviet Paradise' at Berlin's Lustgarten. During its run, 1.3 million Germans shuffled in to view a historical narrative of 'Jewish–Bolshevik' connivance to dominate the world and laud Hitler's invasion of Russia, presented as a crusade of Pan-European liberation from Bolshevism:

> He who has seen this understands the historic conflict in which we are now engaged, a conflict in which there can be no compromise. There are only two possible outcomes: Either the German people will win and ensure the survival of the world and its culture, or it will perish and all the peoples of the world will fall into the barbarism of the Soviet state that has reduced millions to powerless starving slaves. To stop that from happening, the best elements of Europe are fighting under German leadership at the side of our soldiers to destroy the fateful threat to the life and culture of Europe. Our battle is to free the East, along with its vast and inexhaustible riches and agricultural resources, and to save Europe from the nightmare that has threatened it for millennia.

Those who caught sight of the official forty-eight-page brochure were treated to pictures of poverty, misery, decay and hunger in Russia. 'This is true both of the countryside and the cities,' it informed the reader. 'The atmosphere of Bolshevist cities, too, is grim and depressing.' Many visitors sarcastically quipped that they hardly needed an exhibition to recognise a grim existence or a bombed-out landscape. Barbarossa's fallout could be seen everywhere; in Berlin alone, thousands grieved the loss of sons and husbands. After one year of fighting, the High Command announced that from June 1941 to June 1942, 271,612 officers, NCOs and men of all parts of the armed forces had died 'a hero's death' on the Eastern Front. The number missing during the same period stood at 65,730, and many more suffered life-shattering injuries. Meanwhile, those relatives of soldiers lingering an 'unduly long time' in spas and health resorts were accused of 'working against the common good'.

In an effort to cut traffic, the Reichsbahn started demanding express train travellers show proof from their employer of the necessity of their trip, while access to first- and second-class sleepers was restricted. As shortages of goods needed to serve the tourist trade began to mount, retailers in some holiday towns proved reluctant to serve visitors at the expense of residents. To make matters worse, the Gestapo was bemused by the behaviour of many visitors at resorts:

> The unbridled conduct of these persons (gluttony, regular drunken excesses, moral laxity) shows that they do not comprehend the seriousness of the time. Moreover, the unity of the home front is endangered through the disadvantageous effect on the mood of the working population if this activity is not brought to a stop. The chief of the Security Police and the Security Service has therefore ordered that this danger is to be opposed with all [their] energy.[5]

Such reports were not lost on Robert Ley, who thought it 'impossible to allow trains to run carrying workers on vacations'. He furiously declared that the German Labour Front was undergoing its baptism of fire and faced its members 'not as a giving but as a demanding agency'.[6]

Remarkably, during those chaotic days of 1942, grandiose plans for new motorways stretching from Trier to Paris and Calais to Cologne continued to be sketched out by Nazi planners and their allies.

Up north, whilst the Norwegian civilian population endured an almost starvation diet, Vidkun Quisling, the Nazi puppet leader, was busy building himself a 'northern Berghof' sprawling along the Bygdøy peninsula outside Oslo, protected by 150 guards. Described as a 'rambling forty-six-room structure with bulletproof stone walls', the property also boasted an underground air raid shelter and a high tower where Quisling could see for miles around. Although cloaked in secrecy, a force of 200 men worked on twelve-hour shifts to complete the structure. When finished, the residence was officially known as Gimle, but locals sarcastically referred to it as the 'mini Berghof'. Its extensive grounds included the entire shore at the tip of the peninsula with its rocky coves and pristine white beaches. 'Premier Quisling,' noted one report, 'was said to have fitted up a small astronomical observatory in the tower of the house, where he spends much of his spare time observing the stars.' The ground floor included a sauna, library, wine cellar and outdoor area with patio to entertain guests. Nearly 10 square miles of land around the building was controlled by local police, the airspace above was restricted and the coastguard did not allow boats within 2 miles.

Wasting money on such extravagance seemed remarkable given the plight of the Norwegian population. Details of a meat shortage in occupied Oslo were inadvertently revealed to the wider world by *Fritt Folk*, the Norwegian fascist daily, which reported a growing culinary demand for crows despite such birds having never before figured in Norwegian cuisine. Seemingly detached or unbothered about the plight of the locals, Hitler continued to sketch grand plans for Norway, which, he imagined would again provide a vacation spot served by a 'superhighway' stretching from Berlin to Trondheim. Germans could explore the northern reaches of their new empire on a four-lane autobahn with a hundred exits, allowing them to enjoy lush pine forests, grassy meadows, and, as they inched closer to the coast, dramatic fjords and lakes. *Fritt Folk* gushed about the economic advantages of such a scheme. 'The autobahn,' it said, was a 'magical ribbon of space that made driving fast and fun and would reshape the geography of Europe putting Trondheim next door to Constantinople.'[7] Hitler insisted the motorway was better than the railway, 'which has something impersonal about it, it's the road that will bring peoples together'. Just as the autobahn caused the inner frontiers of Germany to disappear, 'so it will abolish the frontiers of the countries of Europe'.

Extraordinarily, in the hope of better days to come, the Norwegian Travel Agency kept an office on Berlin's Unter Den Linden throughout the war; the *Deutsche Zeitung in Norwegen* predicted an increase in tourism after the war, 'because the occupation had acquainted thousands of Germans (soldiers) with Norway's scenic attractions.'[8] Business traffic was certainly increasing, aided by Lufthansa's scheduled Oslo–Stockholm and Trondheim–Tromsö services. Over time, the Oslo–Stockholm route was extended to Rovaniemi in Finland and expanded south with a flight to Saloniki and Athens on a regularly scheduled basis, along with the Vienna–Graz–Agram (Zagreb) route, later connecting to Sarajevo. As the war spread, so did Lufthansa's network, with the following routes:

Berlin–Copenhagen–Oslo
Berlin–Munich–Venice–Rome (in joint operation with Ala Littoria)
Berlin–Vienna–Budapest–Belgrade–Sofia
Sofia–Bucharest
Berlin–Stuttgart–Lyon–Marseille
Barcelona–Madrid–Lisbon
Berlin–Vienna–Budapest–Bucharest (in joint venture with the Hungarian Malert and the Romanian Lares)
Hamburg–Copenhagen

Albert Speer was instrumental in pushing for better air connections with Norway to facilitate his plans for Neu Drontheim, a base for the German navy in the North Atlantic south-west of Trondheim. Encouraged by Hitler, Speer envisioned 55,000 apartments for military personnel built in tight, classical, monumental symmetry, while docks, shipyards and submarine pens would hug the coastline. Hitler also talked excitedly about transforming the Channel Islands into KdF holiday resorts after the war. 'With their wonderful climate, they constitute a marvellous health resort for the Strength through Joy organisation,' Hitler explained. 'The islands are full of hotels as it is, so very little construction will be needed to turn them into ideal rest centres.'[9] Unable to resist a jibe at his Axis partners, he added, 'The Italians could have got hold of a similar prize, if, on entering the war, they had occupied Cyprus.'

27

A CHANGE OF FORTUNES

The beginning of 1943 saw four fundamental factors in play. First, a humiliating German retreat in North Africa left Italy exposed to the Allies. Second, RAF air raids and firestorms reduced cities across the Reich to rubble. Third, a critical manpower shortage slowed down arms production. Finally, although the makings of the tragedy to come were not yet clear, the Wehrmacht in Russia were bogged down in defensive fighting.

As events tumbled quickly, Robert Ley marked his fifty-third birthday crouched in a bomb shelter shouting angrily that millions of people were still working in jobs unconnected with the war. 'There is no one at home too good to put his shoulders to the wheel,' he thundered to armaments workers in East Prussia. 'Unconditional toughness must seize our nation. This we owe to our fallen heroes. He who already works a lot must work still more. Everybody has to make arms.' For some listeners already used to working twelve-hour shifts, his speech seemed little more than a mockery.

Ley was increasingly fragile. Just after Christmas on 29 December 1942, his wife Inga had placed the barrel of a small pistol to her temple and pulled the trigger. Her private secretary, Hildegard Bruninghoff, told how she had become addicted to painkillers following a riding accident a few years earlier and was drinking heavily. In despair, Robert Ley plumbed the depths of his grief by ordering that Inga's parents be granted custody of their three children.

From here on, his public performances were increasingly shaky. Factory workers were horrified to hear him deliver joyless and dispiriting rallying cries, often while inebriated. 'Our common privilege is only to be Germans. In future we know only these things – guns, arms, munitions, discipline, obedience, devotion to Germany.'[1] Goebbels found Ley's rinse-and-repeat cycle of orations embarrassing. 'His amateurism is painfully apparent,' he complained. 'Idealism alone is not enough.' Another time, the Minister of Propaganda fumed after Ley delivered a 'pretty unfortunate' speech in the Mosaic Hall of the Reich Chancellery. 'The minute he opens his mouth he puts his foot in it.'[2]

Surprisingly, though, Hitler appointed Ley Housing Commissioner, a powerful post with executive authority. However, any fantasies he harboured of building social housing were scotched as he navigated the challenge of sheltering bombed-out families. 'That for once gives Dr. Ley the chance to do something with a big assignment,' Goebbels noted. 'In the past, he has always been concerned about being clothed with authority. He fought energetically for authority. Once obtained, however, he would fail to use it, but would start another fight for authority.'[3]

As Ley tackled new responsibilities, management of the KdF troop entertainments and other relief projects fell to lower-level officials. By this point, such operations stretched from Tobruk in Africa to Rovaniemi in Finland, and from Rome to Krasnodar deep in the Soviet interior. By the beginning of 1943, more than half of all KdF artist troupes were playing gigs on the Eastern Front and in Finland.[4]

Artists at the very bottom of the pecking order could find themselves entertaining foreign workers in one of more than 8,000 camps spread throughout Germany and the occupied areas, where industries propping up the German war effort included car chemical plants in Belgium making synthetic gasoline, Europe's largest photographic plant in Antwerp, Dutch shipyards building barges and submarines, and French factories producing planes. Such places were served by KdF in several ways. The organisation arranged excursions, stocked small libraries and arranged the occasional live performance, cinema show or sports tournament. Over in Germany, however, foreign workers endured vastly different experiences, depending on where they were billeted, but most accounts describe decrepit environments and casual violence. Ukrainian Pavel Cherevatenko never forgot being billeted in rat-infested, cramped barrack rooms where food was prepared and eaten in appalling conditions.

> The food was bad, 200 grams of very poor quality bread, like clay and coated with sawdust. Soup in the evenings, mostly from vegetables. Goods trucks from the Silesian station came to the works and we found remains of vegetables or corn in them – that was extra rations.[5]

Those suffering the least hardship, relatively speaking, were Western Europeans: French, Dutch and Belgians. Czechs and Serbs occupied a middle position, and Poles were low down on the racial ladder, but considerably lower were the Soviet citizens, who were branded *Ostarbeiters*. The system also determined that supposedly higher-quality people like Western Europeans earned the same basic wage as the Germans, whereas the Eastern workers received a pittance. *Ostarbeiters* alone had no safety regulations; however, they had to do the most dangerous work. Galina Vertashonok from Belarus was one of them:

> I worked in a factory where condoms were manufactured. The air was very damp and musty because of the rubber fumes ... There was a master craftsman in our shift who was very good-hearted ... He was very good, never yelled at us ... We called him the 'grey master' because he wore a grey coat ... There was a second master. He wore a yellow coat and we called him the 'yellow master' ... He behaved very badly towards us, constantly shouting at us and punishing us.

Only western Europeans received home leave – until further restrictions like longer hours, shorter breaks, and more severe punishments were introduced. Arbitrary racism prevailed in local matters, too, with German colleagues normally calling the tune and forced labourers having to dance to it.

In the spring of 1943, Robert Ley returned to the spotlight to personally welcome soldiers and armaments workers to the Bayreuth Festival as honoured guests of the Führer. As usual, he delivered a pep-talk to Party functionaries, describing the event as a 'visible manifestation for all to see of our people's holy faith in the Fatherland'[6] and praising the 'unbending will' of the people to determine their own lives'. A police report sarcastically noted that, unlike in previous years when KdF beneficiaries fell asleep during performances or exchanged tickets for liquor, the crowd was generally enthusiastic. 'From the many spontaneous declarations of participants at the festival, they really consider their experience in Bayreuth a gift from the Führer and that this great experience has made them feel personally indebted and grateful to the Führer.'[7]

As the war dragged on, the popularity of KdF entertainments on the home front had caused mounting concern for the DAF. In 1942, the management of the Krupp steelworks didn't mince words in complaining that they had 'great trouble selling the tickets for concert events we had bought from you, despite ... having been very engaged in advertisement and the tickets being offered at greatly reduced prices ... Regrettably, we also had to observe that in more than a few cases tickets we had given out for free remained unused.'[8] Concerned about increased vulgarity and extortionate wages, Goebbels lamented that the standard of KdF troop shows on the Eastern Front had 'dropped gravely ... but right now, I do not see any way to change that'.[9]

Meanwhile, despite the privations of war, the public continued to demand holidays. Traffic for Pentecost in 1943 was heavier than in any year since 1939, but discomfort was predictably felt on the railways as a reduction in the national timetable caused overcrowding. As the RAF took an increasing interest in targeting rail infrastructure, panicked passengers not only poured into shelters from the platforms but also from the neighbouring streets during raids. In some areas, trains had to wait in sidings for hours until given the all-clear. The actual journeys could be equally frightening. While every engine driver knew the terrain along the railway lines – knowledge essential for seeking shelter on wooded stretches or in tunnels – there was no official rules for what passengers should do during an alert (most, learning by experience, jumped out of carriages and took shelter in shrubbery or woodland). If the tracks were damaged, passengers often had to trudge (with their belongings) to the next station for medical help or to catch a replacement train.

With the RAF busier than ever, 'shelter life' assumed a regular form as the public spent more evenings barricaded in basements and cellars as air raids intensified. 'We sat pretty close together. It was dark, it was stuffy, it wasn't nice,' says Berliner Hans-Joachim Loll, who was then a seven-year-old schoolboy. 'The windows were walled up, the air holes were plugged with newspaper, the paper often flew out in the event of detonations.'[10] Dr Zitterlein, a medical adviser at the German Ministry of Health, outlined a treatment for an epidemic of cellar sickness in Berlin, caused by long hours in shelters and similar to Spanish flu.[11] As the situation worsened, many holiday resorts including Misdroy, Ahlbeck and Swinemuende were ordered to clear their hotels in order to shelter evacuees from Stettin. Elsewhere, hotels and restaurants were told to eliminate the storage of food and wines in cellars, which were only to be used as shelters for guests: 'It is an emergency room and has no other purpose.' Under mounting pressure, authorities directed that cellars should be frequently aired, boxes and barrels should be available for use as chairs, and the 'owners of the business are to ensure that the air-raid shelter is well looked after. They should also procure air raid beds if possible.'

As this was happening, evacuation measures for entire families also increased, with over 700,000 Berliners leaving the capital in 1943 alone. For Silvia Koerner, along with her mother, two brothers and sister, the sudden departure from their dingy apartment in Berlin-Tempelhof to the unpolluted beauty of a farm in Prenzlau, 60 miles north-east, seemed like a holiday:

> It was strangely quiet and peaceful in the country; instead of the noise of air raids and bombs, for the first time, I heard natural sounds like the mooing of cows, the cackling of chickens, the crowing of roosters and the bleating of sheep, and the discovery of animals like rabbits zigzagging between the sugar beets, and little garden mice.[12]

News of some other 'peaceful holidays' reached the shores of the United Kingdom that year, prompting the British press to speculate on whether the Germans were embarking on a propaganda stunt or were anxious to make a favourable impression. These questions were raised by two letters which twenty-four-year-old British prisoner of war John Roland Hazel sent to his father, disclosing that some prisoners were being given holidays. Not in the most tactful style, and clearly written at the behest of his captors, Hazel's first letter was positively enthusiastic about the development.

> You will be surprised to hear that I together with thirteen other lads were chosen to go for our holidays from three to four weeks. We are at the camp now. This is a new scheme by the German authorities, the idea being to see a little of Germany after three years work. It is a great thing for us and is doing us a world of good. We have been here just over a week and are having a capital time. The German officer in charge of us is doing all he can to see that we get a good time and is very successful. We even get beer.

The second letter runs:

> I am still at (name deleted), enjoying myself tremendously. I could tell you lots about the fine places we have visited, but I am afraid that isn't allowed, so you will have to wait until the end of the war. We have nothing to worry us, and it is the nearest to home life we have had for three years.

Commenting upon this odd communication, the father stated, 'I have an idea that the lads must be about 12 miles from Berlin. I don't know what they have been taken there for. My idea is that they have either been taken there to be within bombing range, or that the Germans have got the wind up, just as they did towards the end of the last war, when they wanted to make the best possible impression.'[13] Indeed, with the tide of war changing in the Allies' direction, many Germans looked to their own long-term preservation, especially after the defeat at Stalingrad in February 1943 and the subsequent Axis defeat in Africa. From then on, the German people were told to shed any illusions that life at home could continue on the old lines in view of the menacing military situation. 'To cherish illusions of tranquillity in face of the united efforts of our enemies is suicidal', the *Völkischer Beobachter* opined. 'With such battles raging in the East, and such issues at stake, the home front has no right to lead a peaceful existence.' A writer in the *Borsen Zeitung* tried to draw some reassuring historic parallels: 'Germany has suffered its worst setback. The position of Germany today is as critical as that of Rome during Hannibal's attack or England's during the Battle of Britain. The British took their setbacks with courage and fortitude. We must show the same power of resistance as the British did in 1940.'

'Over the coming weeks (after Stalingrad), the street scenes changed visibly,' schoolgirl Marianne Gartner reflected. 'Bars, dance halls and many shops and restaurants closed; older men were called up, women without young children and within a certain age group were drafted to into factories, sent to farms or trained in defence units'.[14] The situation was so desperate that even the Nazi party made cutbacks, shedding employees at the Teachers' Association, Public Welfare Office, the Medical Association and the Organization of War Victims.

At first, the new wave of mobilisation was pursued half-heartedly as some women 'played the system' by using exemptions to escape their obligation to work. However, for those unfortunate enough to be bundled off to factories, the cacophony of noise, noxious vapours and mind-numbing tasks could be too much to stomach. Workers doing seventy-hour weeks gratefully accepted the government-supplied stimulant Pervitin, an 'alertness aid' to 'maintain wakefulness'. Over 35 million of the pills had been issued to troops during the French campaign and, although classified as a prescription drug due to the danger of addiction, curbing misuse became impossible. It is now known that Pervitin was in fact a neatly packaged iteration of the highly addictive drug methamphetamine, often known nowadays as 'speed'. After popping a few pills, soldiers felt that they could defy danger and fight furiously without rest or nourishment. Even better, Pervitin releases the feel-good hormone dopamine, making users euphoric. In some cases, tablets were mixed into food at communal restaurants in working-class districts. Curiously, an article by Dr Josef Siefert, Professor of Pathology at the University of Tuebingen, managed to avoid the censors and warned that the continuous doping of war workers would have disastrous results for the national health.

For all the effectiveness of Pervitin, however, even doped-up workers couldn't fail to notice the tide of war had turned. For the Soviets, Stalingrad represented its greatest victory to date over the Nazi invaders and shifted momentum in their favour. From then on the Red Army would push westward, their sights set firmly on Berlin.

In an effort to stiffen resolve, Goebbels whipped up a battle call for 'total war' which was not only heard across the Reich but also in Vienna, where pubs and nightclubs closed to free up more labour; luxury shops were also shuttered. A Swiss visitor complained that Vienna was a far cry from the beautiful cosmopolitan city it had once been. Restaurants were crowded and dirty, service was almost non-existent, and yet nobody seemed to care. 'There was enough to eat for everyone but the joy had gone out of it. A glass of wine was hard to get and required a "relationship" with the waiter or the owner.'

Unquestionably, the picture wasn't much rosier over in Poland where hospitals struggled to cope with dispirited Wehrmacht soldiers arriving for recuperation. An emerging resistance soon set its sights on the Nazi occupiers, making the fragile situation worse. Officers enjoying local cafes reserved for Germans alone were targeted by crude bombs and explosives. In one incident, several German officers were killed. The good times were over.

More terrible news arrived when Allied troops smashed Axis forces in North Africa, ending the German adventures in the desert and paving the way for the invasion of Sicily. As if that wasn't bad enough, at sea most Kriegsmarine submarines steamed home from the Atlantic due to heavy losses in the face of new Allied anti-sub tactics, which sent forty-three U-boats to the ocean floor and left thousands of families heartbroken back in the Reich. Soon after, the Italian island of Lampedusa, between Tunisia and Sicily, surrendered to the Allies.

Tourism continued amid this instability, but the war caused further restrictions. There was dismay when the Reich Department of Chemistry prohibited the production of films, plates and photographic paper as well as the development of film for amateur photographers – a decree which ended travellers taking 'holiday snaps'. However, astonishingly, given the national situation, resorts remained jam-packed that summer. During July, Hermann Esser complained that the railways were creaking and spas and recuperation resorts were too crowded – a situation, he said, that was dangerous and unmanageable. 'Every unnecessary journey is in opposition to the spirit of total warfare. People are therefore warned against making these trips,' he hissed.[15] In a futile effort to prevent civilians hop-scotching around the country the Reichsbahn cut all reduced fares and offers, and encouraged the public not to travel unless absolutely necessary. On one occasion, the self-righteous Goebbels stood open-mouthed after witnessing female travellers 'sunburnt from holiday' refusing to give up their seats and sleeping compartments to troops wounded in battle.[16] A year earlier he had fumed to the Führer 'about the disgusting incidents at German railway stations and in German express trains, and explained that better situated people simply will not heed our advice and our requests'. According to Louis P. Lochner of the Associated Press, Goebbels was referring to the fact that society women and people of wealth were able to use sleepers and first-class seats whereas German servicemen had to put up with inconveniences of every kind. Lochner notes, 'Goebbels on one occasion, on arriving from outside Berlin, tried to argue with the better situated to make room for servicemen, but was snubbed.'[17]

After his angry outburst, Goebbels claimed Hitler authorised him to 'invoke concentration camp punishment to put an end to this nonsense'.[18] Other than this account, Hitler's precise views on tourism at this point are difficult to pin down. Probably he was himself unsure of his position, as was the case for most of his administration (except, as seen, Goebbels and Esser, who were both hardening their views on all forms of unnecessary travel).

28

CRUMBLING HOME FRONT

Throughout the spring and summer of 1943, news from the Eastern Front became increasingly bleak. In what seemed half a world away, the Battle of Kursk in western Russia was fought near the railway embarkation point, where, in happier times, KdF bands played as German troops excitedly left for home leave. For rifleman Hans Roth, the scene resembled paradise lost. 'Railroad Station Kursk – this was the dream of a hundred thousand German soldiers,' he sighed. 'This is where the bliss of four weeks of indescribable vacation began; it is here where I climbed onto the train with a pounding heart yearning for my home, Germany!'

> The terrain is now covered with deep bomb craters; the barracks where we received our food supply is burned out; the sign advertising 'vacation trains to Germany' has been torn to shreds by the bombs. Isn't this like a symbol, or maybe an admonishment to wipe away all sweet thoughts about vacation, homeland, wife and children, to open the heart for the horrible fight for our very existence?[1]

On the home front, Germans were told that they would have to 'grin and bear' yet another cut in meat rations which went down by a 100 grams per week. For the creative, there were many inventive ways to supplement meagre food supplies. Rabbits – which became known as 'balcony pigs' – often made up the main course on family occasions, while it was also rumoured – but never really proved – that cats were nicknamed 'rooftop rabbits' for obvious reasons. There is some anecdotal evidence of a dish named Civet de Chat (cat casserole) in France becoming popular in leaner times, while other enterprising chefs supposedly set up rattraps on balconies and gutters to snare pigeons.

The lure of lucrative, easy catches prompted two teenagers in Göttingen to steal a crate of army hand grenades to blast hundreds of fish from a lake. As always, black market racketeers flourished with every new set of restrictions selling coffee, butter, claret and chocolate for more than ten times their retail value. Even the most law-abiding citizens, tempted by Scotch whisky or French goose liver pâté, were prepared to enter into the occasional illicit transaction.

Although police took a hard line with black marketeers, the screw was really tightened on looters caught stealing from bombed-out properties. In one such case, the death sentence was handed to Hans Dobroszczyk, a thirty-six-year-old factory worker with a second job collecting tickets at the UFA cinema on Nollendorfplatz in Berlin. In the early hours of 2 March 1943, he was reported for having picked a handbag from the ruins of a building after an air raid. Immediately accused of looting, he was arrested, charged and sentenced to death that same day. On the morning of 3 March, Dobroszczyk was hung at Plötzensee prison. His farewell letter read:

Dear wife and daughter,
I have been sentenced to death although innocent. I cannot write why. Stay healthy and happy. Yours Papa.

A decade after launching a crusade against homosexuals, police were still displaying implausible enthusiasm in staking out meeting spots. To grasp the nature of such operations, police noted darkness worked in favour of those being monitored, as an intelligence report from Munich illustrates:

On Saturday 3 July, 1943 at 11pm, a group of nine men gathered in an unlit public lavatory who, at the switching on of a torch, were alarmed and fled the location. A raid on this location would certainly be successful. From my observations, the best time for a raid would be a Saturday at around 11pm.[2]

As Berlin continued to attract troops on leave, Goebbels fretted that prostitution was causing 'many a headache'. 'During a raid we found 15 percent of all women arrested had VD, most of them even syphilis,' he recorded. 'We must certainly do something now about it. In the long run we certainly cannot avoid setting up a "red light district" in the capital similar to those in Hamburg, Nuremberg, and other large cities. You simply cannot organise and administer a city of four millions in accordance with conceptions of bourgeois morals.'[3]

Police were also busy chasing wayward teenagers, as 54 percent of serious thefts were attributed to juveniles in an increase of 120 percent since 1939.[4] Prison sentences for theft shot up, rising from 48,252 in 1939 to 82,828 in 1943. Sentences also increased for receiving stolen goods, gambling, illegal association with prisoners of war, breaches of consumer regulations, and breaches of the War Economy Decree. The number of people sentenced for sexual offences with children under the aged of fourteen fell from 6,285 in 1939 to 2,480 in 1943. Likewise, prison sentences dished out for pimping, unnatural intercourse and rape also fell during the same period. At the same time, with the birth-rate plummeting, punishments against abortion stiffened as the Nazis cried that abortionists 'injured the vital needs of the German people' and threatened the death sentence for both the professional abortionist and women who had undergone the operation more than once.

On 13 August, American bombers made their deepest thrust into Austria yet, to targets near Vienna, where they dropped nearly 200 tons of high explosives on an industrial site south of the city. Until this point, the city had long been regarded as a possible centre for the German capital if air raids made it necessary to evacuate Berlin.[5] For months prior to the attack, authorities had set up a special commission for commandeering hotels and boarding houses to serve as offices for administrative departments for the Reich, while thousands of wealthy Germans fled to Vienna from bombed areas.

Perversely, after the first bombing, the *Völkischer Beobachter* asserted 'this first enemy air raid in Vienna also had its good side ... it finally called the sleepiest of people to remind them that there is only one total battlefield in this total war'.[6] Over in Berlin, Robert Ley sounded the opening notes of his death song. In an article for *Der Angriff* accompanied by a photograph of factory workers holding aloft a banner saying 'One Reich, One Leader', Ley declared that what the English could take 'we can take as well', adding that air attacks on Berlin proved 'our air defence is very powerful, and the bearing of the people exemplary'. The reality, though, was quite different as the number of civilians being killed by bombs assumed significant proportions. 'We just cannot stand air warfare indefinitely,' Goebbels noted in his diary 129 days after his 'total war' speech. He knew that Germany was in a position of almost helpless inferiority and 'must grin and bear it'.

His fear that Berlin would suffer the same fate as Hamburg, which had been pulverised by the RAF, became reality on Monday 22 November. After flying through storm and cloud, 764 aircraft of Bomber Command opened a raid of great intensity and ferocity, laying waste to the city centre. Journalist Konrad Warner was eating dinner when the alarm sounded and dashed to the zoo bunker, where scores of people were already engaged in lively conversation. Suddenly, the building shook violently, and the lights went out – every conversation fell silent. Warner saw women begin to cry as men sat rigid, staring straight ahead.[7]

Across the road from the zoo, the majestic Kaiser Wilhelm Memorial Church – where Marlene Dietrich had been married twenty years earlier – was ripped to pieces. 'Everything was burning,' Warner recalled. 'A firestorm swept through the streets, tearing through cars and passers-by and spreading black, stinking clouds of smoke.' The State Opera House, National Theatre, National Gallery, Romanische Café, Charlottenburg Palace,

Technical University, Hotel Bristol and Charite Hospital were all destroyed. Norwegian journalist Theo Findahl watched the central district of Hansaviertel burning: 'In Altonaer Strasse the water mains burst, leaving the road like a lake … it is impossible to move forward this way to Hansaplatz. The Tiergarten is like a jungle. Branches sting your face as you move forward over the fallen tree trunks.' Missy Vassiltchikov also tried to navigate a route through the mud and ashes of the Tiergarten, which she thought looked like a Great War battlefield in France. 'The trees stark and gaunt and broken-off branches everywhere, over which we had to clamber. I wondered what had happened to the famous rhododendrons and what it would be like in the spring.'

A few hundred feet away at the zoo, Lutz Heck stood paralysed as a direct hit destroyed the aquarium. 'Water was already rushing towards me on the stairs,' his memoirs relate, as he faced a picture of wild confusion. A bomb had fallen through the glass roof into the 30-metre-long tropical-themed crocodile hall, where a bamboo bridge hovered over a mock jungle river housing the alligators and crocodiles. 'Every single inch of glass of the roofs, windows, aquariums and terrariums was shattered by the air pressure and the building interior was completely destroyed,' Heck recounted.

> Like a vision from Dante's inferno, the sight of these mighty giant lizards, internally injured by the air pressure, crushed by collapsing walls, wounded by explosives and writhing in pain, writhing in the foot-deep water of the hall or rolling down the visitor stairs.
>
> With difficulty, I made my way to the huge fresh water aquariums where twenty-five large, metre-long and high display basins and just as many smaller ones had given the fairy-tale impression of a strange, wonderful animal world. Everywhere the water spilled from the tanks, shattered into a thousand shards of glass. Countless fish wriggled in the rubble. I saw a catfish that came from the Havel, and when I noticed that it was still gasping for air, I dragged it – it was just as big as me, namely eight feet long – down into a pond in the garden. The tropical fish species, including the largest, most beautiful rarities, all perished.

A third of the animals were killed by bombs, explosions or subsequent fires. 'The losses in large animals are seven elephants and one African rhino, one chimpanzee, one orangutan, three lions, two tigers, a pair of giraffes and half of the antelopes and deer,' the zoo secretary announced. However, two Malayan pointed-snouted crocodiles, some giant tortoises, two pythons, a few alligators, water turtles, four pike, four giant salamanders that could endure the cold, one vulture and a Hawksbill sea turtle survived. Among the sea of carcasses, the pygmy hippopotamuses were found to be unharmed and temporarily squeezed into the gents' toilets at the train station across the road, where the heating still worked.

In his memoir *Animals: My Adventure*, Heck described how the carcasses of deer, buffalo and antelopes provided hundreds of meals for hungry Berliners – bear bacon and sausage became a 'particular delicacy'.

> The crocodile tails were very tasty; soft-boiled in large containers, they tasted like fatty chicken. The perished deer 'buffalo and antelope provided hundreds of meals for humans and animals. Later on, bear ham and bear sausage were a special delicacy for us. Above all, in the first few days it was a matter of clearing away the animal corpses lying around in animal houses and in many enclosures in the garden. What a task alone to get the seven dead elephants out from under the rubble of their house, from between the bars of their destroyed sleeping stalls and to transport them away! A veterinary squad worked on it for a whole week. The stench that developed grew worse day by day. The half-charred animal giants were carved-up on the spot, with the men handling mountains of intestines behind which they almost disappeared themselves.

As Berlin smouldered, trucks straining under the weight of paperwork continued shunting the machinery of state out of the city. During the bombing campaign, departments of the Reich Chancellery, the Foreign Office and Air Ministry moved to Vienna while the city archives were shifted to Bohemia,

Moravia and Silesia. Remarkably, Germany celebrated the tenth anniversary of the KdF movement at the end of November with a special broadcast in which it was noted that the purpose of the organisation had adapted to the 'cultural caretaking of the bomb-battered population and our soldiers'. Swedish journalist Gunnar Pihl observed increased disorganisation everywhere, especially in industry:

> You find proof of this wherever you look in Germany today. Eyewitnesses from the Blohm and Voss shipyards at Hamburg have told me of how whole eight-hour shifts of workmen have remained idle because Krupps of Essen could not deliver steel plates for the U-boats they were building. In the beer halls of Wedding, Berlin's working quarter, men from the great Rheinmetall Borsig armament works at Tegel have complained to me of the poor quality of tools and the delays in the supply of coal, spare parts and raw materials from the Ruhr and Rhineland. You have only to travel in the rickety old carriages of the crowded trains to realize how near the German state railways are to breaking under the strain.

29

1944

On 20 January 1944, the Royal Air Force unloaded 2,400 tons of bombs on the German capital. For the common people of Berlin, the life of peace and stability they knew before 1939 was now beyond imagination. 'No face ever lit up in a warming smile, no friendly kiss or hug,' Danish reporter P. E. von Stemann observed. 'There was still the sky ... but then it was often effaced by the stinking and greasy carpets of voluminous black smoke.'

The deterioration of the economy saw Berliners begin shopping on a barter basis at twenty-three new 'exchange marts', two of them nestled in the wealthy Kurfürstendamm shopping district. Foodstuffs, live animals and books were the only banned currency, while articles bartered were valued to assure fair exchange and to enable customers to bank points for future purchases.

As the Third Reich tumbled into disarray, Marie Vassiltchikov continued to live life at full sprint – but the 'good times' were no more than a memory, she recorded, portraying Berlin as a drab and diminished place, especially for food or entertainment. 'We tried Horcher's, hoping to get some wine; it was closed,' she grumped. Eventually, after traipsing across town, she found herself tip-toeing through the wrecked bar of the Hotel Eden:

> It was a shambles: chandeliers on the floor, bits of splintered furniture, debris everywhere. Managers and waiters, their napkins

tucked under their arms, were running about in the street, trying very inefficiently to clear away bricks and mortar. In the middle of the street there was a huge crater where a bomb landed near the exit of the cellar. As all the water pipes had burst, people trapped in the cellar were now swimming their way across the crater. So many bombs have fallen in Berlin again that the streets are half-submerged. The town also smells heavily of gas.

Ten days later, Vassiltchikov recorded stomach-turning scenes of horror after a heavy raid hit the Hotel Bristol. 'Sixty people were buried alive, including several well-known generals. It took fifty hours to dig them out and by then most of them were dead.' The smell of fire, burnt human flesh and putrefaction that lay over the city for days after the air raids lingered in the nostrils.

At midnight on 30 January, the KdF building at 25 Kaiserallee was blown to smithereens in an air raid. The entire artists' index, contracts and other vital documentation went up in flames, disrupting the routines of the organisation. Over the coming months many full-time employees were laid off or deployed to war duties, leaving much of the administration and actual entertainment in the hands of a motley command that limped on with the 'cultural caretaking of the bomb-battered population and soldiers'. Given scant resources, entertainment mostly involved one-man shows and small groups performing at new 'KdF am Sonntag Vormittag' concerts on Sunday mornings for military personnel, the bombed-out and factory workers. The KdF hiking department also muddled along with a weekly programme of rambles and walks in the Berlin area.[1]

Amazingly, given the circumstances, Goebbels set his sights on comedians and vaudeville performers making a career out of near-the-knuckle comedy routines. In July 1944, he complained that several incidents at troop shows had shown 'cleanliness' was often not adhered to and warned performers using 'sexual unsavoriness and vulgar and dirty jokes' would be 'inhibited in the future by any means necessary'.[2] Edgy comedy was usually performed before hardened soldiers at the front lines or at concentration camp social evenings (the KdF managed to arrange fifty-one shows for Waffen-SS guards and staff at the notorious Auschwitz death camp from the summer of 1944 until Christmas).[3] Dieter Borsche was a member of a KdF troupe that performed before SS guards at Auschwitz in the winter of 1943. 'We actors received prodigal hospitality and were waited on by prisoners – long columns of whom we saw with our own eyes. We were greatly astonished at their wearing only striped prison smocks in mid-winter.'[4]

It is amazing to think that as the military situation deteriorated, German troops in France continued to enjoy a largely carefree existence. Weekly pleasure tours to Chantilly, Rambouillet and Fontainebleau operated unhindered as late as April 1944[5] and soldiers took advantage of holiday leave in Prague, a destination covered by a new edition of *Greiben's Travel Guide*, which – other than making a special note of the tight food situation – painted an idyllic picture:

> Restaurants. Food stamps. In addition to the domestic stamps, only travel notes from the Altreich or Sudetengau and Ostmark are valid. In all restaurants in Prague you eat according to the menu. Bohemian cuisine is known to be excellent. All larger restaurants have a German-Czech menu. Better Ostmark wines are the Vöslauer, Gumpoldskirchner and Weldinger (white). Best Bohemian varieties: Melniker (red), Czernoseker (white). Slovak varieties: Palugyay, Gereduan and Modra. Among the beers, besides the numerous Prague beers, the Pilsner is particularly popular. The lunch time falls between 12-noon and 3pm. Evening meals are served from 7pm onwards.

Over in the Reich, the Sauerland experienced an influx of tourists from the Ruhr seeking respite far from the wail of sirens and the blast of bombs – their presence increased tourism figures by 2,000 per cent. At the same time, during his legendary late-night conversations, Hitler continued to wax lyrical about future tourism prospects while lamenting that Germans knew little of their own country. 'Since 1938 the number of beauty spots within the boundaries of the Reich has increased considerably,' he declared with pride, saying that in addition to Austria, the countryside of Bohemia and Moravia was a closed book to all but a few Germans.

> Some of them may have heard of the virgin forests of Bohemia, but how many have ever seen them? I have a collection of photographs taken in Bohemia, and they remind one of the vast forests of the tropics. To visit all the beauties of his country, a German today would require to take a holiday in a different district each year for the rest of his life.[6]

Rene Schindler, a student from Switzerland, was absolutely determined to see Germany in all its decrepitude in 1944. While gasping for air in filthy Reichsbahn carriages he was consumed by a 'indefinable unpleasant odor, a smell of decay. A typical smell that was to stay with us and, at times, became intolerable.' The conductress, when asked what time his train would arrive in Munich, did 'not even know how far the train will be able to get today'. However, it did arrive and Schindler decided it was safe to go out and tour the ravaged city, where 'piles of rubbish, metres high' extended along the sidewalks:

> Notices carry the warning 'Caution, rat poison sprayed on this site!' and newspapers publicize the 'War on rats!' For the rats in these unhappy cities can find plenty to feed on, and have become a dangerous plague.

He took in all the unfamiliar sights of the wrecked buildings. People were reopening shops amid the rubble, messages were scrawled on walls in chalk from relatives seeking next of kin, and signs everywhere pointed to shelters and bunkers. As he navigated a path through the filth, Schindler observed 'pieces of furniture, a rusty typewriter, candelabras and files, radiators and bathtubs, pipes, cables, burnt out and rusted safes, parts of a sewing machine, splinters of glass and roof tiles'.

The scene wasn't much better up north, where Ursula von Kardorff, a journalist at the *Deutsche Allgemeine Zeitung*, stood aghast outside the oriental buildings of Berlin Zoo. 'Every now and then I peered through cracks in the wall, but could only see crows. Sheep bleated at one point and smelled of horse manure.' Shaken by the increasing frequency of the RAF raids, 237 mammals and 149 species of birds had been packed off to Alsace for safe keeping. Remarkably, the zoo did manage a much-heralded reopening but some animals were simply too frightened to see humans again. 'It will take some time before they accustom themselves to visitors,' the German Overseas News Agency reported.[7]

After an air raid on 8 May, the Hotel Adlon, Hotel Kaiserhof, Hitler's chancellery and around fifty other well-known buildings collapsed into fire and rubble. With Berlin in disarray, Robert Ley skipped his annual jaunt to Bayreuth to watch musicians strum through their last major wartime performance. Although it was a shadow of its predecessors, the *Munchener Neueste Zeitung* gave a customary gushing review:

> In the great tradition of the German race whose people find their national essence expressed in the works of art and over many generations have entrusted these documents of German culture to the younger generation, which has the historic task of protecting the ideas and heritage of centuries from the threat of destruction.[8]

During the blistering summer of 1944, it became apparent that KdF troop assistance was slowly disintegrating along with the DAF and KdF education programmes, including vocational education and correspondence courses, which ceased to function, while adult education classrooms closed for good. The termination of the last KdF activities was announced in August 1944 and the organisation (in Germany, at least) appears to have been disbanded by October that year. Thus, after eleven years of operations, the most conspicuous creation of the Nazi party practically vanished from sight.

Any last vestiges of optimism for a victorious outcome were spoiled for Robert Ley when his magnificent Berlin residence crumbled under a barrage of RAF bombs. Not long after, he stumbled through a broadcast speech, recorded in all its embarrassing glory by a Reuters reporter. At times he spoke slowly, pausing in the middle of words and making mistakes, then suddenly broke out into hysterical shrieks. Towards the end his breath was coming in gasps. 'I have never seen a greater optimist than I am today,' Ley slurred. 'Taking all circumstances into account, I am now fairly convinced that events have occurred both in the German and enemy camps which guarantee German victory.'[9] Sensing which way the war was turning, Ley had already provided his secretary, Hildegarde Bruninghoff, with phials of poison and sent her to Bavaria with his children with the order: 'Take this if the Russians close in on you and be certain that my children get it.'

As a distraction, Ley soothed his jangled nerves with many fanciful plans such as developing a 'death ray' gun based on sketches which came through the post from an unknown inventor. 'I've studied the documentation,' he cooed to Albert Speer. 'There's no doubt about it. This will be the decisive weapon!' It wasn't. After consultation with experts, Speer found that the 'death ray' gun was a chimera. Ley was, according to Speer, 'one of the biggest cranks we had; especially in the final phase ... one could not help noticing that he was truly irresponsible'.

Allied plans for liberating Europe with a naval, air and land assault on Nazi-occupied France had tentatively been underway since 1941. When it finally happened on 6 June 1944, Allied troops landed along a 50-mile stretch of Normandy coastline in the first stage of an audacious bid to free Europe from Hitler.[10] That day, an armada of destroyers, minesweepers, landing craft and merchant ships made up the largest maritime force ever assembled.

In the skies above the sleepy French coastline, the busy drone of RAF planes could be heard preparing to 'soften up' the Germans. In salvo after salvo the planes swooped overhead, dropping bombs and firing at machine-gun nests on the famed Atlantic Wall. At the end of the first day, along with more than 150,000 men, some 22,000 jeeps, cars and tanks had been landed. The Allies were in France.

As is well known, following D-Day, a growing number of voices outside – and, significantly, inside – the regime believed the war was lost. Some led a failed assassination attempt on Hitler at his field headquarters near Rastenburg on 20 July. 'When I heard the news that there had been an attempt on Adolf Hitler a cold shiver ran down my back,' Robert Ley wearily divulged to radio listeners. 'I am certainly no mystic, and I do not believe in miracles, but here one must admit the Almighty has had a hand in it.'[11] Ley's nervous state worsened a few days later, when British agents discovered the KdF Volkswagen factory was being used as one of the main assembly points for the notorious V1 flying bomb. 'Our bombers were sent out and the factory was totally destroyed,' a British report noted.[12]

From here on, catastrophe piled on catastrophe. In late August, Romania became first of the satellite states to abandon Germany, followed soon after by the liberation of Paris on Saturday 26 August when the French 2nd Armoured Division marched down the Champs-Élysées. Children were boosted onto great tanks by American soldiers as the liberators were showered with embraces and kisses. By September, Allied troops had made a triumphal entry into Brussels in tanks, trucks and armoured cars. 'Never have troop carriers had so many lovely girls aboard; never have jeeps been so gracefully draped in flowers,' American correspondent Austin Hatton observed. 'The frenzy that possesses these people must be seen to be believed.' Accordingly, the Allied headquarters moved to the Belgian capital, where venues like the Blighty Café, YWCA, and the 21-Club moved into former KdF and Wehrmacht welfare buildings. Holiday tycoon Billy Butlin redecorated the 21-Club, an enormous dance venue, to mirror his Skegness holiday camp ballroom with a vast dancefloor, orchestra stage, bar, restrooms and lobby area.

The scene couldn't be more different in Germany, where Goebbels shut down theatres, music halls, cabarets and drama academies. Every day, newspapers carried new directives such as a general suspension of all holidays, a new sixty-hour working week for office workers and the mobilisation of tens of thousands of students.[13] Moreover, on 12 September, the KdF movement wound down its military branches, along with the tourism department of the Ministry of Propaganda. 'German troops have no time for recreation anyway,' was the reaction of one commentator on German radio.[14]

The only domestic travel pamphlet published in 1944 was commissioned by the SS and dropped by plane over the advancing

US armies. Designed to lower morale (and encourage defections), the mockingly titled *Go South to Sunny Germany* leaflet – based on the design of pre-war tourism material – featured a smiling, bikini-clad beauty plugging the seductive line, 'A land of sun and smiles awaits you.' However, on the opposite panel of the pamphlet, the tone changed:

> ACCOMODATION: The sport folk prefer air-conditioned trenches, foxholes and blood-baths on tap. Extremely healthy!
> ENTERTAINMENTS: Continuous performances day and night. New gadgets: Invasion flowerpots throwing out artistically hand carved wooden crosses with name and birthdate. Very Funny. Everybody laughs!
> DANCING: Latest creation: The super doodle-bug swing. Most fashionable. Lessons for everyone. (Reduced rates for front-liners.)
> SOUVENIRS: Highest grade steel bullets, shrapnel and other amusing articles fit perfectly into head, chest, arm, belly, legs and other parts of the body. Very pretty. Especially enjoyed by young ladies. Method of application extremely simple.

In contrast, on the flipside titled 'Germany from within', life in the Reich was portrayed as being normal and contented:

> ACCOMMODATION: Rest in quiet and comfort during the whole season. Regular decent meals. Perfect sanitary installations (Laundry, warm baths regularly).
> ENTERTAINMENTS: Indoor-outdoor games of all types. (Football, Hockey, Cricket, Athletics, Bowling, Billiards, Ping-Pong, Chess and Draughts etc). Libraries, Debates, Lectures, Cinema, Theatre, Orchestral Concerts, Dance Bands, Latest News from the Wireless and Newspapers, Magazines.
> RECREATION: Work Optional. Studies for all professions up to university standard. Periodical examinations. Internationally recognized.
> MEDICAL TREATMENT: Only by specialists, most modern equipment (expert surgeons).

MAIL COMMUNICATION: Unrestricted reception of parcels and letters from home. 7 replies per month.
REGULAR CHURCH SERVICES: For all denominations.
RETURN TICKET: Gratis, as soon as the season ends.

The pamphlet probably raised a smile for GIs as they battled their way into Aachen. Their encroachment into the Reich, coupled with the Russian advance toward East Prussia, spelt the end for Germany. All through this, the bombings took their toll. On 3 October, the ornate Hotel Deutscher Hof, scene of Hitler's most lavish receptions in Nuremburg, burst into flames when a high-explosive bomb hit the corner of the building, destroying the gable and roof and gutting the interior. Meanwhile, new restrictions on postal and telephone services killed off any last signs of tourism or domestic travel. Telephones not serving the war effort were disconnected, and phone bills were to be sent only every third month or at even longer intervals.

With the onset of winter, the economy began to grind to a halt as bad weather piled woes on top of the troubled transportation network. In Vienna, the local KdF (which had managed to continue despite the bombing) tried to cheer spirits by organising a 'homemade presents' show, featuring wooden toys, paper dolls and handbags fashioned from twisted straw. 'It's not what is given but how – with love and devotion, as tokens of affection,' the *Völkischer Beobachter* opined.[15] Across the Reich, exhausted doctors faced a brutal workload treating cases of influenza and pneumonia while patching up those who had slipped and fallen, hurt themselves shovelling snow or been frost-bitten. Such patients came in addition to endless cases of depression, exhaustion and anxiety. The civilian illness and death rate was rising because of longer working hours, lower living standards and segments of the population doing work for which they would ordinarily be judged unfit.

30

DOWNFALL

By the start of 1945, Adolf Hitler had become a shadow of his former self, victim to ulcers, high blood pressure, headaches, flatulence, irritable bowel and mood swings. Those close to him thought it was remarkable he managed to wake up every morning. Over the coming months, the doddering dictator sought refuge in military fantasies as the noose tightened around Germany faster than expected. Twelve days into the New Year, the Red Army opened its winter offensive from the east, causing millions of Germans to flee west and creating a tidal wave of refugees from East Prussia and the Polish Corridor.

Hollow-eyed from a lack of sleep, Robert Ley was also getting worse. He is said to have wept uncontrollably on learning a Russian submarine had sunk the KdF's *Wilhelm Gustloff* on 30 January off the coast of Pomerania, killing thousands of refugees being ferried to safety on the former holiday ship. Three Soviet torpedoes, launched in darkness, sealed its fate. There were only 903 survivors. Women, children and pensioners crowded the ship, and many had only standing room. On the same night as the *Gustloff* slipped beneath the waves, Hitler, cocooned from the din of pounding shellfire, used his last radio address to call on Germans to make 'every sacrifice that is demanded'.

From here on, one shock followed another. At dawn on the last day of January, Soviet soldiers crossed the River Oder 70 kilometres from Berlin. In the absence of any significant military force, Goebbels took on the lackadaisical defence of the city using thrown-together army units, poorly equipped *Volkssturm* pensioners and, regardless of the state of their health, Hitler Youth members. For all his bombast, however, Goebbels was also forced to call up 6,000 green-uniformed boys to reinforce 'rear defensive lines' while an all-female battalion was approved on a trial basis. The 'total war' Goebbels promised in February 1943 was now, two years later, being waged in the countryside outside Berlin. All the while, the air raids continued: 'During the night the cursed Englishmen returned to Berlin with their Mosquitos and deprive one of the few hours' sleep which one needs more than ever,' Goebbels complained as his energy ebbed away.

Moreover, evenings could be unnerving as crooks emerged from the ruins and deserters increased, aided by a flood of false identification papers. Looking to escape Berlin was pointless – traveling any distance was impossible. Services run by BVG, the Berlin transport company, were virtually non-existent given that only 420 trams – out of a fleet of 2,000 – could still move, while on the underground just 150 tube cars struggled to maintain services.

In the midst of this turmoil, the twenty-fifth anniversary of the promulgation of the Nazi party programme was marked in Munich, where Hermann Esser – 20 pounds thinner and worse for wear – forecast a 'historic turnaround' and final victory. Remarkably, after managing to whistle up a crowd to hear his appeal for courage, he insisted the 'only answer' to the mighty blows from the enemy was to throw every last ounce of strength into battle with the 'utmost fanaticism'.[1] For the long-suffering residents of Munich, where about 90 per cent of the Altstadt, or Old Town, was reduced to rubble, there was little left to fight for.

Shortly thereafter, in mid-March, as bombs rained down, Hitler shuffled into his hermetically sealed, splinter-proof bunker under the Old Reich Chancellery, protected by SS guards. Although communications from his tiny radio room were patchy, impeded by Allied jamming and broken phone lines, news arrived on 11 April that the Russians had captured all districts of Vienna south of the Danube. The city fell two days later, leaving Hitler deathly pale and stunned into silence.

Another message delivered that same night relayed that Potsdam – the ancient town on the border of Berlin – had been flattened by the RAF. After pulling himself together, Hitler asserted that 'Berlin would remain German, Vienna will be German again and Europe will never be Russian', adding the familiar nostrum that the Jews and Bolsheviks were to blame.

As many former Nazi officials fled to the Bavarian Alps and the Tyrol, Russian troops wasted no time in exploring their new Austrian conquest. Vienna was basking in sweltering heat when Soviet lieutenant Boris Martschenko took the opportunity to indulge in a spot of sightseeing. 'This is not just a city – it is an architectural fantasy,' he enthusiastically wrote to his wife. 'Budapest is a dirt-heap compared to Vienna.'

> I visited the Opera House. The back of it had burned down – but it remains a remarkable building. Who would have thought that I ever would have had a chance to see it. And, it is amusing to say, Vienna now resembles one of our own cities in holiday mood! From the windows of the houses red flags can be seen, hanging everywhere! The civilians are cautious – they wait until they are in groups of 5–10 people before they approach us. But when they find I can speak some German, and make myself understood in conversation with them, they vie with each other in helpfulness![2]

Whilst Martschenko explored Vienna, Rex North, one of the most visible reporters embedded with the British Army during their onward advance, was busy shooting off accounts of how the people of the industrial cities had been bombed into sullen resignation. As the days wore on, his party rolled into Emsdetten, a small town near Munster in North Rhine-Westphalia, where North was shocked to discover 'another side to the picture of this defeated Germany'. Emsdetten, he wrote, was far from any target of military importance. 'It has never had a bomb. Not one.' Conditions in the town were in such violent contrast to his first experiences of Germany that he wondered if he had been transported to another part of the world:

> You would like an alarm clock? Here they are in abundance. A British soldier has seen them, too, and taken one to send home. He also left the money for a watch – a sum which I estimate roughly equals five shillings. Cameras, films, glassware, almost anything you can think of, is all here. Let's move on to the food. Here is a butcher's shop with a particularly nice ham in the window. On the shelves is a goodish assortment of tinned food. I found there was some horse meat there as well. 'What do you think?' I asked Corporal Reid – he's from Barrhead in Glasgow. 'They seem to have had a much better time than the folks in Main Street,' he said. 'I'm surprised – I thought the Germans were starving.'

In fact, anxiety was rising in Berlin, which faced yet another rations cut which left residents to survive on 1,700 grams of bread, 250 grams of meat and 125 grams of fat a week – in desperation, authorities recommended the public brew spruce needle shoots for vitamins and eat frogs for protein (advice originally dispensed by Dr Werner Bockhacker during his KdF woodland tours a decade earlier). Clean water was pumped from carts, the only electricity came from small generators and almost every shop was closed.

Inside the narrowing limits of Berlin, residents were thinking about life after the fighting. Those with an eye on survival stocked up food, valuables and alibis. Everyone formulated schemes for what they would do when the Russians arrived. Some planned to shelter in the huge, sprawling Grunewald forest near Wannsee, while others reckoned the best option was to batten down in cellars until the crisis had passed. For many in the tattered Nazi hierarchy, it was time to leave. 'Robert Ley has become somewhat hysterical under the impact of recent developments,' sneered Goebbels in his diary. 'It shows he is not naturally a strong personality. Moreover, he oscillates like a windsock when times are serious and critical.'[3]

Indeed, Ley's face was lined with worry when he met Hitler for the last time on the night of 19 April. During their brief, emotional encounter, the Führer ordered him to go south, promising he would follow. Then, at half-past midnight, Hitler made his excuses and returned to other business. Carrying a pistol for protection, Ley, joined by SS commander Sepp Dietrich, slogged along on his final journey to the Alps. Luck saw the pair narrowly avoid Russian artillery, which began bombarding Berlin a few hours later, leaving vast craters above Hitler's bunker. In the clear spring air, the sound of explosions carried for miles. As the end inched closer, gallows humour shone. Berliners made sarcastic comments about how it was possible to travel by tram from the Eastern Front to the Western Front. In fact, a gentle stroll could have covered the entire front line in a matter of hours.

By the time Ley had made his retreat, Albert Speer described life in the bunker as a bizarre mixture of hope and despair as Hitler, seemingly entranced, sat poring over a map, talking about victory and moving non-existent divisions. The map was not of the world, Europe or even of the fronts – it just covered Berlin, the suburbs and Potsdam.

By 24 April, Belorussian and Ukrainian troops completed the encirclement of the city. Surprisingly, the *Berliner Morgenpost* appeared the following morning boasting that while the Russians may have penetrated into individual city districts 'we will chase them away again'. Even 'allotment gardeners,' it claimed, had 'prepared themselves in cold-blooded calm for the fight against the Bolshevik mortal enemy'.

The truth was that even the might of allotment gardeners couldn't stop the Red Army steamrolling through the southern suburbs and Tempelhof Airport, where they set up a makeshift camp in what had been the departures terminal. Fighting also raged in the western district of Charlottenburg, Moabit, near the main rail terminal, and in Schoenberg. 'Wilma D', a sixth-grade pupil from Prenzlauer Berg, felt the full horror of the onslaught when 'a Stalin Organ [a kind of rocket] struck our yard; my mum was standing there with seven other women when the grenade hit. Her legs were ripped off.'[4] Faced with this terrifying military might, the *Volkssturm* defence quickly degenerated into a confused melee, as Russian tanks rolled across the city. The scene at Berlin Zoo was like the setting for an Armageddon film. On a hill by the old donkey garden, a dozen forced laborers groaned and strained as they dug shallow trenches, dismantled railings and cut trees to use as anti-tank barriers. 'Zookeepers and craftsmen who lived outside the zoo were not available due to the heavy artillery fire, those who live in the zoo lived in small ground bunkers at Elephant Gate,' noted employee Katherina Heinroth. Keepers could only take care of the animals at night during the lulls in shellfire.

More bad news arrived on Hitler's desk on 25 April. His beloved Berchtesgaden Berghof, the site of so much holiday fun and happiness, had been blown to smithereens by RAF bombs. Reconnaissance photographs showed the famous sitting room with the enormous window, where he often admired the hills beyond, was an empty shell of brickwork and masonry with not a scrap of furnishing or panelling left – even the window framework had gone. Göring's house was in even worse condition. One end sagged to the ground and the remainder was a tottering wreckage.

After this, Hitler abandoned his posture as fearless defender of Germany and married his long-time girlfriend Eva Braun just after midnight on 29 April. Soon after, he dictated his last will and testament. What happened next is history. On 30 April, Hitler and his wife of forty hours ended their lives with a cyanide pill and a gunshot. Within an hour, their corpses were smouldering on a narrow strip of open ground outside the bunker. As for Goebbels, his sputtering defence ended a day later by his own hand inches from Hitler's funeral pyre.

Even in war, news travelled fast. Fifteen-year-old Brigitte Eicke remembered a neighbour turning up at their cellar at 3 a.m. yelling, 'The leader is dead, the war is over!' On cue, the local *Volkssturm* threw down their weapons and scarpered. When dawn broke, Brigitte joined an orgy of theft at a nearby department store:

Men broke open door after door; everything was there – cigarettes, wine, schnapps, card games and boots. I was able to pick up some pants in the hurry instead of maybe taking boots. Then we went upstairs ... I took baby clothes and toys. I gave it all away on the street afterwards.

Meanwhile, over at Berlin Zoo, secretary, Katherina Heinroth was in a state of panic as Russian tanks rolled over the grounds, laying waste to the gardens and tearing up the paving. 'Artillery shelling destroyed all the roofs and killed most of the animals,' she tearfully recounted. 'The management, Professor Heck and all of his close aides left the zoo grounds shortly before the arrival of Russian troops on 30 April.' At the end of the fighting, bodies were gathered and buried in a mass grave at Elephant Gate (they were later transferred to cemeteries).

On 9 May, the war ended with a whimper as German commanders signed their approval for the total and unconditional capitulation of the armed forces. Around 5 million Germans, including half a million civilians, had been killed, and 4 million had been wounded. Another 4 million homes had been destroyed, and 13 million people were homeless.

31

A NEW TYPE OF TOURIST

Just like in 1918, when British troops marched into Cologne, Allied forces became Germany's first post-war tourists.

Once they found something better than bombed-out ruins, the new occupiers began to feel the holiday mood. Hitler's mountain home quickly came to rank among the most popular GI sightseeing spots in Europe after Berchtesgaden was taken over by the US Army as a rest-and-recreation centre. Among other sites they requisitioned was the Berchtesgadener Hof, the luxury hotel which Hitler reconstructed to house favoured guests and where Neville Chamberlain stayed during the 1938 talks. A visiting reporter described how its deeply upholstered comfort and magnificent mountain views were 'now enjoyed by American and Allied officers, nurses, Red Cross workers, and visitors to the area'. Other hotels housed enlisted men who arrived for a few days' leave. Among other activities, the Americans organised tours to see the ruins of the Berghof, and the residences of Göring and his other accomplices. Four or five times a day, supervised convoys ran from the Berghof settlement up the skilfully engineered road to the Tea House.

Meanwhile, the British Military Government embarked on the wholesale requisitioning of buildings in Hamburg, including the plush harbourside Atlantic Hotel, which they converted into an officers' club, while the famous Laeiszhalle concert hall – once Hamburg's cultural centre – was taken over by the British Forces Network. Local Germans, barred from the promenade at Neuer Jungfernstieg, stood aghast as British soldiers nailed a 'Piccadilly Circus' sign to a building on the Grosser Allee, one of Hamburg's oldest commercial streets. In the fanciful words of the British occupation forces, Hamburg was transformed into a 'huge holiday camp' for British troops. 'This maze of rubble must have been one of the gloomiest places in Europe,' the *Liverpool Echo* observed. 'Within a few weeks it will be one of the brightest spots on the Continent.' By mid-June, three cinemas, a theatre and more than six sports clubs were in operation. There were plans for yachting and golf, and neon lights were installed above several cinemas 'ready for autumn'. By summer, football, hockey, cricket, boxing and athletics games were being run and local swimming pools – two indoor and one outdoor – were made available to the troops in the city. A circus and a funfair on the outskirts of the city were also being considered.

Some 35 miles south-west of Berlin at the UFA film studios in Potsdam, a canteen and rest centre was set up in the building where Marlene Dietrich had filmed *The Blue Angel* fifteen years earlier. Nearby, nestled deep in lush green woodland, three lakeside cafes at Wannsee served coffee and cakes. Inspired by booze-fuelled parties held for demobbed troops, one of them came to be called the Café De Mob, while another provided customers with a full range of water sports, fishing gear and even trips on a pleasure steamer, as the *Daily Mirror* reported on 25 July 1945:

> NAAFI is running a showboat for British troops in Berlin; she will take 350 soldiers on her first cruise on the Havel See, one of Berlin's great lakes today. Beer, tea and cakes will be served by German waitresses, destined later to wear navy uniform with bellbottomed trousers and sailor caps bearing the NAAFI badge. The pleasure steamer, to be named *Pettit's Packet* after Major Pettit, commanding NAAFI in Berlin, will be christened by Junior Commander Mary Churchill. Then ENSA will give a performance of *Blitz and Pieces* under the spacious covered passenger deck.

Meanwhile, the architects of German misfortune were being hunted. That summer, a large group of former Nazi leaders fell into Allied hands including Göring and Rosenberg along with generals and admirals like Dönitz, Kesselring, Rundstedt, Busch, Guderian, Schörner, Weichs, Leeb, List, Kleist and Falkenhorst. Diplomats Papen and Schmieden, industrialist Krupp and, finally, Funk, Speer, Darre, Backe, Dorpmüller and Seldte were also picked up. In the final reckoning, Robert Ley was captured 50 miles south of Berchtesgaden when American forces received a tip-off from a talkative local. Wearing labourers' clothes and a newly grown beard, Ley had been hiding in a peasant's cottage. Babbling and gesturing incoherently, he told his captors they had got the wrong man. 'I am ignorant of political subjects,' he explained, before being driven into custody. Hermann Esser was also arrested but released after being considered an 'unimportant official' – no doubt a personal relief, but an insult to his self-importance.

As Ley settled into prison life, his planned KdF complex at Timmendorfer Strand on the shores of the Baltic became a transit station for Allied forces. A journalist noted that the British were billeted in hotels and luxury villas but 'the sandy beach which provides ideal bathing is the great attraction, and motor boat trips to damaged German submarines and the wrecked *Deutschland*, Hitler's 'Strength Through Joy', cruiser are popular features of the off-duty hours'.[1]

Eventually, Ley was indicted by the International Military Tribunal on three counts: (1) promoting the accession to power of Nazi conspirators and consolidation of their control over Germany; (2) promoting preparations for war; and (3) organizing and participating in crimes against humanity. In a scream of protest, he complained he had not committed murder and had not ordered any. He recorded his feelings in a long and desperate letter to his dead wife, Inga:

> I did not start a war. I had no power to do so, I did not even know about it. To the contrary, for me the war came at the most inopportune moment. I was in the midst of my social

reconstruction, which I now had to interrupt. God in heaven, what have I done that I am treated under such conditions as a criminal? Lord God, give me an answer, I have a right to it.

By this point, Ley was tired of the world and tired of life. 'I cannot stand this shame any longer. I was with Hitler in the good days, and now I want to be with him in the black days. We have forsaken God and therefore we were forsaken by God.'

Soon after, in a state of despair, the creator of the DAF and KdF strangled himself in his prison cell using a thin strip of bath towel; to speed up his suffocation he stuffed his mouth with material from his underpants. His body was taken away from the cell and buried in a nearby field. The location of his grave remains unknown.

ENDNOTES

1 Enchanted Land

1. Granville, A. B. *The spas of Germany*. 1838. p. 117.
2. Hapag since 1905.
3. Riesel's also offered a 45-day self-conducted excursion to the 1892 Chicago World's Fair, with the itinerary including New York, Philadelphia, Baltimore, Washington. Pittsburgh, Chicago, Milwaukee, Lake Michigan, Detroit, Niagara, Suspension Bridge, the Canadian lake, Queenstown, Buffalo and back to New York by Pacific Express through the valleys of the Delaware and the Susquehanna. *American Register*, Saturday 26 November 1892.
4. *Morgen Post*, 29 August, 1874.
5. *Die Presse*, 30 August, 1873.
6. *East London Observer*, 18 May 1872.
7. Ibid.
8. Jaffe, F. 'San Francisco', *Stangen's illustrierte Reise- und Verkehrs-Zeitung*, 1895.
9. 'White-Chapel', *Stangen's illustrierte Reise- und Verkehrs-Zeitung*, 1895.
10. Zit. nach Gyr, *The History of Tourism*.

11. Karl Baedeker issued the first volumes of his guides from Koblenz, where he died in 1859. His son, Fritz, moved the business to Leipzig in 1872, and by the time the Nazis took power the business still flourished, directed by Karl's grandson.
12. *Northern Daily Mail*, 12 October 1929.
13. By the mid-1930s, the Reichsbahnzentrale for German travel had offices in Budapest, Havana, Helsinki, Gothenburg, Copenhagen, London, Milan, New York, Paris, Prague, Rotterdam, Vienna, Zurich, Amsterdam, Asuncion, Belgrade, Buenos-Aires, Bucharest, Chicago, Cairo, Kobe, Lima, Rio de Janeiro, San Francisco, Santiago de Chile, Shanghai, Toronto, Genoa, Monte Carlo, Riga, Sao Paulo, Sofia and Stockholm.

2 The Nazis Arrive

1. Statistisches Reichsamt, *Statlstlsches Jahrbuch fur das Deutsche Reich*. 1933.
2. *Yorkshire Post and Leeds Intelligencer*, 23 May 1933.
3. *Aberdeen Press and Journal*, 29 May 1933.
4. *Truth*, 7 June 1933.
5. *Leeds Mercury*, 8 August 1933.
6. *Western Gazette*, 14 July 1933.
7. *Daily Herald*, 15 January 1940.
8. DAF, which by a Hitler Decree of 24 October 1934, became a Party affiliate. Power over industrial relations was consolidated with astonishing speed as Ley broke the unions into three groups: workmen, white collar workers, and employers. 'Then the finances of these three groups were unified into one,' he later explained. 'And so eventually there was no differentiation between the workman, the white-collar workers and the employer'.
9. Cited from Guérin, D. *The Brown Plague*. Duke University Press Books, 1994. p. 125.
10. DAF special circular, 27 June 1933. 2336/PS.
11. In fact, after 1933, the great majority of workmen in German industry had no effective means of voicing grievances.
12. *New York Times*, 13 June 1937.
13. Kelley, D. *22 Cells in Nuremberg*. p. 153.

Endnotes

14. Whetton, C. *Hitler's Fortune*. p. 197. The finances of the DAF were put under the supervision of the Nazi Party Treasurer, Franz X. Schwarz.
15. 'Strength through joy! The new after-work organization of the German Labour Front'. Front page and page 2 (excerpt) *Berliner Morgenpost*, 28 November 1933.
16. *Der Deutsche*, 28 November 1933.
17. Fröhlich, E. *Die Tagebücher von Joseph Goebbels*. Munich. p. 324.
18. *Der Deutsche*, 28 November 1933.
19. *Werkszetischrift der Betriebsgemeinschaft Focke-Wulf Flugzeugbau*. June 1939. p. 12.
20. Sopade report, July 1935.
21. *Dundee Courier*, 27 June 1938.
22. Dressler-Andress, H., *Three Years of the National Socialist Community*. Berlin, 1936.
23. Speer, Albert. *Inside the Third Reich*. Simon & Schuster. 1979. p. 57.
24. *Dundee Evening Telegraph*, 3 January 1939.
25. Klaus Behnken. *Sozialdemokratische Partei Deutschlands*. Reports, vol. 5 (1938). p. 173.
26. *Der Deutsche*, 28 November 1935.

3 The Cultured Worker

1. Buchholz, W. 'Die Nationalsozialistische Gemeinschaft "Kraft durch Freude": Freizeitgestaltung und Arbeiterschaft im Dritten Reich.' PhD dissertation, 1976. p. 20.
2. Ibid, p. 22.
3. Zandt Moyer, L. 'The Kraft durch Freude Movement in Nazi Germany: 1933–1939' (Dissertation, North-western University, 1967).
4. Dressler-Andress, H. *Three Years of the National Socialist Community*. Berlin, 1936.
5. Ibid.
6. Shafer, Y. 'Nazi Berlin and the Grosses Schauspielhaus' in *Theatre in the Third Reich, the Prewar Years*. Greenwood Press, 1995.

7. *Midland Daily Telegraph*, 25 November 1937.
8. *Arbeitertum*, August 1938.
9. *Aufbruch 1933, Neubau des deutschen Theaters: Ergebnisse und Forderungen.* Berlin, 1934. p. 52
10. Rühle, G. 'Schlageter von Hanns Johst – eine Uraufführung zu Hitlers Geburtstag' in *Theater heute*, August/Sept. 2002.
11. Ihering, H. "Staatliches Schauspielhaus: 'Schlageter,' *Börsen-Courier*, 21 April 1933.
12. Michael H. Kater, 'The Raul Hilberg Memorial Lecture', The University of Vermont. 2007.
13. This came in addition to regular events by the NS-Sinfonieorchestra. Misha Aster, *The Reichs Orchestra*, Mosaic Press; 2010. p. 135.
14. Reichsbahnzentrale pamphlet *Welcome to Germany*, 1936.
15. Lagebericht der Staatspolizeistelle Potsdam für Dec. 4 1935. Cited from *Hitler's Happy People: Kraft durch Freude's Everyday Production of Joy in the Third Reich*. Julia Timpe, Brown University, 2007.
16. *Und morgen gibt es Hitlerwetter! – Alltägliches und Kurioses aus dem Dritten Reich.* p. 102.
17. As the 'Commissioner for the supervision of the intellectual and ideological education', Rosenberg had few admirers in the clergy or the Party.
18. *Der Deutsche*, 1 December 1933.
19. *The Scotsman*, 7 September 1934.
20. Buchholz, 1976, p. 179.
21. Deutsche Heraklith A.G. paid KdF RM15.701.56 to arrange keep fit programmmes. National archives: 1561456.
22. *Lancashire Evening Post*, 21 December 1935.
23. Ley, *Deutschland ist schöner geworden*, p. 94.
24. DAF Information Sheet, 9 January 1935.
25. *Der Deutsche*, 29 November 1934.
26. *Arbeitertum*, 15 December 1936. p. 6.
27. *Sunderland Daily Echo and Shipping Gazette*, 2 July 1937.

4 Beauty and Horror

1. Within a few short months of Hitler's appointment as Chancellor, the Norddeutscher Lloyd, and Hamburg-America lines expelled all Jews from their board and management positions.
2. The Nuremberg Laws of 1935 forbade most hotels to accept Jewish guests. A decree of the Ministry of Interior from July 1937 posed extreme restrictions on the presence of Jews in spas; an additional decree from June 1939 made participation impossible. Confino, A. *Traveling as a culture of remembrance: Traces of national socialism in West Germany, 1945-1960.*
3. *Yorkshire Post and Leeds Intelligencer*, 26 July 1935.
4. *Nordische Rundschau*, 8 August 1935.
5. Hilde Rohlén-Wohlgemuth *Att vara flykting i Sverige under 30-talet*, Stockholm.

5 Hooray for KdF!

1. *The Times*, 19 February 1934.
2. On 3 January 1934, Hitler published a 'thank you' note addressed to Robert Ley in the *Völkischer Beobachter* – a clear sign of his satisfaction with the DAF and KdF.
3. *Siemens Mitteilungen*. Dec. 1934 p. 254.
4. A term for ethnic Germans commonly used by the Nazis.
5. Postcard from Berchtesgaden, June 25 1935 (Author's private collection).
6. Baedeker 1938, 6, 35. The property even had an approving review in 'What is not in the Baedeker,' a paperback guide which provided a tongue-in-cheek alternative directing the reader's gaze behind the tourist facades.
7. A winding road was driven for five miles up the mountain under the direction of the engineer Fritz Todt, the builder of the new autobahns. At lower levels, luxurious villas for leading Nazis, including Göring and Speer, and a colony of barracks and administrative offices sprang up.
8. U.S. National Archives, Washington National Records Center. Letter from Martin Bormann to Dr. Friedrich Wolffhardt, Führer Headquarters, 27 December 1941.

9. A documentation centre, which now occupies a nearby site, shows family snapshots on the Berghof path became a ritual. Surviving photos – and there are thousands of them – show a hugely diverse portrait, ranging through intimate family gatherings, works outings to lone travellers rigidly saluting. From the mid-1930s, the huge machine of government had offices and departments based in Berchestsgaden, which became the de-facto second capital.
10. In the summer of 1933, the Berchtesgaden market only had 50,103 guests, in 1935 it was 64,330 and in 1937, 80,145.
11. This image was distributed millions of times by the illustrated press, by books, illustrated journals and the then popular cigarette-picture albums. Collectors albums like 'Hitler away from everyday life', 'Hitler, as nobody knows' and 'Adolf Hitler – pictures from the life of the leader' exploited the leader cult for commercial purposes and thereby strengthened it. A popular postcard showed Hitler lounging on a deckchair on the terrace, with the caption: 'A quiet moment at Berchtesgaden.'
12. *Eckington, Woodhouse and Staveley Express*, 27 August 1938.
13. Hunt, I. *On Hitler's Mountain: Overcoming the Legacy of a Nazi Childhood*. Harper Perennial. 2011. p. 95.
14. *To the 1930 Passion Play via Cunard Line*. Pamphlet, 1930.
15. Reichsbahnzentrale pamphlet *Welcome to Germany*. 1936.
16. *Der Deutsche*, 13 June 1934.
17. *Völkischer Beobachter*, Munich edition, 13 September 1934.
18. *NS-Freizeitorganisation vor 80 Jahren gegründet, Deutschlandfunk*.

6 A Mixed Bunch
1. Schulz-Luckau 1937, p. 10.
2. *Coventry Evening Telegraph*, 25 November 1937.
3. Sopade 5, Nr. 2 (February 1938), p. 34.
4. Semmens. p. 108.
5. Sopade 5, Nr. 2 (February 1938), p. 34.
6. *Der Fermdenverkehr*, 15 January 1938.

Endnotes

7. *LFV Württemberg-Hohenzollern Rundverfügung*, 6 August 1937 as cited by Kristin Semmens in *Seeing Hitler's Germany*. 2005. p. 104.
8. *NS-Freizeitorganisation vor 80 Jahren gegründet, Deutschlandfunk*.
9. Over the coming years, household accommodation became vital to KdF providing much needed capacity during the summer months.
10. *Achentaler Nachrichten*, 24 July 1934.
11. *Kraft durch Freude, Rothenburg ob der Tauber*. 1935.
12. *Völkischer Beobachter*, 21 February 1935.
13. *The Sphere*, 9 July 1932.
14. General rules, as cited from *KdF.-Urlaub: Die Deutsche Arbeitsfront, Gau Sudetenland* (Trip number 209).
15. *Dundee Courier*, 7 March 1938.

7 *Trample on the Hills*

1. *The Sphere*, 16 July 1932.
2. *Northern Whig*, 14 September 1940.
3. Horst Dressler-Andress. *Three Years of the national Socialist Community Kraft durch Freude: Aims and Achievements*. Berlin, 1936.
4. 1935 *Oberstdorf Allgauer Alpen* travel brochure.
5. *Coventry Evening Telegraph*, 25 November 1937.
6. Ibid.
7. Newspaper cutting, undated. Probably 1934-35.
8. Gay, P. *My German question: growing up in Nazi Berlin*. Yale, 1998.
9. Ibid.
10. His company 'Volksreisen für den kleinen Mann agency'. In 1935, the tiny village of Ruhpolding recorded 9,000 arrivals, but by 1938 that number had shot up to 13,000 vacationers from the Degener travel agency.
11. *Truth*, 13 June 1934.
12. Schön, Heinz. *Die KdF-Schiffe und ihr Schicksal*. 1987, p. 29.
13. Ibid.
14. *Manchester Guardian*, 13 September 1937.

15. Tooze, A. *The Wages of Destruction: The Making and Breaking of the Nazi Economy.* Allen Lane, 2006.
16. Ibid.
17. Tooze, 2006, p. 168.
18. Shelly Baranowski quotes the reaction of travellers to this illusion of evaluation (2004, p. 195).
19. Frommann. *Reise mit KdF.* 1992. p. 250.
20. Guides to German Records, microfilmed at Alexandria, VA. No. 39. Records of the Reich Leader of the SS and Chief of the German Police (Part 3).
21. Frommann p. 311.
22. Spode, *Arbeiterurlaub im Dritten Reich.* p. 311.
23. Frommann p. 271.
24. Ibid.
25. 'Als Hitler lr die Har küßte'. *Neue Zeit*, 2 June, 1993.
26. The incident happened on the afternoon of 20 June 1934. Passengers were moved to the Norwegian steamer *King Haakon*. Immediately after the accident had become known, the steamer *Stuttgart* was sent from Bremerhaven to take off the passengers and crew of the *Dresden*.
27. *Manchester Guardian*, 5 November 1935.
28. Ibid.

8 Prora

1. Hitler's secretary Martin Bormann provided the remedy: The area was cordoned off and guarded and was then only accessible with proof of authorization. The pilgrimages that testified to Hitler's popularity were now organized by the party. Hitler received groups from the Hitler Youth and BDM and delegations from other party organizations, but also non-party groups and associations. The visits followed the same ritual: marching, line up in front of Hitler, singing a song, shaking hands, marching off. After 1936, Hitler increasingly used the backdrop of the Obersalzberg for high-profile diplomatic receptions, and a functioning seat of government, a second center of power next to Berlin. Pre-war visitors included Prince Regent Paul of Yugoslavia, the

Duke of Windsor who had abdicated in December 1936 as King Edward VIII, Italian Foreign Minister and son-in-law Mussolini's Count Ciano, Aga Khan, the leader of Indian Muslims, to name a few.
2. *New York Times*, 19 January 1937.
3. *Joe et Travail*, February 1938. p. 13.
4. Schroeder, Christa, *Er war mein Chef*, p. 171.
5. Therese Linke, unpublished handwritten memoir, p. 9. Cited from Görtemaker, Heike B., Eva Braun, *Eva Braun: Leben mit Hitler*. Verlag C. H. Beck, Munich, 2010.
6. *On Hitler's Mountain* p. 95.
7. 'Hitler's holiday dream lives on', *Observer*, 29 December, 1996.
8. 'Hitlers Riesenklotz für sein nervenstarkes Volk', *Die Welt*, 3 May, 2016.
9. These never got beyond the planning phase. Königswinter on the Rhine was also earmarked to be transformed into a 'KdF town' of unprecedented size. Although smaller than Prora, its overall concept was comparable. With a planned capacity of 5,000 and around 1,000 employees, the hotel was to run over 200 meters along the Rhine. In addition to the hotel, numerous facilities such as cinemas, theatres, music pavilions, parks and even a fleet of cruise boats were planned for the entertainment of the guests. 'Königswinter – größtes Landerholungsheim der DAF', *Westdeutscher Beobachter*, 5 August 1937.
10. H. Heiber and B. Heiber, *Die Rückseite des Hakenkreuzes. Absonderliches aus den Akten des Dritten Reiches*. 1993. p. 193. (As cited in Frederic C. Tubach. *German Voices: Memories of Life during Hitler's Third Reich*. University of California Press.)
11. In later reports, Kolberg is no longer mentioned as a possible location, but Köslin further east did emerge as a candidate.
12. Interrogation of Albert Speer, former Reich Minister of Armaments and War Production / Supreme Headquarters / Allied Expeditionary Force / Office of Assistant Chief of Staff, G-2 / SECRET.
13. Ibid.
14. Alfred Rosenberg's memoirs. Skull Press Ebook Publications. 2013. p. 65.

9 Luring the British

1. Dressler-Andress, H. *Three Years of the national Socialist Community Kraft durch Freude: Aims and Achievements.* Berlin, 1936.
2. Letter from the Germany Embassy in London to the Foreign office in Berlin, 29.7.1935, (Landrat des Siegkreises, Rundschreiben vom 17.8.1935).
3. Landesstelle Köln-Aachen des Reichsministers für Volksaufklärung und Propaganda an den Land- rat des Siegkreises, Köln, den 15.8.1935, Anlage zu: Landrat des Siegkreises, Rundschreiben vom 17.8.1935, in: StAKw, Bestand Oberpleis 1937.
4. *LFV Rhineland*, circular no. IX, 2 August 1937. KASb, Siegkris District Office.
5. *Penistone, Stocksbridge and Hoyland Express*, 9 June 1934.
6. *Aberdeen Press and Journal*, 9 November 1934.
7. *Sunderland Daily Echo and Shipping Gazette*, 22 February 1935.
8. *Yorkshire Evening Post*, 1 August 1935.
9. Reichsbahnzentrale pamphlet *Welcome to Germany* 1936.
10. *Arbeitertum*, December 1935.
11. Horst Dressler-Andress, p. 14.
12. *I Shall Bear Witness: The Diaries Of Victor Klemperer 1933-41.*
13. *Portsmouth Evening News*, 1 October 1935.
14. Waln p. 117.
15. *Aberdeen Press and Journal*, 9 November 1934.
16. Hamburger, Ernest. 'Significance of the Nazi Leisure Time Program' *Social Research*, 12 (2), 1945. p. 244.
17. 'Das schöne / beautiful / la belle Berlin' Tourist Brochure. Berliner Verkehrsverein, Berlin C2. 1935
18. Higham, Charles. *Marlene*. Granada, 1977. p. 62
19. 'Topography of terror, Berlin'. 2021 exhibition.
20. The Nazi moral crusade to rid the nation of homosexuals was written into law in 1935. Known as clause 175 of the penal code, it ensured that over 15,000 gay men would be packed-off to concentration camps over the coming decade, where many perished.
21. *Leicester Evening Mail*, 17 June 1930.

22. Control of the beach was taken over by staunch Nazis. Scouting troops of the NS welfare looked for Jewish bathers and chased them away. In December 1938, Jews were officially banned from indoor and outdoor swimming pools.
23. Verwaltungsbericht der Stadt Köln 1933/34, S. 30, in: StAK, Ce 21/1933-34. The Cologne Municipal Council also opened a Travel Bureau, opposite the Cathedral and prepared weekly programmes of entertainment, amusements, restaurants, times to visit Churches and Museums in their *Kolner Woche* guide. *Vertrauliche Mitteilungen der Fachschaft Verlag*, no. 36. 26 July 1938. As of late 1938, the publication of travel guides and city guides required official permission.
24. *Montrose Standard*, 2 August 1935.
25. Ibid.
26. *Birmingham Daily Gazette*, 22 August 1935.
27. *Sevenoaks Chronicle and Kentish Advertiser*, 4 October 1935.
28. *Aberdeen Press and Journal*, 5 August 1937.

10 Soaring Above: Aviation

1. Goebbels' Diary, 10 April 1933. Doubleday, 1948.
2. Budapest, Havana, Helsinki, Gothenburg, Copenhagen, London, Milan, New York, Paris, Prague, Rotterdam, Vienna, Zurich, Amsterdam, Asuncion, Belgrade, Buenos-Aires, Bucharest, Chicago, Cairo, Kobe, Lima, Rio de Janeiro, San Francisco, Santiago de Chile, Shanghai, Toronto, Genoa, Monte Carlo, Riga, Sao Paulo, Sofia and Stockholm.
3. During 1931, 123,000 arriving and departing passengers were accounted for at Tempelhof; in 1935 there were 174,000; and in 1936 no fewer than 220,000. These were impressive figures compared with the 9,000 air passengers counted at the same airport in 1925.
4. *The Scotsman*, 26 March 1936.
5. Lufthansa, 'The German Airways', May–August 1934 Timetable.
6. *Aberdeen People's Journal*, 16 December 1939.
7. 1A/ABC/48 Imperial Airlines Brochure. Return tickets were valid for fifteen days for the Cologne–London route at the price of

RM144 and could be used at any time within the period of validity.
8. Dan Grossman interview with Nathan Morley, 8 April 2021.
9. 'The Hindenburg First Atlantic Crossing'. *The Sphere*, 18 April 1936.

11 The Lucrative Olympics

1. The curtain for Olympic year opened with a dramatic firework display above Munich, followed by the inauguration of the 'Olympia-Strasse' autobahn which cut through the mountains from Munich to Garmisch, the venue of the Winter Games. Over 42,000 KdF tourists visited the Winter Olympics which was considered the 'warm up' show for the Summer Games slated to take place in Berlin during August 1936.
2. 'Travel to Germany', *Die Reichsbahnzentrale für den Deutschen Reiseverkehr* (RDV) 1936 p. 3.
3. Ibid.
4. *Belfast News-Letter*, 31 July 1936.
5. Olympic Documentation, p. 146; 'Topography of terror, Berlin'. 2021 exhibition.
6. Sausages and ale were dished out to day-trippers ferried in by a charabanc rattling between the village and Stadium. From dawn to dusk, families with kids, veterans and swarms of Hitler Youth's jostled among the aroma of stale beer and sweaty punters. Tented accommodation on a field opposite offered families a cheap bed and washing facilities.
7. *New York Times*, 27 July 1936.
8. *Westdeutscher Beobachter*, 31 July 1936.
9. Olympic Documentation, p. 107.
10. *OZ Ausgabe* 1,1936. p. 4.
11. *Bradford Observer*, 1 August 1936.
12. Olympic Documentation, p. 371.
13. *Bradford Observer*, 1 August 1936.
14. Dorothea Günther (1914–) from Berlin, June 2010. LEMO.
15. Werner Viehs (1924 -) 'What a life!' *My Century*. LEMO.

Endnotes

16. Esther Wenzel. 'I, Witness to History'. Wesley Retirement Communities, 1996.
17. Socolow, Michael. *Six Minutes In Berlin*. University of Illinois Press. 2016.
18. *Fleetwood Chronicle*, 14 August 1936.
19. As well welcoming visitors to Germany, Anhalter had already become the starting point for many fleeing into exile including author Klaus Mann, who fled Berlin just as Hitler came to power. 'I left berlin very early in the morning on 30 January 1933, as if driven by a bad premonition. On the way to the Anhalter Bahnhof, the streets were still virtually devoid of people. Tired and foul tempered, I virtually disregarded the sleepy morning city. It would have been my last view of Berlin, my farewell. I left berlin without saying goodbye.'

12 Let the Games Begin

1. The plan was to accommodate the infantry school and the 1st battalion of the infantry training regiment. The dining house became a hospital – one of the most modern of its time. The headquarters, staff and officers' quarters were housed in the reception building.
2. *Bradford Observer*, 13 January 1936.
3. *Hastings and St Leonards Observer*, 8 August 1936.
4. To add to the fun, Across the city, the games were accompanied by numerous theatre, opera and sports productions, the German exhibition and several art exhibitions – a total of three million visitors reacted enthusiastically, as did the vast majority of international press representatives.
5. *Berlin 1945: A Documentation*. p. 82.
6. *Der Athlet*, der Hitler düpierte, SZ. 31 March, 2020. https://www.sueddeutsche.de/sport/jesse-owens-todestag-olympia-berlin-1936-1.4851867.
7. Brown made the observations in the university journal *Granta*, cited by the *Yorkshire Evening Post* 8 October 1936.
8. *Leeds Mercury*, 28 August 1936.

13 Special Presentations

1. *Daily Mirror* –16 August 1937.
2. *Hartlepool Northern Daily Mail*, 28 February 1938.
3. *London Times*, 4 July 1939.
4. Armin Zweite, *Franz Hofmann und die Staedtische Galerie*. 1937, p. 284.
5. *Belfast Telegraph*, 29 July 1938.
6. *Bradford Observer*, 27 January 1938.

14 Hamburg

1. Postcard 2.9.1935 from Hamburg to John Banta, Grantwood, New Jersey. (Author's private collection)
2. Ibid.
3. *Norwegen Kleiner Schiffs-Reiseführer für KdF. Reisen Hamburg Schiffsfahrten*. 1930. p. 3.
4. 'Auf der Reeperbahn, nachtsumhalb eins'. *Hamburger Fremdenblatt*, 18 July 1939.
5. Handel und Schiffahrt, Hamburg. 1936.
6. Interview with Nathan Morley, 2020.
7. Ibid.

15 Nuremburg's Jolly Gathering

1. *Aberdeen Press and Journal*, 5 August 1937.
2. During the conferences, Munich station hosted many small-scale sideshows including the 'World Enemy Number 1: Bolshevism,' exhibition shunted into a siding on a special train. 'In each van, material is displayed to call attention to the extent of hunger, executions, Atheism, Jewry, and rearmament in Soviet Russia,' noted a *Morning Post* reporter. 'The last section is designed to show the fight of Adolf Hitler and the National Socialist movement against this Red world pest.'
3. *Belfast News-Letter*, 4 September 1936.
4. The unluckiest visitors could find themselves huddled under tarpaulin on local farmland without sanitation, heating or

food. To feed 24,000 guests, 1.5 million lbs of meat, and about 800,000 lbs of sausages were ferried into the city along with beer and bread.
5. *Sunderland Daily Echo and Shipping Gazette*, 4 September 1937.
6. *Sunderland Daily Echo and Shipping Gazette*, 27 August 1938.
7. Paavolainen, Olavi. *Kolmannen Valtakunnan vieraana*. 1936.
8. *Dundee Evening Telegraph*, 8 September 1936.
9. *Coventry Evening Telegraph*, 11 September 1936.
10. Baker White, J. *Dover–Nuremberg Return*. p. 16.
11. Speer pp. 140-41.

16 The Tide Turns
1. *Bradford Observer*, 16 March 1938.
2. Magistrat Linz an Reichsstatthalter Wien, 27 July 1938.
3. *Derry Journal*, 18 March 1938.
4. 'Im Haus des Terrors', *Die Zeit*, 1 February 2019.
5. Anti-Jewish pogroms in Vienna and the Austrian federal states saw National Socialists and sympathizers storm Jewish institutions. They drove through the streets in trucks, looted, destroyed, pillaged and detained men and women they believed were Jews. In Vienna alone, 42 synagogues were ransacked and set on fire, thousands of shops and homes of Jewish citizens were destroyed, and families were arrested.
6. *Britannia and Eve*, 1 August, 1943.
7. In September 1937.
8. *Anglo-German Review*, August 1938. p. 281.
9. The Austrian integration into the German Reich led to an overhaul of its tourism policy, with local tourist associations merged into the German network. Although passport and visa between the German Reich and Austria was repealed, the Reichsausschuss für Fremdenverkeh (Reich Committee for Foreign Traffic) oversaw traffic to and from Germany.
10. *Österreich 1938-1945*, LEMO, Deutsches Historisches Museum, Berlin.
11. Göllner, Siegfried. *Die Stadt Salzburg 1938*.
12. *The Scotsman*, 17 June 1938.

13. The press trumpeted the advantages which the new regime was bringing to Austria. Newscasts were stocked with wearisome injections of slum clearances, free meals for the poor and a reduction in the price of beer – all achievements in the country's marvellous National Socialist destiny. However, a series of well-directed campaigns failed in deflecting attention form the subtle rise in prices coupled with a sudden drop of supplies, given Austria had previously received more than 20 percent of raw materials and foodstuffs from the British and French Empires. Whilst greengrocers struggled to stock up with apples, oranges and almonds, items including butter, sugar and sardines became luxuries. In rubber, wool, cotton, nonferrous metals, oil and fats Austria was even poorer than Germany.
14. *Joie et Travail*, October 1938.
15. Ibid.
16. State Police Station Kiel to the Secret State Police Office Berlin. 1 August 1938.
17. Sonnemann. p. 88.
18. Monthly Work Report Garmisch-Partenkirchen, 2 March 1938 StA Mü, LRA 61 616. Cited from 'The Jews in the Secret Nazi Reports on Popular Opinion in Germany, 1933–1945' ed. Otto Dov Kulka and Eberhard Jäckel.
19. *The Scotsman*, 28 May 1938. Addressing the International Tourist Alliance in Berlin during May 1938. Moreover, a minor item of interest is that Germany had become a land of congresses. During 1938, no fewer than 83 international conferences were held within the frontiers of the Reich.
20. In a preamble to the 1938 edition of the *Reichs-Handbuch Der Deutschen Fremdenvekehrs-Orte*.
21. *Larne Times*, 28 May 1938.
22. Arrival figures for summer 1938. *Und morgen gibt es Hitlerwetter! – Alltägliches und Kurioses aus dem Dritten Reich.* p. 80.

17 Follow the Sun

1. The following events were planned for the day on 17 February 1939. Schön, Heinz. *Die KdF-Schiffe und ihr Schicksal.* 1987. p. 96.
2. Ibid, p. 95.
3. Frommann p. 184.
4. 'Auf dem Weg nach Tripolis', *Der Angriff*, 22 March 1938.
5. *Anglo German Review*, May 1938.
6. Except from the journal of Elizabeth Dietrich. https://www.wilhelmgustloffmuseum.com/maiden_voyage.html
7. Ibid.
8. Schön p. 38.
9. Schön p. 134.
10. 'Wir deutschen Arbeiter in Madeira', NS Gemeinschaft Kraft durch Freude, Gau Sachsen, Kraft durch Freude (May 1935). p. 24.
11. 'Silvesterfahrt mit Kraft durch Freude', *Arbeitertum*, 15 February 1939.
12. Buchholz, W. 'Die Nationalsozialistische Gemeinschaft „Kraft durch Freude": Freizeitgestaltung und Arbeiterschaft im Dritten Reich.' PhD dissertation, 1976; Frommann 1992.
13. *Völkischer Beobachter*, No. 317, 1937.
14. The trip took place on 7 November 1938. *Arbeitertum*, 15 December 1938.
15. Bundesarchiv. R 58/950.
16. *Britannia and Eve*, 1 July 1941.
17. *Chelmsford Chronicle*, 2 September 1938.
18. *Joie et Travail*, January 1938. p. 64.
19. Deutschland-Berichte der Sozial-Demokratischen Partei Deutschlands, 1935.
20. PSFA0319 / US National Archives.
21. Schön p. 39.
22. Frommann p. 231.
23. *Daily Herald*, 6 June 1939.
24. *Birmingham Daily Post*, 21 January 1939.
25. *Neue Zeit*, 1 November 1949.

18 1939

1. However, economic interests at times trumped ideology and for the sake of tourism, foreign Jews were exempt from the ban.
2. Kaplan, Marion. *Between Dignity and Despair*. Oxford, 1999. p. 146.
3. Ibid.
4. *Dundee Courier*, 7 January 1939; *Nottingham Journal*, 10 January 1939.
5. *The Scotsman*, 4 April 1939.
6. *Dundee Evening Telegraph*, 22 March 1939.
7. There was a growing distaste for the fascist regime in Berlin. Indeed, at a Transport and General Workers' Union meeting in September 1937 in the UK, a Mr. J. Porter from Distributive Workers, Manchester, recommended a boycott on holidays in Germany by British people. 'My advice to this Congress is to tell affiliated members to keep out of Germany until a decent moral standard of government is in force there.'
8. Some tourists stranded in Germany in 1914 ended up in squalid internment camps, such as the notorious Ruhleben near Berlin.
9. *Daily Gazette for Middlesbrough*, 8 August 1939.
10. M. Hoffmann and W. O. Reichelt, *Reiseverkehr and Gastlichkeit im neuen Deutschland*. Hamburg, 1939. pp. 25–26.
11. *Milngavie and Bearsden Herald*, 5 August 1939.
12. *Leeds Mercury*, 2 September 1939.
13. Ibid.
14. The MER, allied with the German Reichsbahn, increased its turnover from 142 million Reichsmarks in 1932 to 217 million Reichsmarks in 1939. Hachtmann. *Tourismus-Geschichte*. p. 128.
15. *The Bystander*, 19 July 1939.
16. Schumann, W. *Being Present, Growing up in Hitler's Germany*. Kent State, 1991. p. 32.
17. 'Der Reisesommer 1939 – Verheißungen vom Süden', *Die Welt*, 1 September 2009.
18. *Larne Times*, 20 May 1939.
19. *Yorkshire Post and Leeds Intelligencer*, 5 September 1939.
20. *Thanet Advertiser*, 21 July 1939.

21. MER given its experience in moving people around the country, reaped additional revenues by transporting 7,900 forced labourers from Bohemia and Moravia to Germany in an early act of willful complicity in crimes against humanity.
22. *Sheffield Evening Telegraph*, 24 March 1939.
23. *Aberdeen Evening Express*, 24 March 1939.
24. *Lincolnshire Free Press*, 21 August 1939.
25. *Edinburgh Evening News*, 6 January 1939.

19 The End of an Era
1. Soviet Union and Germany inked a 'nonaggression' pact. Germany invaded Poland on 1 September 1939. Stalin's invasion of Poland followed a fortnight later.
2. The exodus of Americans was more orderly than was the case in 1914, when many left baggage in hotels and on railway platforms in the dash to get home.
3. *Bristol Evening Post* –12 September 1939.
4. *Northern Whig*, 24 August 1939.
5. Kertesz, G. A. *Documents in the political history of the European continent 1815-1939*. Oxford, 1968. p. 504.

20 War
1. BA Berlin, R58/146, SD mood report, 13 December 1939.
2. Even now in 2021, is considered to be the largest architectural legacy of the Nazi era, surpassing the Nuremburg Rally Grounds and the Reich Chancellery. But like many grand plans, the full vision for Prora never materialized – not a single holidaymaker ever went on vacation there.
3. *Kraft durch Freude*, Düsseldorf edition, November 1939. p. 1.
4. The Dutch vessel *Simon Bolivar* had struck a German mine in the North Sea, sinking with the loss of over 120 lives. The transatlantic liner SS *Athenia* was torpedoed by the German navy just hours after Britain declared war; 117 civilian passengers and crew were killed.

21 1940

1. V. E. Baghdasaryan. 'Through the Looking Glass'. Moscow, 2007.
2. *Kinematograph Weekly*, 30 November 1939. Over in London at the German Railways Information Bureau on Lower Regent Street, a golden German eagle remained in place inviting passers-by to visit 'The Land of Healing Spas'.
3. The War Economy Decree prompted a spate of angry protests in Vienna, where a sharp rise in insubordination, absenteeism and anti-Nazi remarks was duly noted by police.
4. SPD Report Jan 1940 cited from *Berlin 1945, A Documentation.* p. 84.
5. Heinrich Hauser, *Battle Against Time: a Survey of the Germany of 1939 from the Inside.*
6. Ibid.
7. Bundesarchive Reichskanzlei, R 43-II/768A. File: Verkehrswesen, Hebung des Fremdenverkehrs, 1940-1944.
8. Pamphlet *Pauschalriesen im Sommer 1940*, Berlin.
9. See the list in IfZ, MA 737, and Buchholz, W. 'Die Nationalsozialistische Gemeinschaft „Kraft durch Freude": Freizeitgestaltung und Arbeiterschaft im Dritten Reich.' PhD dissertation, 1976, p. 308–21.
10. *Arbeitertum*, March 1940.
11. Werner, I. *So wird's nie wieder sein.* p. 111; Dermota, A. *Tausendundein Abend: Mein Sängerleben.* Vienna 1978. p. 143.
12. Künneke, E. *Mit Federboa und Kittelschürze. Meine zwei Leben.* Frankfurt, 1991. p. 65.

22 Drunk on Victory

1. Just prior to the invasion, German agents – surreptitiously masquerading as tourists – had booked hotels in Trondheim (the Hotel Phoenix (Fønix) in Munkegata). There job had been to feed intelligence back to Germany in the weeks prior to the attack.
2. *Belfast News-Letter*, 30 May 1940.
3. *Birmingham Daily Gazette*, 6 May 1940.
4. *Leicester Evening Mail*, 14 May, 1940.

23 Hitler's Tourists

1. SD Report 100, 27 June.
2. Andreas-Friedrich, R. *Der Schattenmann: Tagebuchaufzeichnungen. 1938-1945.*
3. *Suddeutscher Zeutung*, 25 December 2015.
4. Berger, E. *Auf Flügeln des Gesangs. Erinnerungen einer Sängerin.* Zürich, 1988. p. 59.
5. 'German Railroads Make Bid for Foreign Tourists: Paris Office Reopened to Help Travellers Visit Reich'. *New York Herald Tribune*, 6 August 1940.
6. Confino, A. *Traveling as a culture of remembrance: Traces of national socialism in West Germany, 1945-1960.*
7. Quoted in. Ousby, I. *Occupation*. p. 57.
8. According to *Der Deutsche Wegleiter*, a biweekly German-language guide to occupied France, by May 1941 one million Germans had been served by the unit.
9. *The Scotsman*, 6 August 1940.
10. 'KdF.-Arbeit im Elsass: Die Schaffenden des Kreises Hagenau lernen auch hier den Unterschied zwischen einst und jetzt kennen.' *Der Gaubrief*, 20 March 1943. p. 19.
11. Junger, E. *A Journals from Paris, 1941 – 1945.*
12. Kageneck. 2012. pp. 70–71.
13. *Diary of the Dark Years, 1940–1944.* p. 71.
14. Mork, W. *Soldatenleben in Frankreich 1940-1941.*

24 A New Europe

1. As cited in the *Manchester Guardian*, 21 February 1942. p. 6.
2. The strain of preparing for the invasion of Russia was also taking its toll on the Reichsbahn (In the period from February 15 to June 19, 1941, a total of 11,784 trains with around 200,000 wagons travelled over an average distance of 800km for the deployment against the USSR. Amazingly, it was possible to carry out these movements in addition to the normal timetable.)
3. *New York Herald Tribune*, 20 August 1941.
4. Smith, Howard. *Last Train from Berlin.* 1942. p. 95.

5. Ibid.
6. *Aberdeen Press and Journal* –19 February 1941.
7. 'House That Peter the Great Built Attracts Few These Days'. *New York Times*, 19 August 1941.
8. *Warschauer Zeitung*, 3 July 1940.
9. Ibid.
10. National archives: 1537395.
11. The territory of the former province of Posen was annexed by Germany and made part of Reichsgau Danzig-West Prussia and Reichsgau Wartheland in 1939. A Woerl guidebook for Posen was published in 1940.
12. Boberach, H. (ed.). *Meldungen aus dem Reich: Die geheimen Lageberichte des Sicherheitsdienstes der SS 1938–1945*. 1984.
13. Zylberberg, M. *A Warsaw diary, 1939-1945*.

25 Barbarossa

1. 'Hitler's Table Talk', p. 5.
2. Latzl, K. 'Tourismus and Gewalt: Kriegswahrnehmungen in Feldpost-briefen' in Heer, H. and Naumann, K. (eds). *Verniehtungskrieg: Verbrechen der Wehrmacht, 1941-1945*. Hamburg, 1995. pp. 448–49.
3. But, while in hospital Inga was given morphine for pain relief which she was soon to become dependent on for the remainder of her short life.
4. Noakes. *Nazism*. p. 308.
5. Smith, H. *Last Train From Berlin*. London, 1942. p. 72.
6. Ibid.
7. *Hartlepool Northern Daily Mail*, 31 July 1941.
8. Morris, along with his staff and the American press corps, were rounded up and held in detention until German diplomats had been safely repatriated from the United States.

26 1942

1. Juno was abruptly withdrawn after their factory, not far from Alexanderplatz, was destroyed by a British bomb.

2. Many 'spiv' cigarettes in packets without a name or address of the manufacturer appeared on the black market, but as time pressed on, people were content to buy any make or brand.
3. Harald Endemann to his wife Charlotte, 7 October, 1942.
4. On 20 September, 1942.
5. Simmons, p. 176.
6. *Arbeitertum*, 15 December 1942 p. 2.
7. *Fritt Folk*, 28 October, 1940.
8. *Deutsche Zeitung in Norwegen*, 15 April 1943.
9. 'Hitler's Table Talk', 22 July 1942. p. 584.

27 A Change of Fortunes

1. *Aberdeen Evening Express*, 13 February 1943.
2. Smelser, R. *Robert Ley: Hitler's Labour Leader*. Berg. 1998. p. 289.
3. Goebbels' Diaries, 15 September 1943.
4. Vossler, F. *Propaganda in die eigene Truppe*. p. 322.
5. Letter by Pavel Cherevatenko to the Berlin Geschiehtswerkstatt, Kharkiv (Ukraine), 1998 Dokumentationszentrum NS Zwangsarbeit Berlin-Schonewerde Sig. Berliner Geschichtswerkstatt.
6. Volsing, E. 'Bayruther Kreigsfestpiele 1943'. *Deutsche Dramaturgie*. September 1943, p. 165.
7. SD Domestic Issue Report. 27 September 1943.
8. Historisches Archiv Krupp, Essen WA 41/ 73-125, P. 268; Krupp Management letter to KdF branch in Essen October 1942. Cited from Timpe, J. *Hitler's Happy People: Kraft durch Freude's Everyday Production of Joy in the Third Reich*. Brown University, 2007.
9. Goebbels' Diary, 12 January 1943.
10. https://www.berliner-zeitung.de/politik-gesellschaft/hitlers-vorspiel-zum-untergang-li.78969
11. *Yorkshire Post*, 2 August, 1943.
12. Silvia Koerner: Evakuierung aus Berlin 1943, LEMO.
13. *Aberdeen Press and Journal*, 10 September 1943.
14. Marianne Gartner in *The Naked Years: Growing up in* Nazi *Germany*, p. 125.

15. *Nottingham Journal*, 27 July 1943.
16. Semmens, K. *Seeing Hitler's Germany: Tourism in the Third Reich*. p. 158.
17. Ibid.
18. Goebbels' Diary, 20 March 1942. p. 134.

28 Crumbling Home Front
1. Roth, H. *Eastern Inferno: The Journals of a German Panzerjäger on the Eastern Front, 1941–43*. Casemate, 2013.
2. Staatsarchiv München, Polizeidirektion München, Nr. 7975, Schutzpolizei Report, 6 July 1943.
3. Goebbels' Diary, 8 April 1942.
4. Blau, *Die Kriminalität in Deutschland während des zweiten Weltkrieges*, p. 61.
5. It was also rumoured that the Czechoslovak spa of Carlsbad, in Bohemia, was earmarked to be the new capital 'acting capital'.
6. *Völkischer Beobachter*, 14 August 1943, p. 3.
7. 'Zweiter Weltkrieg: Luftangriffe auf Berlin', *Der Spiegel*, 10 October 2012.

29 1944
1. A surviving pamphlet for April 1944 (Berlin district) shows where to meet on what date, at what time, and the name of the person in charge of the hike (the Wanderführer). Above the words 'HEIL HITLER!' is the announcement for the next area, Heimabend, on 4 May 1944 and at the bottom of the A4 sheet are the names of two Nazi Party members responsible, Kreiswanderwart Erich Bothe and Kreiswart Pg. Walther.
2. BArch R 56 I/37.
3. USHMM RG.11.001 Zentralbauleitung Waffen SS Auschwitz, reel 23. Cited from Timpe, J. *Hitler's Happy People: Kraft durch Freude's Everyday Production of Joy in the Third Reich*. Brown University, 2007.
4. Grunberger, R. *A Social History of the Third Reich*. W&N, 1971. p. 473.
5. Confino, Alon. *Traveling as a culture of remembrance: Traces of national socialism in West Germany, 1945-1960*.

6. Hitler's Table Talks, p. 717.
7. The zoo reopened between 3 p.m. and 9 p.m. The number of visitors was limited to the capacity of the nearby bunker which was used in air-raids.
8. *Munchener Neueste Zeitung*, 18 August 1944.
9. *Dundee Evening Telegraph*, 10 January 1944.
10. D-Day was originally set for 5 June but had to be postponed for a day because of bad weather.
11. *Aberdeen Evening Express*, 22 July 1944.
12. 'Report on the Flying Bombs', British Information service. September 1944.
13. *Aberdeen Press and Journal*, 25 August 1944.
14. *Daily Herald*, 25 August 1944.
15. Weyer, T. *The Setting of the Pearl*. Oxford University Press, 2005. p. 263.

30 Downfall
1. *Lancashire Evening Post*, 26 February 1945.
2. Jones, M. *After Hitler*. John Murray, 2015.
3. Goebbels' Diaries, 27 March 1945.
4. Ichschlugmeiner Mutter die brennenden Funken ab: Berliner Schulaufsätzeausdem Jahr 1946 – Annett Gröschner / Rowohlt Taschenbuch Verlag. In 1946, in the immediate aftermath of the war, Berlin students described their personal wartime experiences in essays. In these authentic documents they talk of fear of death, horror and lucky escapes.

31 A New Kind of Tourist
1. *Dundee Evening Telegraph*, 16 June 1945.

BIBLIOGRAPHY

Baranowski, Shelley. *Strength through Joy: Consumerism and Mass Tourism in the Third* Reich. Cambridge, 2004.
Binion, Rudolf. *Hitler among the Germans*. New York, 1976.
Bleuel, Hans Peter. *Strength through Joy: Sex and Society in Nazi Germany*. London, 1973.
Brendon, Piers. *Thomas Cook: 150 Years of Popular Tourism*. London, 1991.
Brook-Shepherd, Gordon. *Austrian Odyssey*. London: Macmillan, 1957.
Engelmann, Bernt. *In Hitler's Germany: Everyday Life in the Third Reich*. New York, 1986.
Evans, R. J. *The Coming of the Third Reich*. London, 2004.
Frei, Norbert. *National Socialist Rule in Germany. The Führer State, 1933–1945*. Oxford: Blackwell, 1993.
Glaser, Hermann. *The Cultural Roots of National Socialism*. London, 1978.
Grunberger, Richard. *The 12-Year Reich: A Social History of Nazi Germany, 1933–1945*. New York: Da Capo, 1995.
Harlan, Veit. *Im Schatten meiner Filme*. Gütersloh: SigbertMohn, 1966.
Hart-Davis, Duff. *Hitler's Games: The 1936 Olympics*. London, 1986.

Bibliography

Heiber, Helmut. *Adolf Hitler: Eine Biographie*. Berlin, 1960.

Heiden, Konrad. *Der Fuehrer: Hitler's Rise to Power*. Boston, 1944.

Kershaw, I. *Popular Opinion and Political Dissent in the Third Reich: Bavaria 1933–1945*. Oxford, 1983.

Kershaw, I. *The Nazi Dictatorship: Problems and Perspectives of Interpretation*. London, 1985.

Kershaw, I. *The Hitler Myth*. Oxford, 1987.

Kershaw, I. *Hitler, 1889–1936: Hubris*. London, 1998.

Kershaw, I. *Hitler, 1936–1945: Nemesis*. London, 2000.

Knox, MacGregor. *To the Threshold of Power, 1922/33: Origins and Dynamics of the Fascist and National Socialist Dictatorships*. Cambridge, 2007.

Longerich, P. *Heinrich Himmler*. Oxford, 2010.

Moeller, Felix. *Der Filmminister: Goebbels und der Film im Dritten Reich*. Berlin: Henschel, 1998.

Morley, Nathan. *Radio Hitler: Nazi Airwaves in the Second World War*. Amberley, 2021.

Mühlberger, Detlef. *Hitler's Followers: Studies in the Sociology of the Nazi Movement*. London, 1991.

Mühlberger, Detlef. *Hitler's Voice: The* Volkischer Beobachter, *1920–1933*. 2 vols. Bern, 2004.

Noakes, Jeremy (ed.). *Nazism 1919–1945, vol. 4. The German Home Front in World War II*. Exeter, 1998.

Noakes, J., and G. Pridham. 'Democracy and Social Structure in Pre-Nazi Germany' in Parsons, T. *Politics and Social Structure*. New York, 1969.

Peukert, Detlev J. K. *Inside Nazi Germany. Conformity, Opposition and Racism in Everyday Life*. New Haven/London: Yale University Press, 1987.

Pulzer, Peter. *The Rise of Political Anti-Semitism in Germany and Austria*. New York, 1964.

Rupp, Leila. *Mobilizing Women for War: German and American Propaganda, 1939–1945*. Princeton University Press, 1978.

Riding, Alan. *And the Show Went on: Cultural Life in Nazi-occupied Paris*. New York: Alfred A. Knopf, 2010.

Schirach, Baldur von. *Ich glaubte an Hitler*. Hamburg: Mosaik Verlag, 1967.

Schoenbaum, David. *Hitler's Social Revolution; Class and Status in Nazi Germany, 1933-1939*. New York: Doubleday, 1966.

Schulte-Sasse, Linda. *Entertaining the Third Reich: Illusions of Wholeness in Nazi Cinema*. Durham, NC: Duke University Press, 1996.

Shirer, W. L. *The Rise and Fall of the Third Reich: A History of Nazi Germany*. New York, 1960.

Spode, Hasso. 'Der deutsche Arbeiterreist: Massentourismus im Dritten Reich' in Huck, Gerhard (ed.). *Sozialgeschichte der Freizeit*. Wuppertal, 1980.

Spotts, Frederic. *Bayreuth: A History of the Wagner Festival*. New Haven, 1994.

Stachura, P. *Nazi Youth in the Weimar Republic*. Santa Barbara, California, 1975.

Staub, E. 'The Psychology of Perpetrators and Bystanders', *Political Psychology*, Vol. 6, No. 1. March 1985.

Vossler, Frank. *Propaganda in die eigene Truppe: Die Truppenbetreuung in der Wehrmacht 1939-1945*. Paderborn: F. Schöningh, 2005.

Weingartner, J. J. *Hitler's Guard: The Story of the* Leibstandarte SS Adolf Hitler *1933–1945*. London, 1974.

Weyr, Thomas. *Vienna under Hitler*. Oxford, 2005.

Weys, Rudolf. *Cabaret und Kabarett in Wien*. Vienna and Munich: Jugend & Volk, 1970.

Widdig, Bernd. *Culture and Inflation in Weimar Germany*. Berkeley, California, 2001.

INDEX

A

Gunter Adam 109
Adlon Hotel 97–8, 155, 174, 181, 184, 197, 237
Allgemeine Deutsche Gerwerkschaftsbund 13
Hans Ammon 38
Amt Reisen, Wandern und Urlaub 47
Lale Andersen 187
Anhalter Bahnhof 99, 104, 211
Anglo-German Review (AGR) 135
Arbeitertum 28, 35, 77, 143, 146, 147, 153, 168, 186, 192, 193, 206

B

Lida Baarova 39
Baedeker 12, 44, 201, 202, 254
Barbarossa 204–08
Djuna Barnes 82
Norman Bayles 149
Bayreuth 30, 31, 45, 158, 219, 237
Samuel Beckett 119–21
Berchtesgaden 42–7, 65, 66, 75, 122, 134, 137, 177, 247, 249, 251
Erna Berger 186
Berghof 43–7, 65–7, 122, 247
Berlin Philharmonic 17, 30
Martin Bormann 44, 88
Botanischer Garten 84
Brandenburg Gate 106, 185
A. G. K. Brown 110
Hildegarde Bruninghoff 238
Bund Deutscher Madel 86, 126–27
Karl Busch 55

C

Neville Chamberlain 134, 162, 183, 249

Winston Churchill 183
Hermann Clajus 85
Sydney A. Clark 74
Bertram de Colonna 28, 49, 57
Thomas Cook 7, 10, 52, 74
Archibald Crawford KC 144

D

Édouard Daladier 134
Walther Darre 36, 138, 251
Carl Degener 59, 195
Degenerate Art 112–14, 171
Deutsche Arbeitsfront 18
Deutsche Oper 30
Deutsche Reichsbahn 14, 42, 59, 72, 96, 99, 122, 139, 166, 176, 195, 210, 213, 224, 236
Deutsche Verkehrsbücher 14
Deutsche Wegleiter 189
Elisabeth Dietrich 143–45
Marlene Dietrich 82, 229, 250
Engelbert Dollfuss 15–16, 59
Dopolavoro 20
Horst Dressler-Andress 24
W. E. B. Du Bois 30, 125
Jean Merril Du Cane 91
Duke of Windsor 121

E

Elbhattan 118
ENIT Tourismus Reisen 195
Hermann Esser 15, 51, 64, 140, 151, 160, 178, 182, 224, 225, 243, 251
Eternal Jew 114

F

Negley Farson 134
John Feardon 86
Feldherrnhalle 124
Karl Fierler 195
Theo Findahl 230
Harry Flannery 176, 181, 187, 197–98
Theodor Fontane 11
Henry Ford 90
Ruth Andreas-Friedrich 185
Willi Frischauer 17
Bella Fromm 62, 109
Gustav Frohlich 39
Walther Funk 177, 251
Wilhelm Furtwangler 30

G

Garmisch 9, 87, 139, 144, 160, 200
Karl Gebhardt 109
Anton Gerriets 68
Germania 90, 130
Philip Gibbs 141
Harry Giese 185
Joseph Goebbels 21, 39, 52, 57, 67, 76, 89, 98, 107, 108, 114, 120, 121, 137, 137, 139, 151, 154, 155, 174, 179, 180, 198, 211, 212, 217, 219, 223–25, 228–29, 234, 239, 243, 245, 247
Hermann Göring 29, 88–90, 107, 127, 130, 133, 138, 139, 159, 249, 251, 257
Graf Zeppelin 93

Index

Martha Graham 98
Alexander Gray 74, 78
Dan Grossman 92
Gustav Grundgen 108
Dorothea Günther 101, 184
Wilhelm Gustloff 142, 145, 172, 242
Konstanty Gutschow 118

H
Henry Hall 152
Hamburg America Line 12, 38
Hapag 12, 72, 116, 195
Haus Vaterland 125, 181
Heinrich Hauser 175–76
Edward Heath 129
William Randolph Hearst 96
Lutz Heck 37, 230
Katherina Heinroth 247–8
Rudolf Hess 121, 199
Hindenburg (airship) 92–4, 106
Adolf Hitler 14–19, 44–5, 47, 65, 66, 74, 76, 79, 88–90, 106, 112, 117–18, 122–23, 124, 126–27, 128, 130, 132, 133–37, 153–56, 162, 184, 186–87, 192, 204–05, 214–15, 217, 235, 238–39, 242–44, 246–47, 248, 252
Hofbräuhaus 124
Horcher's 233
Irmgard Hunt 46, 66

I
Herbert Ihering 29
Imperial Airlines 89, 91–2
Christopher Isherwood 81, 83

K
KaDeWe 101
Kaiserhof Hotel 89, 98, 126, 174, 197, 237
Karl Kaufmann 118
KdF-Wagen 153–54, 168, 173
John F. Kennedy 85
King George VI 121
Victor Klemperer 77
Clemens Klotz 67
Kraft durch Freude (KdF) *passim*
Carl Vincent Krogmann 118–19
Kurfürstendamm 39–40, 81, 101, 197, 233

L
Bodo Lafferentz 47, 60, 62
Hans Lammers 65
Anton Lang 46
Kenneth Lawson 114
Ernst Lehmann 93
Robert Ley 18–21, 24–5, 27, 32–4, 42, 47, 59, 63, 67, 69–71, 79–80, 121–22, 125, 148–49, 154, 172–73, 179, 182, 193, 200–01, 205, 213, 216–19, 229, 237–39, 242, 245–46, 251–52
Charles Lindbergh 90
Heinz Linge 44, 186
Lufthansa 89–91, 103, 174
Lustgarten 212

M
Ramsay MacDonald 104
Klaus Mann 81

Yosuke Matsuoka 104
Yehudi Menuhin 31
Herybert Menzel 76
MER 135, 159–60, 211
Unity Mitford 67
Mitropa 152
Vyacheslav Molotov 104, 162
Herbert Morrison 95
Leonard Mosley 66
Benito Mussolini 104, 134, 148, 159

N
Nationalsozialistische Kulturgemeinde 32
Norddeutscher Lloyd 12, 60, 72, 105, 163, 170–71

O
Oberammergau 46
Olympic Games 96–111, 126, 154
Jesse Owens 108

P
Ignatius Phayre 45
Eric Phipps 121, 130
Pablo Picasso 114, 171, 190
Andre Francois-Poncet 106
Grace Morrison-Poole 96
Alexander Powell 45
Prora 65–70, 122, 169, 173
Corrado Puccetti 20

Q
Roswitha Quadfliegm 119–20
Vidkun Quisling 213–14

R
Reichsamt Deutsches Volksbildungswerk 26
Reichsbahn *see* Deutsches Reichsban
Reichsbahnzentrale 31
Reichstheaterzug 28
Reichszentrale für Deutsche Verkehrswerbung 14
Leni Riefenstahl 109
Max Reinhardt 114
Sidney Rogerson 93
Alfred Rosenberg 32, 69–70, 88, 154, 251
Rothenburg 52
Marie-Louise de Rothschild 16

S
Hjalmar Schacht 18
Kurt Schaaf 147
Christa Schroeder 66
Gustav Schrökl 10
William Shirer 98, 155, 174
Anton Silberhuber 10
Howard K. Smith 197, 199, 205, 207
Hans Söhnker 187
Emmy Sonnemann 29, 88, 139
Albert Speer 24, 39, 69, 79, 128–31, 186, 215, 238, 246
Carl Stangen 10–12
Richard Strauss 31, 106
Julius Streicher 23, 115, 138
Sudetenland 134, 138, 160, 195–96, 200

Index

T
Richard Tauber 114
Tempelhof Airport 90, 103, 130, 220, 246
Theater des Volkes 27
Tiergarten 82–3, 130, 141, 230
Fritz Todt 75–6, 186, 257
Otto David Tolischus 174
Arturo Toscanini 104
Ferdinand Tuohy 147–48, 194

V
Marie Vassiltchikov 181, 230, 233–34
Miriam Verne 67
Völkischer Beobachter 29, 41, 47, 52, 99, 134, 147, 183, 193, 196, 206, 222, 229, 241

Volkswagen 79, 153–55, 168–69, 239

W
Richard Wagner 30–31, 180
Robert Walser 83
Wandervögel 55, 158
Wannsee 22, 39, 84, 107, 211, 245, 250
Herbert Warning 22, 40, 72, 148, 182, 236
Paul Wendel 83
Hugh R. Wilson 107
Thomas Cuthbert Worsley 81
Martin Gustav Wilhelm Wronsky 91

Z
Zoological Gardens 37

Also available from Amberley Publishing

Radio Hitler
NAZI AIRWAVES IN THE SECOND WORLD WAR

Nathan Morley

Available from all good bookshops or to order direct
Please call **01453-847-800**
www.amberley-books.com

Also available from Amberley Publishing

'With his soldier's instincts Trigg has brought the grit, grime and guts of the German experience to life to show just what total war means'
PATRICK MERCER OBE

THE BATTLE OF STALINGRAD THROUGH GERMAN EYES

THE DEATH OF THE SIXTH ARMY

JONATHAN TRIGG

Author of *D-Day Through German Eyes*
'Fascinating' *Daily Mail*

Available from all good bookshops or to order direct
Please call **01453-847-800**
www.amberley-books.com